BOOKS BY

Stanley Edgar Hyman

THE CRITIC'S CREDENTIALS   1978
Essays and Reviews edited by Phoebe Pettingell

IAGO   1970
Some Approaches to the Illusion of His Motivation

FLANNERY O'CONNOR   1966

STANDARDS   1966
A Chronicle of Books for Our Time

THE PROMISED END   1963
Essays and Reviews, 1942–1962

NATHANAEL WEST   1962

THE TANGLED BANK   1962
Darwin, Marx, Frazer and Freud as Imaginative Writers

POETRY AND CRITICISM   1961
Four Revolutions in Literary Taste

THE ARMED VISION   1948
A Study in the Methods of Modern Literary Criticism

The Critic's Credentials

THE CRITIC'S CREDENTIALS

Essays & Reviews by

STANLEY EDGAR HYMAN

Edited by
PHOEBE PETTINGELL

Atheneum New York

1978

Some of the essays and reviews have previously been published as follows:

ATLANTIC MONTHLY: *Richard Wright Reappraised; A Darwinian Sidelight*
BOSTON HERALD TRAVELER: *Really the Blues*
CENTENNIAL REVIEW: *Jessie Weston and the Forest of Broceliande*
KENYON REVIEW: *Myths and Mothers*
THE NEW LEADER: *Kenneth Burke at Seventy; A Multitude of Lieblings;
    The Art of Joseph Mitchell; Mark Twain, Half Twain; Truths
    from the Grave; Anthropologist of Gopher Prairie; Prince Myshkin
    in Hollywood; Couplings; The Book of the Year?; Germ's Choice,
    Shame's Voice; The Lawrence Mob; Playing Doctor, Playing War;
    The Bulging Pockets of Anthony Carson; Waiting for Bakayoko;
    The Oldest Story; Salad Days, Green and Cold; A Trap Named
    Hope; Varangian Times; A Scythian Humanist; Nabokov's Distort-
    ing Mirrors; Images of Sigmund Freud; Illumination for the Un-
    churched*
THE NEW YORKER: *A Blow with a Maize Stalk; Sad Encounters; Fable
    Italian Style; Counting the Cats*
SHENANDOAH: *Ideas in Fiction*
TRIQUARTERLY: *The Handle*

Library of Congress Cataloging in Publication Data

Hyman, Stanley Edgar, 1919–1970.
    The critic's credentials.

    1. Literature, Modern—History and criticism—
Collected works. I. Pettingell, Phoebe.
II. Title.
PN710.H95 1978   809   77–88902
ISBN 0–689–10847–8

For Howard Nemerov

Introduction

BY PHOEBE PETTINGELL

I

IN *The Armed Vision*, that audaciously militant scrutiny of literary criticism, the twenty-eight year old Stanley Edgar Hyman hypothetically constructed "out of plastics and light metals," an ideal critic: one who would command all branches of learning and all tools of his profession in "a fearful assumption of personal capacity." Reluctantly admitting the improbability of such a Platonic archetype, he suggested instead that we must settle for "pluralist criticism," arguing that any single approach is inadequate, while the greatest diversity casts the most light. Conflict would be inevitable—even welcomed as part of a refining process which would discover a new golden age of critical sensibility:

> From the interplay of many minds, even many errors, truth arises, as our wise men have known since Plato's dialogues. This synthesis of critical method is not simply multiplicity or plurality or anarchy, but a genuine dialectic contest or *agon*. From it, too, truth will arise. We may get it within the individual critic, in an integrated method, or outside the individual critic, in the group symposium, but in some form or other we must get it. And "we" here stands for the whole world, for where truth is at issue, we are all of necessity critics.

"The razor's edge," wrote Samuel Taylor Coleridge, "becomes a saw to the armed vision." The human eye fortified by technology (in this case, the microscope) was, for Stanley, a powerful metaphor of the potency of new critical techniques, capable of holding their own in an increasingly scientific world.

Fifteen years later he wrote "The Critic's Credentials" as a mature revision of this conclusion. During a symposium in 1963 (at which this essay was presented for discussion) he humorously confessed that what had most excited him in his twenties was "a work criticizing a work criticizing a work criticizing a work criticizing a work; then I thought I had something really quite rare and purified and serious." He added resolutely, "At least after fifteen years I am able, I hope, to get into bed with a novel without all that in between." This shift of emphasis involved, among other things, the recognition that his own talents were never primarily speculative. Like Dr. Johnson, his strengths lay in judicious excellence of taste and clarity of thought enhanced by a witty, incisive style. Ruefully, he had also come to feel that his paean to a dawning age of criticism now read like a threnody over a few golden years. Kenneth Burke, F. O. Matthiessen, Lionel Trilling, I. A. Richards, and William Empson had not been heralds of a new sensibility, but its innovators; their followers, capable of reproducing the letter of method but not the spirit of lively genius, had dwindled into fossilizing relics of a dead era, or were swept away by blood-dimmed tides of literary yahoos and charlatans.

Shortly after completing his final speculative work in 1961, Stanley began writing a bi-weekly book column for *The New Leader*. He regarded this as "an experiment in regularly confronting the literature of our time with a hard eye, so to speak, insisting on standards of excellence at a time when truth has become unfashionable in literary journalism." This four-year intensive exposure to current fiction probably did more than anything to effect his change of stance. The essays collected in this volume (all written between the early sixties and his death in 1970) represent the most complete exposition of his mature ideas, when his commitment to "standards" was highest.

Stanley's interests were remarkably diverse, his reading prodigious. For many years he belonged to both the American Folklore Society and the American Anthropological Society, participating as an active controversialist in both fields. He was deeply knowledgeable about Freudian psychology, an informed amateur in the social sciences, even trying (on a more popular level) to keep abreast of trends in science. Recognizing that the subjects of poetry and fiction are drawn from an infinite spectrum, he always insisted that the critic cannot afford to be ignorant of that richness. His own sense of richness enabled him to bring a formidable breadth of knowledge and insight to everything he wrote.

II

STANLEY EDGAR HYMAN was born on June 11, 1919, in New York City, and grew up in Brooklyn. His grandfather, who had been a student of *Torah* in Russian Poland, had emigrated to this country to escape tsarist anti-semitism. Stanley was raised in Orthodox Judaism, but after a pious childhood, he suffered a loss of faith which transformed him into a lifelong militant atheist (looking back on it, he admitted to having read "too many English novels about young men who had fatal doubts and left the Church," adding that he had been "so bemused by literature" that he had not distinguished his own religion from the Church of England). His secular education struck him as "savagely competitive," but "I rather liked it, competed with great success, and think it effectively armored me for later life." As a child, his interests were mainly scientific: he hung around herpatologists at the Bronx Zoo, spent hours looking through his microscope, and dreamed of a career in microbiology. His happiest memory of summer excursions to the country was botanizing for mushrooms; this recollection provided him with a lyrical metaphor for poems which move us by seeming to be "without ancestry and descendants, to spring up timeless and beautiful like Indian pipes in deep woods, to delight our minds and refresh our hearts."

Perhaps it was this romanticism that gradually weaned him from science. At Erasmus Hall high school he became increasingly intrigued with journalism, and matriculated at Syracuse University in 1936, firmly committed to writing. At Syracuse, a charismatic teacher, Leonard Brown, introduced him to the writings of Kenneth Burke, and, soon after, to Burke himself, who became his life-long friend, mentor, and intellectual sparring-partner. It was to Burke that he credited his sense of "a literary criticism constituting a passionate avowal of the ultimate and transcendant importance of the creative act."

Stanley was so attracted to a page-long story by another of Brown's students that he prophesied he would marry its author, Shirley Jackson. As a pair, they founded a dissident literary magazine on campus as a forum for their essays, fiction, poetry and drawings. (Although authorities were assured that its title, *Spectre*, had been inspired by Shirley's interest in the occult, of course it derived from Marx.) In 1940, shortly after graduation, they married, and settled in New York. As a winner of *The New Republic*'s college essay contest, Stanley briefly worked there as an editorial assistant. Shirley, who was making up her mind whether to become a writer or a cartoonist, flitted from one uninteresting job to another, subsequently lampooning several of them in her stories.

Later that same year, Stanley became a staff writer at *The New Yorker;* he continued to hold this position until his death. Though never a very successful reporter, he contributed several notable "profiles" in the late fifties on such subjects as vanishing species, the second-hand book business, and the Brooklyn Bridge. In his last years he wrote book reviews. Long after he was no longer living in the city, he continued to visit it twice a year, establishing a temporary office at *The New Yorker,* and he wrote all his letters on its stationery as a sign of the deep attachment he felt for its world.

After several years of financial struggling, Stanley was invited by Kenneth Burke to join him on the literature faculty of Bennington College—a faculty then consisting of such luminaries as Theodore Roethke, Francis Fergusson, William Troy, and W. H. Auden. Stanley taught only for a year, then resigned to finish *The Armed Vision*. It appeared in 1948 to a storm of controversy (just at the time Shirley launched her own career with her macabre story, "The Lottery"). Reviewers deplored the "savage attacks" on T. S. Eliot, Van Wyck Brooks, Yvor Winters, and especially Edmund Wilson (one critic expressed a common opinion in calling that chapter "one of the least tasteful bits of venom that has appeared in a long time."). Many seemed equally outraged by the book's adulation of Burke, Richards, and Empson whom they sideswiped as "crafty manipulators," purveyors of "unwieldly paraphernalia," altogether "an unfortunate esoteric trend in literary criticism," as well as "suspiciously Marxist." In some moods, Stanley depreciated his talents (comically) as "mainly of a destructive order with a highly developed instinct for the jugular," but *The Armed Vision* proved him equally adept at the one quality he admired in Wilson: "the function of translation or interpretation, of explaining the work's paraphrasable content" for readers who would have been unable to attempt *The Philosophy of Literary Form*, *Principles of Literary Criticism*, or *Seven Types of Ambiguity* unaided. Surprisingly, few reviewers paid any serious attention to the plea for pluralist criticism, and Stanley continued to carry the standard of that cause throughout his writings. In later years he was often asked if he repudiated any of his early judgments of those critics whose work he had dealt with in this study. Very privately, he admitted to feeling that he had somewhat overrated the importance of Maud Bodkin, Christopher Caudwell, and R. P. Blackmur. However, he staunchly defended the justice of all his attacks.

The Hymans found the Bennington community so congenial that (except for a brief defection to Westport in the early fifties) they made it their permanent home, and raised their four children—the "Laurie, Jannie, Sally, and Barry" of Shirley's *Life Among the Savages* and *Raising Demons*—in a large gothic house recognizable from many of her novels. The house was filled with Stanley's library of 30,000 books: predominantly literary criticism, modern fiction and poetry, psychology, archeology, folklore, and anthropology. His antiquarian interests were on display in the dining room, where, in his own description, "an Indian miniature from the Rajput Hills jostles an Azande *shongo*, or throwing knife, on the wall, and the shelves are shared uneasily by a group of Australian churingas, a terra-cotta ithyphalic *Silenos* from ancient Thebes, an Iroquois turtle rattle, a collection of Japanese *netsukes*, a Gaboon ship harp, and a Corsican vendetta knife." Numismatics was Stanley's hobby; he particularly loved ancient Greek coins, "whose symbols seem never conventional or allegorical, but always the literal picturings of objects full of *mana*, magical power. The owl *is* Athena, pop-eyed and stern. Alexander does not wear his horns as a king might wear a laurel wreath or crown, as a token of honor or ranks; he *is* Zeus Ammon, and the horns sprout from his head as visible emanations of his godhead." Stanley also collected old blues records, whose lyrics he spent many patient hours transcribing. He was a fanatic sports fan, and a fierce poker player.

In 1953, Stanley rejoined the Bennington faculty, this time to stay. In spite of his reputation for critical harshness, as a writer, he was the gentlest of teachers. Students and colleagues were often startled at how cordial his praise could be, and usually tried to live up to his high valuation. He had a gift for bringing out the best in people he worked with, and he gave his best as a patient, compassionate listener, sage counselor, and a temperate committeeman who demanded gentlemanly behavior in the heat of academic disputes. He lost the lean and hungry look of his *Armed Vision* days to become a stocky, patriarchal figure, running his fingers through his curly beard as he sat perched on a high stool in classes; genially stumping around campus with an outlandish walking-stick made of python vertebrae (once the property of James Joyce); the boisterous life of innumerable parties.

On completing his first book, Stanley had immediately embarked on another equally ambitious project: an examination of four non-literary nineteenth century innovators: Charles Darwin, Karl Marx, Sir James Frazer, and Sigmund Freud. Insisting on the poetic value of these men as radically "imaginative writers," Stanley defined his own perception of literature: "I believe their books to be art, but I believe art itself to have an ethical as well as an aesthetic dimension, in that it is the work of the moral imagination, imposing order and form on disorderly and anarchic experience. That this vision of order and form is primarily metaphoric makes it no less real, since lines of force then radiate out from the work of art and order or reorder the world around, as they do from Wallace Stevens' jar in Tennessee." Ultimately, he claims that "the language of ideas is metaphor, and essentially metaphor. . . . These great enlightenings are humanist; philanthropic in the root sense, for the love of man." This analysis was published in 1962 as *The Tangled Bank* (Darwin's image for the teeming abundance of forms on this earth). Its moving characterization of Darwin, with whom "we rejoice in life," and Freud, whose perception "once again made a tragic view possible for the modern mind," demonstrate Stanley's deeply sympathetic affinity with the spirit of both. He likewise shared their austere devotion to work, regulated by a well-ordered life.

Poetry and Criticism, a very different kind of study, followed the twelve years of labor over *The Tangled Bank*, but was published first (1961). Its subject is the manner in which certain great poems have called new critical theories into being. In spite of the theoretical nature of this thesis, Stanley chose to demonstrate it by a practical examination of four illustrative examples. It was his own admission that he was uneasy as a speculative critic. He loved this book more than any of his others, and in it displayed his versatility with a spectrum of critical methods to best advantage.

Stanley published only one volume in the fifties: a collection of essays by twentieth century British and American critics, *The Critical Performance.* The appearance of *The Tangled Bank* inaugurated his most productive era; the same year he brought out a pamphlet on Nathanael West: 1963 saw a compilation of his miscellaneous essays, *The Promised End,* and a reader, *Darwin for Today.* Together with a former student and close friend, Barbara Karmiller, he edited two volumes of selections from the writings of Kenneth Burke: *Perspectives by Incongruity* and *Terms for Order.* By 1965, poor health and failing eyesight forced him to give up regular reviewing for *The New Leader* (though he continued to write for the magazine). Many of these pieces appeared in *Standards,* and one was expanded into his study of Flannery O'Connor (1966).

Shirley Jackson died in her sleep on August 8, 1965. She and Stanley were devoted to one another, and worked with almost total interdependence. Their effect on each others' writing is too great to be calculated. After her death he edited a reader of her works, *The Magic of Shirley Jackson,* and *Come Along with Me,* a final collection of her stories and essays. During this sad time he also brought together the literary remains of his late colleague at Bennington, the critic William Troy. It was the first book publication of Troy's work and won a National Book Award in 1967.

When I first arrived at Bennington as a student, I had already heard Stanley described as a gleeful savager of literary reputations, and a cynic who derided all forms of faith. I wanted to avoid him as much as possible, so chance or fate promptly assigned me to his freshman course. My surprise at his courtly manner was perhaps less than my astonishment at his intense belief in the redeeming power of literature. He hated superciliousness, conservative elitism (qualities he had attacked in *The Armed Vision*) and anything which smacked of faddism, precisely because they were to him a blasphemy and profanation. In Biblical cadences, he would tell us, "Tragedy reaffirms a nobility and grandeur in the human condition, even Longinus' sublimity. If it is man's fate to go down inevitably into suffering and death, some exultation nevertheless rises to the skies." He never tired of teaching his favorite works: *The Bacchae, Antony and Cleopatra, Walden, Ulysses,* Aristotle and Burke, Coleridge and Richards, the poetry of Yeats—year after year with the same enthusiasm, remarking happily each September that it made the world new again for him. I was sufficiently won over (much to his amusement) to take his most famous course, "Myth, Ritual, and Literature."

The ritual theory of myth was developed by "The Cambridge School," (a group of British classicists and folklorists active during the first half of this century) and most profoundly defined in Jane Ellen Harrison's *Themis,* which insists that myth derives from religious rite, originates, in fact, as "the spoken correlative of the acted rite," and *not* from misunderstanding of historical events or scientific phenomena. Thus, the heroic figures of Greek epic and Arthurian legend, or the doings of incarnate gods (be they Dionysus, the Buddha, or Christ) are the humanized personifications of ritual prototypes: in Miss Harrison's fine phrase, "the reflection, the projection of man's emotions socially reinforced." Stanley insisted that "Since 1912 (the year *Themis* was first published) it has been impossible to talk seriously about mythology in any other terms, or to use the word 'myth' for anything but a narrative of known or presumed ritual origins," and devoted himself to keeping the spark of this theory—once widely accepted, but lately disregarded—alive in his course. He left only fragmentary expositions in his writings, though he always intended someday to write a book on the subject. It was his religion, not just an imaginative spring-board, but gospel too sacred to be tampered with, or even revised. Tragedy was sublime because it preserved the rite of death and rebirth, "the only true immortality" in the repetition of the seasonal cycle, or man's continuing struggle to perpetuate himself, as against what Miss Harrison scathingly calls "heaven's brazen and sterile immutability." His tribute to her in *Standards* as "the great lady who found Greece marble and left it living flesh," is one of the most impassioned things he ever wrote. His admiration for the other great lady of the movement, Jessie Weston, who valiantly quested for ritual origins through the forests of Romance scholarship, was only slightly less intense.

Stanley and I married late in 1966. Failing eyesight had by then made many of his former interests impracticable, and curtailed his strenuous working habits. We traveled; interviewing old jazz musicians in New Orleans, exploring archeological sites in Greece, Turkey, Ireland, and Sicily. During 1968 we lived in Cambridge, England, across the Granta from Darwin House, and a short distance from Newnham College, which, Stanley felt, was still imbued with the doughty spirit of Jane Harrison. It was here that he completed his last book, *Iago: Some Approaches to the Illusion of His Motivation.* In it he once more argued his case for pluralist criticism, examining Iago's "motiveless malignity" from the perspectives of five different critical vocabularies in turn—each inadequate as a single explanation, but all together casting light on the play's dark corners.

Stanley spent 1970 as a visiting professor at Buffalo. Although the job left him with more leisure for writing, than did his demanding schedule at Bennington, he found university life uncongenial, and returned with relief to Vermont at the end of spring term. He died suddenly on July 29, 1970, a few months before the publication of *Iago*, and the birth of our son, Malcolm.

Stanley's last two essays were both on the Bible. When he started writing for *The New Leader* in 1961, his first piece had been a skeptical look at The New English Bible's translation of the New Testament. Several days before his death he completed "Illuminations for the Unchurched" for the same magazine—a somewhat less demurring view of a new version of the

Old Testament. Earlier in the month he had covered related ground in "History and Sacred History," which reiterates his belief in the ritual theory: that "there is no real history connected with the Bible," but that its stories have arisen out of still more ancient forms of worship. This position was not merely a quixotic hobby-horse. He saw mythic origin as a recognition of chthonic presences which cannot be eradicated, but continue to lurk beneath the superstructure of our Olympian civilization, a metaphor akin to Freud's understanding of the unconscious. R. W. B. Lewis once observed that "Mr. Hyman is all for seeds, psyches, and material causes," and it is true that Stanley's method always aims for the heart of things, rather than striving for harmonization or synthesis. In scrutinizing the evidence of our primitive selves, we see "our wriggling ancestor, the bloodstain on our fancy clothes, the corpse from which our grain sprouts, our lustful and murderous wish," but in facing the irrational with an unflinching eye, we also participate in the heroic process of bringing to light what was concealed. "That which was hidden shall be made manifest!" is a universal religious proclamation.

Stanley's last projected book (alas, never begun) was to be a critical study of Bible scholarship, confounding the trivializers of religion who substitute ethical hero-worship for devotion, and undermine the faith they purport to uphold with pseudo-historical or scientific rationalizations. He had a profound understanding of what faith entailed. Had he lived longer, perhaps he might, in his own peculiar way, have ended where his grandfather began as a student of *Torah*.

III

IN "The Critic's Credentials," Stanley insisted that:

Our world is a multiverse and complex one, and our literature accurately reflects it. Unless the critic's equipment is similarly multiverse and complex, he will be turned away at the door of literature, or rather, he will be admitted to what seems to him a drafty ruin, but which reveals itself to the trained eye as Grail Castle.

The armed vision gave way to the quester's vision, but he never lost his conviction that the study of literature demands a tireless and courageous pursuit of truth. It was a sign of Stanley's humility that, believing this, he rejected the role of high-priest to the mysteries, instead choosing to emulate an archetypal figure from Romance—the faithful guide whose lantern enables other seekers to discern the castle. But it was not a sacrificial role. His delight in the illimitable discoveries literature can provide is infectious. Reading him, one realizes that ultimately criticism is one more form of philanthropy.

I am most deeply grateful to my friend and editor at Atheneum, Harry Ford, for boundless assistance and innumerable kindnesses; to Nancy Donaldson Pettingell, who read and commented on every stage of the manuscript; and to Myron Kolatch for his tireless encouragement and advice. Without the support these three have given both to my late husband and to myself, this book never would have seen the light.

P. P.

Contents

I

II

Contents

III

IV

V

I

The Critic's Credentials

WHAT KNOWLEDGE, outside of literature itself, must the critic (and in one fashion or another we are all critics) bring to bear on a work of literature? I tried to answer that question as a problem of critical methodology as long ago as 1948 in *The Armed Vision*. There is no point in my repeating those formulations here, except to note my conclusion that the Ideal Critic would know and do everything, while the Actual Critic, poor fellow, would have to manage as best he could. On this occasion I would like to investigate the problem of extra-literary knowledge from the other end, from the point of view of the work of literature rather than the critic.

Different works make a variety of demands on the critic's learning. Each requires him, in a sense, to display his credentials before it will admit him to its interior reaches. I intend to discuss some of the demands made by specific works of twentieth-century literature. My examples will be taken entirely from fiction, for no better reason than that I have been reading a lot of it recently. They could as readily be taken from poetry or drama, which make very similar demands on the critic these days.

It is a sign of the times that I can assume general agreement that some knowledge outside of literature is requisite. We have come a long way since the literary Know Nothingism of the Forties, when the purist New Critics denied the relevance of any information not in the poem. This ideal of knowing nothing but the poem itself was never practical, since even a New Critic is a man, not a clean blackboard. In any case, it has gone out of fashion. We have swung back from the idea of the critic as a skilled technician, a Steinmetz or a Fleming, to the older ideal of the critic as a broadly educated man of letters, a Coleridge or an Arnold. Obviously we should all know everything —Coleridge and Arnold did—but since we do not, it may be useful to see what specific knowledge some modern novels ask of us.

The following subjects are in no hierarchy of importance, but psychology inevitably comes to mind first when the question is raised. Ours is so markedly an age of psychology, and the psychologist of our age, supremely, is Sigmund Freud. Could the critic function without a knowledge of psychoanalysis? He could, but only as he could function with one eye, seeing things without depth perception. There are novels like dreams in that their deepest meanings cannot be reached without the aid of psychoanalytic concepts.

Nathanael West, who called Freud his "Bulfinch"—that is, the source of his myths—provides a good example. *Miss Lonelyhearts* is about a young man with a Christ complex who takes on the world's burden of pain and suffering. West tried deliberately to use a handbook for the story, William James' *The Varieties of Religious Experience*. But beneath the Jamesian religious agony, motivating it and explaining it, is Freudian case history, a classic Oedipus complex. Miss Lonelyhearts is the sort of man who as a child would have renounced his phallicism out of castration fear, and everything in the book from his pseudonym to his death is symbolic female and sexually passive identification. The Christ or scapegoat role simply masks this deeper renunciation.

Similarly, in Bruce Jay Friedman's *Stern*, a disproportionate reaction to an anti-Semitic remark made by an ogrish figure Stern calls the "kike man," masks Stern's comparable neurotic warp. Where *Miss Lonelyhearts* is partially-conscious Freudian case history, *Stern* is a full-fledged Freudian novel, and I think that a critic innocent of psychoanalysis would find it bewildering.

Other novels demand other psychological knowledge of us.

Fyodor Sologub's *The Petty Demon*, is, among other things, a study in the development of a case of paranoid schizophrenia. We watch the book's protagonist, a repulsive schoolteacher named Peredonov, progress from delusions that the cat has gone to report him to the police, or that an "eyebird" is spying on him, through a series of increasingly mad and violent actions, to the final terrible murder of his friend Volodin. This clinically-accurate case history is not the content of the novel but its form, its dramatic action. Peredonov's galloping psychosis gives *The Petty Demon* its doom and accelerating momentum, in just the fashion that the curse on the House of Atreus operates in *The Oresteia*, or the prophecy about the fate of Oedipus operates in *Oedipus the King*. A critic ignorant of clinical psychology would read a diminished copy of *The Petty Demon*, one lacking the fatedness of tragic drama.

On the other hand, there are novels where the distress of the protagonist is neurotic rather than psychotic, and the possibilities of comic form arise. Such is the case with Walker Percy's first novel *The Moviegoer*. Both the hero, Binx Bolling, and the heroine, his cousin Kate, have considerable emotional difficulties. He suffers from severe apathy and depression, she has an anxiety neurosis and suicidal impulses. Their courage and love for each other nevertheless enable them to manage a feeble affair, then a brave marriage, and at the end they are on their way to a kind of wry and wary happiness. If the critic does not know neurosis from psychosis, his expectations are not properly aroused, and to that extent the book's comic form eludes him.

Nor is that yet enough psychological equipment for the study of twentieth-century fiction. Other novels require that the critic know experimental psychology, and the Gestalt theory that informs so much of it in our time. These novels, like animal learning, are configurational in that the patterning of the experience has a significance not present in any single element in it. The works of Franz Kafka furnish the best examples. Every detail of the arrest, judgment, sentencing and execution of Joseph K. in *The Trial* is irrational, since he is innocent. As a configuration, however, these events make perfect sense. In this context Joseph K. is guilty, because arrest-judgment-sentencing-execution make up the *Gestalt* of guilt.

One sees this more clearly when Kafka overtly uses the metaphors of animal learning. Everything Gregor Samsa and his family do in "The Metamorphosis" is reasonable granted the single mad configuration: that he is learning how to be a giant insect, and that they are learning how to live with one. The narrator of "The Burrow" is similarly a man grappling with neurotic anxiety, but his behavior is meaningful only in the configuration of the life of a defenseless burrowing animal. In a story that uses another sort of metaphor, "In the Penal Colony," we watch one configuration replace another in history. The old official's love for the machine and his sacrificial death are as reasonable within the context of his *Gestalt* as they are sadistic and insane in the *Gestalt* of the new governor's humanitarianism. Gestalt theory here enables the critic to grasp Kafka's fables imaginatively; without it they remain pointless and absurd.

Ralph Ellison's *Invisible Man* is an example of a more recent book that is deepened and enriched by an understanding of Gestalt psychology. The book is a series of wild configurations. The point of the brutal battle royal scene is not the battle royal itself, but the fact that the Negro boys fight blindly in a context that includes a naked blonde girl dancing and the narrator delivering his graduation speech. The Negro sharecropper Trueblood's narrative of incest with his daughter is one story in itself, and a shameful one. It becomes quite another story in a context of white listeners whose suppressed incestuous wishes are symbolically gratified by the act. In this configuration it is a triumphant act, in fact a spirited form of economic self-betterment. So through the book. Every situation is a configuration, and the briefcase the narrator carries is a configuration of configurations. Without a sense of these

Gestalts, Invisible Man never comes together as a meaningful and coherent whole.

So, then, the critic spends years studying psychology, and gets to know it pretty well; not the way the psychologist knows it, but sufficiently well for literary purposes. Isn't that enough? Ah, poor fellow. The next novel he tackles demands that he know all about anthropology. To begin with, there is cultural anthropology. Some novels are about the behavior of primitive peoples. I think of the African novels of Joyce Cary, who was a district officer in the Nigerian bush before he became a novelist. Some of Cary's novels are about Pagan tribes: *Aissa Saved, An American Visitor, The African Witch.* Another, *Mister Johnson,* deals with urbanized and culturally demoralized Nigerians. In both cases the behavior of the Africans can seem mysterious and unpredictable to the reader. If the critic is a student of African ethnology, Cary's Nigeria becomes a world as formal and elegant as Jane Austen's England.

The more important need for cultural anthropology, however, is not to equip the critic to deal with the small proportion of novels about primitives, but to equip him to deal with those novels about forms of civilized behavior that have a primitive analogy. I think here of F. Scott Fitzgerald's *The Great Gatsby*. Gatsby's attempt to win, or win back, Daisy by throwing enormous parties seems a sign of his rather pathetic foolishness. However, a reading of Franz Boas on the Kwakiutl *potlatch*, the ceremonial waste and destruction of goods in a competition for prestige, enormously deepens the critic's understanding of Gatsby's parties. To the degree that our culture resembles that of the Kwakiutl (Ruth Benedict suggests in *Patterns of Culture* that in some respects it is almost indistinguishable from it) Gatsby's parties are neither whimsical nor absurd. The waste of wealth shows that you have wealth to waste; the destruction of wealth shows that you have the power to destroy it; consequently, you are a great chief. Gatsby does make himself a great chief, and he almost gets Daisy. The trouble is that Tom and Daisy are greater Kwakiutl chiefs than he is. Ultimately Gatsby fails and loses his life because he is less callous about waste and destruction than they are.

Other sorts of anthropology are equally useful to the critic. One is the old-fashioned comparative anthropology of the nineteenth century, best represented by Sir James G. Frazer's *The Golden Bough*. William Golding's *Lord of the Flies*, for example, requires that we know all about that Frazerian world of scapegoats, blood rites, totemism, and *mana*. The works of Shirley Jackson similiarly demand a knowledge of Frazerian anthropology. Without it "The Lottery" is inexplicable, the end of *The Sundial* has no point, and the mob scene in *We Have Always Lived in the Castle* seems gratuitous.

As *Lord of the Flies* demands a knowledge of Frazer from us, so Golding's *The Inheritors* requires that we know some physical anthropology and prehistory as well. It tells the story of the extinction of a family of Neanderthal Men, gentle and good, by a band of *Homo sapiens*, ruthless and bloodthirsty. It is clear that these are the last Neanderthals, and that we have been privileged to witness the most significant event of prehistory, the extinction of the only other rival human species. Golding's interest lies not in fictionalizing evolution, but in creating a Platonic myth of original sin: that "Fall" when the evil men from whom we descend, the "Inheritors," wiped out the good men from whom we might have descended, our potential good essence or nature. Nevertheless, without a respectable knowledge of the physical and cultural differences between *Homo neanderthalis* and *Homo sapiens*, the critic cannot even understand the book's events, let alone their significance.

Sometimes a novel appears to demand of us a knowledge of anthropology, but the demand is illusory. Such a novel is Saul Bellow's *Henderson the Rain King*. If I knew more African ethnology, the reader thinks, this lion cult and rain rites, these philosophic conversations with King Dahfu, would make more sense to me. But if he does know more African ethnology, the details make even less sense to him. The truth is that *Henderson* is not set in a real Africa at all, but in a fantasy Africa of German theorizing. As critics have shown, the lion cult comes from Nietzscheland, the rain rites are those of the Reichian tribe, and Dahfu is Big Chief Hippodrome.

Oddly enough, in his short novel *Seize the Day*, Bellow really does function as an anthropologist and demands some anthropology of the critic. When he studies the sub-culture of Upper Broadway hotel life, Bellow brilliantly recreates culture and personality. Tommy Wilhelm and his father are the patterns of cultural alienation and integration, Tamkin is a shaman figure, and the stranger's funeral at the end is the tribal ceremony that initiates and transforms. Here a knowledge of primitive behavior really is useful.

Many contemporary novels demand history of the critic. On a superficial level, this means history in the sense of current history, and the demand is that the critic know some facts about what went on in the world at one time and place or another. One has to know something about ancient Greece and Rome to handle the historical novels of Robert Graves and Marguerite Yourcenar, and the more one knows the richer these novels become. To make any sense out of Ignazio Silone's *Bread and Wine* and Cesare Pavese's *The Moon and the Bonfire* one must understand that the Italian anti-Fascist Underground consisted of revolutionary conspirators, and that the later Resistance to the Germans was a mass movement. Evelyn Waugh's novels and Anthony Powell's *A Dance to the Music of Time* series tell us quite a lot about England between the world wars, but they assume an educated English reader who knows much more that they do not bother to tell us. An American critic had better find out about it.

The novels of François Mauriac steep us in the vinegar of French provincial life, but that souring has a pathology that goes back at least to 1797, and one cannot understand it without the perspective that French political history furnishes. Katherine Anne Porter's "The Leaning Tower" and Christopher Isherwood's Berlin novels show us the Weimar Republic in acute stages of dissolution, but unless we know something about the violent struggle for state power going on behind the facade of café life, we see only a dance of shadows. Putting things at their simplest, Joseph Heller's *Catch-22* tells us that an American flier named Yossarian didn't want to fight in the war, and George P. Elliott's *David Knudsen* tells us that an American photographer named Knudsen didn't approve of thermonuclear warfare. The significance of both novels depends on the degree to which these attitudes are representative, yet that is a question that can only be answered outside the novels, from a knowledge of current history.

There is a much deeper sense, however, in which history is important to the critic. He must not only know some historical facts, he must have a sense of historical process or law. To understand the short stories of Sean O'Faolain's first book, *Midsummer Night Madness*, one has to know when the fighting is revolutionary, between Sinn Feiners and Black and Tans, and when it switches to civil war, between Free Staters and the Irish Republican Army. But to deal *properly* with the stories the critic must know the way Irishmen feel and think about such matters as sex and violence after the many centuries of Roman Catholicism and British rule (what Stephen Dedalus called his "Italian and English masters"), and what that domination and rule did to shape the Irish personality.

Similarly, to understand the short stories of Isaac Babel's *Red Cavalry*, the critic must know quite a lot about the Russian Revolution and Civil War, and about Cossack and Jewish life in Russia, including that ugly institution the *pogrom*. But to deal critically with the mindless brutality of Babel's Cossacks, the ambivalence toward the Revolution shown by Babel's Jews, one would have to understand the historical processes that produced these attitudes and actions; in the case of the Jews, processes going back to the destruction of the Temple in 70 A.D.

We can see this question of historical facts, as opposed to a deeper understanding of historical process, in another form in the treatment of the South in American fiction. The critic has to understand Southern history deeply enough to know that Faulkner is absolutely authoritative on the Civil War and Reconstruction, that Sartoris and Snopes are literally unrealistic but metaphorically true. He must be able to tell that Robert Penn Warren is sharply accurate about Kentucky tobacco farming in *Night Riders*, and quite preposterous about Kentucky slave-owning in *Band of Angels*. As for the New South today, a number of Southern writers have entirely lost touch with it, as Carson McCullers demonstrates in *Clock Without Hands*, while others, such as Flannery O'Connor, continue to tell the truth about it. The critic had better be able to distinguish.

Another area of knowledge that the critic needs is sociology. Marxian sociology no longer has the relevance to English and American fiction that it had in the Thirties, as we may be pleased to observe, but fiction sharing the assumptions of Marxism continues to appear from the Communist countries of Europe, from such Communist faithful as Louis Aragon, and from the new nations of Asia and Africa. The critic needs a familiarity with the writings of Karl Marx and the literature of Marxism, and the world situation today nowhere suggests that this need is apt to diminish.

If Marx is no longer relevant to American fiction, Thorstein Veblen is more relevant than ever, with so many of our current novels centering on the life of the new middle class in the suburbs. An obvious example is the Patimkin family in Philip Roth's novella "Goodbye, Columbus," with their sporting goods tree, their basement refrigerator full of fruit, their unused bar decorated with twenty-three unopened bottles of Jack Daniels, each with a little booklet tied around its neck. The Patimkins are a sermon on a text from *The Theory of the Leisure Class*, and a critic who did not know the role of conspicuous consumption and conspicuous display in our society would be considerably handicapped in dealing with the work of Roth and a number of young writers similarly preoccupied.

Modern sociology, with its newer vocabulary, is equally useful and necessary. Beneath the love story and psychological warfare of D. H. Lawrence's autobiographical *Sons and Lovers* there is sociological fact, the stresses of Paul Morel's upward mobility, as he and his mother strive to pull him up out of the working class. A generation later we get the same autobiographical story, with the same desperate upward mobility, in John Updike's short story "Flight" in *Pigeon Feathers*. In the life-and-death battle between Allen Dow's mother and his girl Molly (the latter characterized by the former as "little hotpants") we can see the familiar Lawrentian Oedipal conflict. But much of the pathos comes from the story's sociological dimension, the impersonality and inevitability of the conflict between a love that insists on social betterment and a love content with what is.

The critic must use the findings of sociology with discrimination, since his subject-matter, literature, is ultimately concerned with truths beyond statistical evidence. The Kinsey reports are an example of the dangers here. James Baldwin's *Another Country* (as the genital pun in its title suggests) is a novel in which almost all the male characters at one time or another have homosexual sex relations. Widespread male homosexual experience is one of the revelations of the first Kinsey report. Nevertheless, sociological correctness does not keep the sex scenes in *Another Country* from being absurd, tractarian, and imaginatively unconvincing.

The love of Frank Alpine for Helen Bober in Bernard Malamud's *The Assistant*, which becomes more and more purely sublimated until at the end Frank is a sacrificial saint who neither sleeps nor eats as he works for his beloved, must be statistically quite a rare case. Not many American males told Dr. Kinsey's researchers that their sex lives were entirely sublimated into spiritual love and sacrificial labor. Yet the Malamud novel has a profound truth to the realities of human passion that can be found neither in the Kinsey works nor in the Baldwin novel. (There *is* a profound sociological truth in *An-*

other Country, that Negro bitterness and race hatred are almost universal in America, but I do not think that sociology has yet demonstrated it statistically.)

A lot that the critic of fiction has to know can be grouped loosely under the rubric of religion. This includes history of religion, theology, and comparative religion. Since we are, historically at least, a Christian culture, the critic must begin by knowing quite a bit about the Christian religion and its texts from the Bible on. Some of the fiction of the twentieth century makes powerful use of Christian myth and symbol in disguised or secular forms, and the critic had better be able to recognize them. (I find that the examples that come to mind here are all by women writers, a fact which may be significant but which I cannot begin to explain.)

Flannery O'Connor's two novels, *Wise Blood* and *The Violent Bear It Away*, as well as a number of her stories, are dominated by the theme of Christian Vocation. Since Miss O'Connor is a devout Roman Catholic, her personal vision of Vocation probably sees it as a call to the holy and useful life of an ordained priest in the Roman Catholic Church. But the vision of Vocation in her novels and stories is the antithesis of this; it is the red-eyed fanaticism of backwoods preachers who find in their primitive Protestant sects no institution adequate to contain the power of their calls. Hazel Motes in *Wise Blood*, who has Jesus in his head like a stinger, preaches the Church of Truth Without Christ, murders and is murdered. Tarwater in *The Violent Bear It Away* is ready to preach his mad Christianity only after he has drowned a child, burned his house and land, and been crazed by suffering a homosexual rape. Henry Ashfield's call to be baptized in "The River" is a call to drown. The Bible salesman in "Good Country People" is a fraud, and his hollow Bible contains only the trappings of fleshly sin.

The great Christian theme of Damnation (which Darwin in his *Autobiography* calls "a damnable doctrine") is secularized in Djuna Barnes' *Nightwood*. The doctor, Nora, Robin, Jenny, and Felix are all damned for their sins, as firmly as any of the sinners in Dante's Inferno, but now infernoes are individual and portable. The doctor is a Virgil who can guide but lacks the power to warn, a spurious priest who can hear confession but cannot absolve. Unless the imagery of hellfire is imaginatively meaningful to the critic, it does not work when Miss Barnes uses it metaphorically, and without it the novel is only an account of some sad neurotics and homosexuals who are more to be pitied than blamed.

Katherine Anne Porter similarly secularizes Christian Betrayal, the betrayal of Jesus by Judas, in the magnificent end of "Flowering Judas," where Laura dreams that the suicide Eugenio is Jesus, the warm bleeding flower on the Judas tree, betrayed to his death by herself as Judas. Much less powerfully, Muriel Spark also uses the imagery of Christian Betrayal in *The Prime of Miss Jean Brodie*, with Miss Brodie as Jesus and Sandy as Judas. If the critic does not know that the Betrayal of Jesus is at once the most atrocious and revolting of human acts, and an act entirely forewilled by God as essential to the salvation of the world, much of the irony and tension of these works dissipates.

Other novels require the critic to know some of the subtleties of Christian orthodoxy and heresy. The heresies are timeless, as Peter Drucker once reminded me, and they recur in every generation in new secular forms. I have space to mention only one orthodoxy and one heresy, but it would be useful and not too difficult to write a whole work of criticism analyzing modern literature in these theological terms. The orthodoxy I have in mind is the official position taken by the Council of Trent in the middle of the sixteenth century against the Donatist heresy, which arose in the fourth century in North Africa and was revived by the Reformation. Donatism argues that sacraments conferred by the unworthy are invalid. Following St. Augustine, the Council affirmed that these sacraments retain their validity, since their true minister is Christ. This Tridentine orthodoxy gives meaningfulness to Graham Greene's novel about a whiskey priest, *The Labyrinthine*

Ways [also known as *The Power and the Glory*], and to J. F. Powers' novel about a worldly priest, *Morte D'Urban*, and his story about a sinful and vocationless priest, "Prince of Darkness."

The heresy I have in mind is Antinomianism, the doctrine that Justification by Grace or Election frees from the Law; or, in its Marcionite form, the doctrine that Love (Christian love, Paul's *agape* of I Corinthians 13) frees from the Law. This heresy is the moral of James Gould Cozzens' *By Love Possessed*, in which love quite literally frees from the law, and it underlies all of Graham Greene's novels in which the sins men commit from motives of love will surely be forgiven. (It should surprise no one that Greene is profoundly orthodox on Donatism and profoundly heretic on Antinomianism. His consistency is not theological but sentimental, since Donatism is hard on human weakness and Antinomianism is indulgent to human weakness.)

A few works of fiction demand that the critic know Judaism similarly. The most interesting of these in our time are the novels and stories of Isaac Bashevis Singer, that remarkable late flowering of Yiddish literature. The reader without a solid grounding in Jewish Messianic beliefs and Jewish demonology will find himself lost in *Satan in Goray*. This tells how the Satanic forces, unleashed by the false messiah Sabbatai Zevi, take over and destroy the little East European Jewish *shtetl* of Goray in the seventeenth century. Singer's "The Black Wedding," in which a bride becomes convinced that she is married to a demon and is bearing a demon child, is a psychological masterpiece. It is not *only* a psychological masterpiece, however. The demons must also be understood in moral and religious terms. If they are simply reduced to the fantasies of repressed sexuality, the story is diminished by half.

The critic must equally know the age-old battle in Jewish theology between the Orthodoxy that developed out of Phariseeism in the first century, and the Reform and Enlightenment that have periodically risen up against it since, to understand

15

Singer's other two romances, *The Magician of Lublin* and *The Slave*. *The Magician of Lublin* is about Yasha Mazur, an infidel Jew and circus performer who is reconverted by misfortune and becomes Reb Jacob the Penitent, an anchorite saint. The book is thus a parable of the failure of the Enlightenment, a capitulation to Orthodoxy and the Law. *The Slave* goes the other way. Jacob, an Orthodox Jew enslaved by a Polish peasant in the seventeenth century, finds happiness married to the peasant's daughter, and deserts Orthodoxy and the Law for a universalist and ethical reform Judaism of his own devising. These two novels thus offer us the full spectrum of Judaism, an equivalent to the orthodoxies and heresies of Christianity.

Other novels require us to know the myths and rituals of Greek religion, or the myths and rituals of primitive cultures. I have written so much on the subject of myth and ritual that I do not want to discuss them here, except to note that again both a superficial and a profounder novelistic use of this material exist. Mary Renault, for example, in such "historical" novels as *The Last of the Wine*, and *The King Must Die*, fictionalizes the Theseus myth. All the critic really has to know is that one myth and its accompanying rites. But in the case of Joseph Conrad's novels, the patterns of myth and ritual are analogies of their actions: they are rites of initiation, fertility, totemic feast, purification and expiation, killing the divine king. From these rites Conrad's heroes emerge transformed and redeemed. To deal with Conrad, the critic would do well to know a great deal about myth and ritual.

In the case of comparative religion, too, some fiction appears to make demands on the critic's learning when it is really only making demands on his patience. The recent stories of J. D. Salinger are good examples of this spurious demand. "Zooey," for example, an account of the miraculous cure of Franny Glass by family love after her collapse in "Franny," offers us Salinger's Big Religious Package. This includes: the Upanishads, the Diamond Sutra, Meister Eckhart, Dr. Suzuki on *satori*, saints, *arhats*, *bodhisattvas*, *jivanmuktas*, Jesus, Gautama,

Lao-tse, Shankaracharya, Hui-neng, Sri Ramakrishna, the Four Great Vows of Buddhism, God's grace, the Jesus Prayer, *japam*, Chuang-tzu, Epictetus, Yama the God of Death, and the Bible. Zooey Glass has studied all this religious jumble, and Salinger may have, but there is no necessity for the critic to know any more about it than that its ingredients compose an indigestible goulash. These sacred symbols are decorative, not organic to the story, and they ask of the critic only that he know when he is being taken on an Eastern Flight.

Still other demands on our learning are made by twentieth-century fiction, but in these latter cases, I am afraid, my own learning is not equal to the demands, and I have to discuss these fields from a position of ignorance. The most important of them is philosophy, a subject largely beyond my comprehension. Some novels are openly based on a philosophic system, refer to it, and require the critic to be familiar with it. The dependence of Marcel Proust's *Remembrance of Things Past* on the philosophy of Henri Bergson is the obvious example here. Other novels utilize a number of philosophies, refer to them, and require the critic to be familiar with their intricacies. Thomas Mann's novels, particularly *The Magic Mountain* and *Doctor Faustus*, are cases in point.

Still a third sort of novel, however, is much trickier. It depends on an implicit philosophy, sometimes one not yet fashionable, and thus it may for a long time be misread. A case in point is André Malraux's *Man's Fate*. When this novel appeared in the Thirties, I read it, as did everyone else so far as I know, as a work inspired by revolutionary Communism, with its hero Kyo the dedicated revolutionary. Rereading *Man's Fate* now, one realizes that it never was such a work. It is and was then an Existentialist and death-obsessed novel, its revolutionary crisis only the occasion for acts of Existentialist commitment to death; and it has no hero. If one had been familiar with the philosophy of Heidegger or Jaspers then, as I was not, or even with the work of such proto-Existentialist thinkers as Kierkegaard and Nietzsche, would it not have been possible to avoid decades of misreading *Man's Fate*? No one did, to my knowledge, but the critic trained in philosophy can at least resolve to avoid similar sheepish misreadings in the future.

I think that something similar is going on in regard to the novels of Iris Murdoch, the Oxford philosophy don who writes comic novels. I suspect that such a work as *A Severed Head*, which seemed to me as it did to most of the reviewers I read, no more than an amusing game of Musical Beds, is a serious demonstration of Heraclitan flux. Since I know nothing about Heraclitan flux beyond the fact that Heraclitus said *"Panta rhei*," all flows, I am obviously not the critic for the job.

One of the things twentieth-century fiction demands of the critic is, obviously, languages. Even if, like myself, he has no skill with languages and confines himself to works written in English and to works in translation, he is never safe. I had an amusing demonstration of that fact not long ago. I reviewed a novel by an English comic novelist, Anthony Burgess. Called *A Clockwork Orange*, the book deals with a listless socialist England of the future, in which the young hoodlums take over after dark. It is a powerful and compelling inside vision of sadism, written by a hoodlum narrator. What I found most interesting about it was the "nadsat" or teenage argot used by the hoodlums, running to several hundred unfamiliar words. I devoted part of my review to complimenting Burgess on this language and explaining how, in my guess, he had formed some of the words. A good deal of ingenuity went into my explanations, and the one that gave me most satisfaction was my discovery that Burgess had obtained "yahzick" for "tongue" quite poetically, from the standard stick-out-your-tongue-and-say-*ah*-when-*zick*. As soon as my review was printed, half the population of the United States wrote to me that my ingenuity might have been better occupied. The "nadsat" words were Russian words, "nadsat" was Russian for "teen" and "yahzick" Russian for "tongue," and I had simply credited Burgess with inventing the Russian language, or tongue.

If, then, the critic must know all the major European languages, or at least enough of them to avoid such scandalous blunders, must he know all languages? Must he learn Norwegian to read Ibsen, as Joyce did, or teach himself Japanese like Seymour Glass? If, for example, he knows French well, must he learn Parisian argot to read Raymond Queneau's *Zazie?* I do not know the answers to these questions, but they are important questions just the same.

Ultimately there is no field of study that some work of literature does not demand, or that would not be useful equipment for the critic. He can hardly understand John Dos Passos' novels and their movement from I. W. W. anarchism to conservative Republicanism without some command of political science. Beneath the surface of Sinclair Lewis' *Arrowsmith* is a debate about the proper roles of the private sector of the economy and the public sector of the economy in the support of such activities as scientific research, but the reader innocent of economics will never even notice that it is there.

Sometimes, again, the demand is false. We do not have to understand modern science to deal with the novels of C. P. Snow. Snow understands modern science, but his novels are about the activities of scientists; they are not themselves embodiments of scientific thinking. On the other hand, a reader of *Labyrinths,* by the Argentine writer Jorge Luis Borges, had better know some physics and mathematics, including the paradoxes of topology, or he may never emerge from the labyrinth.

Similarly, the work of Ernest Hemingway is heavily concerned with sport: bullfighting, prize fighting, hunting and fishing, and others. But we do not need to know anything about sport beyond what Hemingway tells us. Sport is not Hemingway's subject, merely an occasion for a character's moral choice. Robert Cohn could have knocked down Pedro Romero in *The Sun Also Rises* with a shillelagh; Stanley Ketchel in "The Light of the World" could as readily have been Bronco Nagurski; Francis Macomber in "The Short

Happy Life" could have been in Africa to smuggle out Benin bronzes. In the work of Henry de Montherlant, on the other hand, sport really is central, rather than the occasion for something else, and all the necessary information is not there on the page. I cannot imagine a critic dealing with *The Bullfighters* unless he knows quite a lot about bullfighting, or dealing with Montherlant's essays unless that odd sport track-and-field is not an odd sport to him.

Some novels make no demands on our extra-literary learning. Others ask that we know one field, or two. But occasionally there is a novel so presumptuous that it insists that we know everything, and that it will remain closed to us if we do not. Think of what a work such as *Finnegans Wake* requires of us, in addition to command of the world's languages and literatures. It asks all the knowledge mentioned above, from psychoanalysis to sport, and some lores I would never have thought of: the fluvial geography of the world, the topography of Ireland, old music hall turns and popular songs, hagiography, fairy tales, jurisprudence, cookery, and about a hundred other subjects.

It is important to remember that all this knowledge is the beginning, not the end, of literary criticism. Such knowledge has its limits, as I have tried to suggest, and aesthetic truth will often transcend the truths of science or of social science. But our world is a multiverse and complex one, and our literature accurately reflects it. Unless the critic's equipment is similarly multiverse and complex, he will be turned away at the door of the work of literature, or, rather, he will be admitted to what seems to him a drafty ruin, but which reveals itself to the trained eye as Grail Castle.

1963

Ideas in Fiction

They were moved by fear or vanity, rejoiced or were indignant, reasoned, imagining that they knew what they were doing and did it of their own free will, but they all were involuntary tools of history, carrying on a work concealed from them but comprehensible to us. Such is the inevitable fate of men of action, and the higher they stand in the social hierarchy the less are they free.

The actors of 1812 have long since left the stage, their personal interests have vanished leaving no trace, and nothing remains of that time but its historic results.

Providence compelled all these men, striving to attain personal aims, to further the accomplishment of a stupendous result no one of them at all expected—neither Napoleon, nor Alexander, nor still less any of those who did the actual fighting.

WE ALL KNOW that magisterial voice, surely, explaining the role of the individual in history, in the pages of *War and Peace*. It is not Pierre's voice or Andrew's voice, but the voice of Count Leo Tolstoi, the author, interrupting his novel's action to expound his ideas.

Here is a contrasting quotation:

Even if a man were born in humble circumstances, I would require of him nevertheless that he should not be so inhuman toward himself as not to be able to think of the King's castle except at a remote distance, dreaming vaguely of its greatness and wanting at the same time to exalt it and also to abolish it by the fact that he exalted it meanly. I require of him that he should be man enough to step forward confidently and worthily even in that place. He should not be unmanly enough to desire impudently to offend everybody by rushing straight from the street into the King's hall. By that he loses more than the King. On the contrary, he should find joy in observing every rule of propriety with a glad and confident enthusiasm which will make him frank and fearless. This is only a symbol, for the difference here remarked upon is only a very imperfect expression for spiritual distance. I require of every man that he should not think so inhumanly of himself as not to dare to enter those palaces where not merely the memory of the elect abides but where the elect themselves abide. He should not press forward impudently and impute to them kinship with himself; on the contrary, he should be blissful every time he bows before them, but he should be frank and confident and always be something more than a charwoman, for if he is not more, he will never gain entrance. And what will help him is precisely the dread and distress by which the great are tried, for otherwise, if he has a bit of fibre in him, they will merely arouse his justified envy.

This is the idea revealed to us by Franz Kafka's *The Castle*. But it is nowhere stated in *The Castle*. I quote it from Soren Kierkegaard's *Fear and Trembling*, where Kafka found it. Kafka's way of saying it was to embody it dramatically in a novel.

These are the two main fashions in which ideas are expressed in fiction: explicitly and implicitly. But let us look at the matter from another angle. One of the most famous remarks in modern literary criticism is T. S. Eliot's statement about Henry James: "He had a mind so fine that no idea could violate it." I have heard this quoted as a witticism, a joke at James' expense. But the context makes it clear that Eliot means it as high praise, although his tone is not entirely earnest. Let me quote the paragraph, from Eliot's tribute to James in *The Little Review* in 1918, which he never reprinted:

James's critical genius comes out most tellingly in his mastery over, his baffling escape from, Ideas; a mastery and an escape which are perhaps the last test of a superior intelligence. He had a mind so fine that no idea could violate it. Englishmen, with their uncritical admiration (in the present age) for France, like to refer to France as the Home of Ideas; a phrase which, if we could twist it into truth, or at least a compliment, ought to mean that in France ideas are very severely looked after; not allowed to stray, but preserved for the inspection of civic pride in a Jardin des Plantes, and frugally dispatched on occasions of public necessity. England, on the other hand, if it is not the Home of Ideas, has at least become infested with them in about the space of time within which Australia has been overrun by rabbits. In England ideas run wild and pasture on the emotions; instead of thinking with our feelings (a very different thing) we corrupt our feelings with ideas; we produce the political, the emotional idea, evading sensation and thought. George Meredith (the disciple of Carlyle) was fertile in ideas; his epigrams are a facile substitute for observation and inference. Mr. Chesterton's brain swarms with ideas; I see no evidence that it thinks. James in his novels is like the best French critics in maintaining a point of view, a viewpoint untouched by the parasite idea. He is the most intelligent man of his generation.

Clearly, by "ideas" here Eliot does not mean all ideas, but a sort of ideas he dislikes: received ideas, inorganic ideas, unfelt ideas, facile ideas—products of the thought that had been divorced from feeling in the celebrated "dissociation of sensibility" in the seventeenth century. If didactic ideas about politics or religion are improper to the novel (and, we may note, the later Eliot would not have thought so), there are other kinds of ideas that are entirely proper to the novel, and James's novels are full of them.

I propose in the following remarks to discuss, not proper and improper ideas, or even those ideas about form that we call "aesthetic ideas," but some of the ways writers express ideas about human experience, about the world, in fiction, ranging from quite obvious ways to subtler and often ironic fashions. As much as possible, I have tried to avoid drawing my examples from philosophic novels. French literature has been particularly rich in this tradition, from Diderot and Rousseau to Sartre and Camus. There is no point in discussing the way philosophic novels use ideas; the ideas are the *point* of the novel, and the author is apt to be a novelist only secondarily. Instead, I shall talk about fiction that aims primarily at imaginative creation within a form.

The simplest way in which ideas appear in fiction is the author appearing onstage to state them in his own voice, as in the quotation from Tolstoi earlier. This fashion is now somewhat outmoded, but it was for a long time one of the pleasures of the novel. Jane Austen begins *Pride and Prejudice* with a "truth universally acknowledged," that any well-off bachelor surely needs a wife, and the entire novel is a comic working out of the implications of that wishful proposition. Thackeray's *Vanity Fair* concludes with the author echoing the Preacher's melancholy conclusion about the vanity of life, although Thackeray does not seem very melancholy about it. Dickens' novels contain so many ideas about society that Philip Collins recently published two specialized studies, *Dickens and Crime* and *Dickens and Education*, and enough material remains for a dozen similar volumes.

In the older fashion, the novelist would unashamedly insert an essay on any subject that interested him into his novel. Thus the Swiss novelist Gottfried Keller, writing *Green Henry* in the middle of the last century, will have his autobiographical narrator protagonist begin a chapter called "Concerning Free Will":

> Because the man stood so high in my estimation, I set myself the more zealously to reinstate my beloved Free Will, which I considered I had possessed and valiantly exercised all along. Among the few things that have been preserved from those days there is a small note-book. It contains some hasty jotting, and I am now rereading, with more diffidence but not without emotion, the pencilled pages:

He then proceeds to quote pages from Keller's notebook on the subject of freedom of the will.

In our century, novelists speak in their own voices with less abandon. Thus Sinclair Lewis describes George F. Babbitt's bathroom:

> Though the house was not large it had, like all houses on Floral Heights, an altogether royal bathroom of porcelain and glazed tile and metal sleek as silver. The towel-rack was a rod of clear glass set in nickel. The tub was long enough for a Prussian Guard, and above the set bowl was a sensational exhibit of tooth-brush holder, shaving-brush holder, soap-dish, sponge-dish, and medicine-cabinet, so glittering and so ingenious that they resembled an electrical instrument-board. But the Babbitt whose god was Modern Appliances was not pleased.

The point of the details is to convey the idea that Babbitt worships Modern Appliances, and surely they do convey it, but in the last sentence Lewis comes out and says it anyway. Sometimes the author's voice is somewhat subtler than this. Here is Evelyn Waugh in *The Loved One* describing Aimée preparing for a date with Mr. Joyboy:

> With a steady hand Aimée fulfilled the prescribed rites of an American girl preparing to meet her lover—dabbed

herself under the arms with a preparation designed to seal the sweatglands, gargled another to sweeten the breath, and brushed into her hair some odorous drops from a bottle labelled: 'Jungle Venom'—'*From the depth of the fever-ridden swamp,*' the advertisement had stated, '*where juju drums throb for the human sacrifice, Jeannette's latest exclusive creation* Jungle Venom *comes to you with the remorseless stealth of the hunting cannibal.*'

This is funny in itself, but "the prescribed rites of an American girl" is the author's voice, making sure that we recognize the satiric general in the comic particular.

Sometimes the author states his ideas, not in his own voice, but in the voice of a character or narrator not too remote from him. This was the frequent practice of Ernest Hemingway. There is a famous disillusioned passage in *A Farewell to Arms:*

I was always embarrassed by the words sacred, glorious, and sacrifice and the expression in vain. We had heard them, sometimes standing in the rain almost out of earshot, so that only the shouted words came through, and had read them, on proclamations that were slapped up by billposters over other proclamations, now for a long time, and I had seen nothing sacred, and the things that were glorious had no glory and the sacrifices were like the stockyards at Chicago if nothing was done with the meat except to bury it.

We know that this was Hemingway's view because it coincides with other statements of his on the subject. But in the novel it is not spoken by the author but by Lieutenant Henry, the narrator-protagonist, who is *not* identical with the author. Here the idea not only expresses the author, as in the earlier examples, it also serves the novelistic purpose of helping to define the character.

John Steinbeck uses two characters in sequence to articulate his ideas about society in *The Grapes of Wrath:* first the Reverend Casy, then, after Casy's death, Tom Joad; this gives the ideas an effect of complexity that they would not otherwise possess. In "Seymour—An Introduction," J. D. Salinger creates a caricature of himself, Buddy Glass, to articulate Salinger's ideas about the possibilities of sanctity in our time. On the other hand, James Purdy creates an antithesis of himself, the mass rapist Cabot Wright, in *Cabot Wright Begins,* to enable him to be nasty on a wide variety of subjects, among them J. D. Salinger. Cabot defines "New York classic fiction, *The Shepherd in the Pie, Gooey and Girly,* and the Great Boy Writer's Gentile successor, *Your Rarebit is Running*" (read *The Catcher in the Rye, Franny and Zooey,* and John Updike's *Rabbit, Run*).

Sometimes the idea is not articulated by any single character (or by any characters in succession, as in Steinbeck's case), but floats somewhere above a dramatic dialogue. In Cervantes' *Don Quixote,* Don Quixote and Sancho Panza discuss the diet proper to knights, and Sancho concludes: "Hereafter, I will stuff my saddlebags with all manner of dried fruit for your Grace, but inasmuch as I am not a knight, I shall lay in for myself a stock of fowls and other more substantial fare." Sancho is scoring off his unworldly master, but he does not speak for Cervantes. In Cervantes' view, the spirit and the flesh have equal validity, and the knight's triumphant failure is ultimately a scoring off all the worldly. When the canon attacks the books of chivalry as "false, lying, harmful, and lacking in public usefulness," and the knight passionately defends them, neither speaks for Cervantes, whose view of romance literature embraces both comic half-truths in a much larger perspective.

"You can't repeat the past," Nick Carraway tells Gatsby in *The Great Gatsby.* " 'Can't repeat the past?' he cried incredulously. 'Why of course you can!' " Of course you *can't,* as that part of Fitzgerald that is Nick knows. But there is a sense in which Gatsby *has* succeeded by an act of will in repeating the past, and that part of Fitzgerald that is Gatsby knows that you can and must, and that greatness lies in this quixotic determination. In complex novels, such as Dostoevsky's *The Brothers Karamazov*, the dialogue becomes a symposium. What the novel ultimately has to say about man's destiny and God's providences is said not by Dmitry, or Ivan, or Alyosha, but by all three of them, not to speak of Father Zossima and Smerdyakov, Christ and the Grand Inquisitor. As each idea is provisional, limited, or overstated, so the provisional, limited, and overstated ideas of the others balance and correct it.

There is one sort of novel, the *Bildungsroman* or novel of initiation into the world, in which the ideas are generally not stated by the protagonist, whether unified or split, but are stated *to* him; are fought over him in fact. Thomas Mann's *The Magic Mountain* is a classic example. The debates between Naphta and Settembrini, to win the allegiance of Hans Castorp, are not simply the intellectual exercises that they seem. Neither Naphta's Authoritarianism nor Settembrini's Liberalism is offered by Mann as true, nor is truth to arise out of any combination of them or mediation between them. Ultimately they educate Hans Castorp to go elsewhere—to the sensuality of Clavdia, the inarticulate vigor of Peeperkorn, finally to less rarified heights and the battlefield of the First World War. In this, Castorp embodies Europe and European history, and ideas in *The Magic Mountain* serve as a form of historical causation, and the test is ultimately pragmatic: not, are they true or not, but, what effect did they have?

Often ideas appear doubly in a work of fiction, dramatized in the action *and* articulated in the words. "Awakening," by the Soviet writer Isaac Babel, is a comic story of the narrator's escape from the closed Jewish world of his childhood, with its concentration on culture in an absolute denial of nature. The symbolic poles of the story are the violin lessons with Mr. Zagursky that the narrator's parents try to force him to take, and the informal instruction in swimming that he gets instead from a kindly Russian physical culturist. This antithesis of ideals is fully embodied in the story, but in addition Babel articulates it, with style and wit. He writes:

To learn to swim was my dream. I was ashamed to confess to those bronzed lads that, born in Odessa, I had not seen the sea till I was ten, and at fourteen didn't know how to swim.

How slow was my acquisition of the things one needs to know! In my childhood, chained to the Gemara, I had led the life of a sage. When I grew up I started climbing trees.

But swimming proved beyond me. The hydrophobia of my ancestors—Spanish rabbis and Frankfurt money-changers—dragged me to the bottom.

Here the implicit and the explicit support one another. In the work of less skillful writers, the explicit sometimes seems didactic. The point of John O'Hara's first novel, *Appointment in Samarra* is that you cannot evade fate, and that point is made painfully clear by the brief sad life of Julian English. But O'Hara must have felt that it was not, since the title is explained on the title page with a long parable about a man who encountered death in Bagdad and promptly fled to Samarra; Death had of course been surprised to see him in Bagdad, since she had an appointment in Samarra with him that evening. We get a similar crude underlining of the idea in the title of George Orwell's *Nineteen Eighty-four*. The novel warns: This is the nature and power of totalitarianism. The title shrieks: Watch out, here it comes!

Sometimes the idea is fully dramatized in the work of fiction but never articulated, as Kafka used Kierkegaard's idea in *The Castle*. This is the fashion in which James characteristically allowed his mind and work to be violated by ideas (although he *is* sometimes explicit about them, as in Strether's life-affirmation to Little Bilham in *The Ambassadors*). A good example is the main idea in *The Wings of the Dove*, the ironic nature of sacrifice. Milly Theale, the dove, dies in a passion of sacrificial goodness, leaving her beloved, Merton Densher, the wealth that will enable him to marry her rival, Kate Croy. But the beautiful selflessness of the gesture itself comes between the

survivors and makes their marriage unlikely, and Milly's pure
sacrifice for their happiness may turn out to be the only thing
that could have won Densher away from Kate. "We shall
never be again as we were!" Kate says ruefully in the last line
of the novel. Nowhere in the novel does James state his ideas
about the effects of perfect sacrifice in an imperfect world (the
Christian analogy is obvious); the action states them.

A similar theme is rather differently treated in a novella, "A
Portrait of Shunkin," by the Japanese master Junichiro Tanizaki. Shunkin is a blind female musician, cruel and imperious,
and Sasuke is her devoted male disciple. When Shunkin is
horribly disfigured by an enemy as she sleeps, Sasuke blinds
himself with a sewing needle in order never to see her as less
than beautiful, and to join her in isolation. What does Tanizaki think of the ironies of such a sacrifice? We are never told,
except insofar as the monstrosity of the act tells us. Instead,
the narrator of the novella, who is not Tanizaki but a rather
simple-minded person, concludes his tale:

> It seems that when the priest Gazan of the Tenryu
> Temple heard the story of Sasuke's self-immolation, he
> praised him for the Zen spirit with which he changed his
> whole life in an instant, turning the ugly into the beauti-
> ful, and said that it was very nearly the act of a saint. I
> wonder how many of us would agree with him.

Another ironic way of presenting ideas in novels is to imply
them by stating their opposites. This requires a community of
assumption with the reader that cannot always be assumed. In
Stendhal's *The Charterhouse of Parma*, Conte Mosca explains
to the Duchessa Sanseverina:

> The essential quality of a young man of the present day,
> that is to say for the next fifty years perhaps, so long as we
> remain in a state of fear and religion has not been reestab-
> lished, is not to be liable to enthusiasm and not to show
> any spirit.

In addition to making a point about Mosca, Stendhal wants the reader to understand from this remark that precisely what the times require are young men liable to enthusiasm and showing spirit: bolder and more successful Fabrizios, in fact. (Stendhal was so little sure of that community of assumption that he saw himself as writing for our century rather than his, and he dedicated *The Charterhouse*, at the end, "To the Happy Few" who would understand.)

Mark Twain, perhaps rightly, had more faith in his readers. A famous scene in *Huckleberry Finn* states its idea in just this fashion. It is Huck meditating about helping to free Jim from slavery. He thinks:

> It would get around that Huck Finn helped a nigger to get his freedom; and if I was ever to see anybody from that town again I'd be ready to get down and lick his boots for shame. That's just the way: a person does a low-down thing, and then he don't want to take no consequences of it.

Helping Jim, he concludes, is not only shameful and low-down, it is wicked and sinful. Huck decides to "do the right thing and the clean thing." He writes Miss Watson telling her where Jim can be found, and after that: "I felt good and all washed clean of sin for the first time I had ever felt so in my life, and I knowed I could pray now." But he gets to thinking about Jim's humanity and kindness, he weakens, and he topples back into the pit. "All right, then, I'll *go* to hell," he thinks, and tears up the letter. It is uproarious, but it is profoundly serious in addition. In a comic transvaluation of values, the scene not only reveals Twain's true ideas about slavery and humanity, but it comments on the civilization and the Christianity that have taught Huck to call his humane impulses shameful and sinful, and to call enslaving and betraying, acts of Christian virtue.

Graham Greene is another writer fond of this sort of negative statement. His whiskey priest in *The Labyrinthine Ways* dies affirming the cowardice, uselessness and inadequacy of his life and death, which is Greene's way of assuring us that the priest was a brave martyr and perhaps a saint. Similarly, in Flannery O'Connor's *Wise Blood*, we have Hazel Mote's creation of a Church Without Christ. "I believe in a new kind of jesus," he says, "one that can't waste his blood redeeming people with it because he's all man and ain't got any God in him." In Hazel Mote's life and death, with no word of comment, Miss O'Connor affirms another blood that redeems and atones, another Jesus who incarnates God, and a Church *with* Christ (not unlike the Roman Catholic Church) that is institutionally able to contain and channel the burning and, in her view, entirely authentic divine calls that tear apart such prophets as Hazel or Tarwater in *The Violent Bear It Away*.

Sometimes the idea in a novel is so complex and profound that it cannot be stated, only symbolized. The best example of this in our fiction, perhaps, is the white whale in *Moby-Dick*. The entire book is devoted to defining the meaning of the whale. A chapter called "The Whiteness of the Whale" explores the ambiguities of his color, at once evil and innocent, and contrasts them with the more reassuring ambiguities of the blackness of darkness earlier. The chapters of whaling lore tell us endlessly about the nature and destiny of whales. We learn the meanings of Moby Dick for Ahab, for Ishmael, for everyone on the Pequod. (In a miniature of this movement, the chapter called "The Doubloon" shows us characters from Ahab to Pip staring at the gold doubloon that Ahab has nailed to the mast and projecting their own meanings into its design, as one projects meanings into a Rorschach blot.) Ultimately, what is *Melville*'s idea embodied in the great white whale? All of these meanings, and many others; it is an idea so complex that it cannot be paraphrased, or expressed in any vocabulary but the symbolism in which it is expressed. Other examples of ideas in fiction that have too complex an intellectual content to be readily paraphrasable are the symbol of the snow in Joyce's novella "The Dead," and, in recent fiction, the female principle V. in Thomas Pynchon's novel of that name.

Less complex ideas in fiction are often suggested in a key image or word, even in a pun. In Ralph Ellison's *Invisible Man*, there is a New York scene in which the narrator buys a hot buttered yam from a street seller for a dime. He thinks about his sudden reversion to the Southern foods of his childhood, and the shame felt by educated Northern Negroes at their secret fondness for chitterlings or hog maws. "They're my birthmark," he tells the yam seller, ordering two more. "I yam what I am!" In the pun of "yam" and "I am," there is far more than an admission of "low" eating habits; there is a whole symbolic acceptance of Negro identity, along with an existentialist idea about essence arising out of existence.

There is a comparable scene in John Updike's *The Centaur*. George Caldwell is lecturing on evolution to a high school class:

. . . the volvox, of these early citizens in the kingdom of life, interests us because he invented death. There is no reason intrinsic in the plasmic substance why life should ever end. Amoebas never die; and those male sperm cells which enjoy success become the cornerstone of new life that continues beyond the father. But the volvox, a rolling sphere of flagellating algae organized into somatic and reproductive cells, neither plant nor animal—under a microscope it looks just like a Christmas ball—by pioneering this new idea of *cooperation*, rolled life into the kingdom of certain—as opposed to accidental—death. For—hold tight kids, just seven more minutes of torture—while each cell is potentially immortal, by volunteering for a specialized function within an organized society of cells, it enters a compromised environment. The strain eventually wears it out and kills it. It dies sacrificially, for the good of the whole. These first cells who got tired of sitting around

33

forever in a blue-green scum and said, 'Let's get together and make a volvox,' were the first altruists. The first do-gooders. If I had a hat on, I'd take it off to 'em.

This is a respectable theory, Wallace's and Weismann's idea of death as an advantageous evolutionary adaption, with a touch of Prince Kropotkin's concept of mutual aid. But the volvox also images Caldwell, altruist and do-gooder: the self-sacrificing teacher who dies to free his son Peter, and is simultaneously the noble centaur Chiron, dying in place of Prometheus. And how nicely the word "volvox" (from the Latin "volvere," to roll) suggests other resonances: "will" and "voice" in Latin, "flight" in French, the sacrificial ox turning on the spit in English.

There is another such scene in Nathanael West's *Miss Lonelyhearts:* the idyllic weekend that the title figure and Betty spend in a farmhouse in Connecticut, in the course of which he deflowers her. It is Miss Lonelyhearts' only experience of happiness in the novel, and perhaps, the reader hopes, Betty's innocence and goodness can save him. But Miss Lonelyhearts is Fallen Man, and Fallen Man cannot return to Edenic innocence except through Christ's Atonement. How does West tell us this? Before Miss Lonelyhearts and Betty go to sleep, they eat an apple; when they wake in the morning, she serves him, among other things, fried apples. After breakfast he drives to town and stops for gas, where he tells the attendant about seeing some deer at the pond. "The man said that there was still plenty of deer at the pond because no yids ever went there. He said it wasn't the hunters who drove out the deer, but the yids." This is the evil of a Fallen world, but beyond that it continues the apple joke: the yids who spoil Paradise, who drive out the "dear," are of course Adam and Eve.

Some of the purest fiction has as its only idea a general statement about life. One of Anton Chekhov's stories, "The Lady with the Pet Dog," introduces its married protagonist, Dmitry Dmitrich Gurov, in the first pages as a man who knows that any extramarital affair "inevitably ends by introducing excessively complicated problems, and creating intolerable situations." In the course of the story he and the married lady of the title have such an affair and fall desperately and tragically in love. In the last sentence of the story we are told: "to both of them it was clear that the end was still very far away, and the hardest and most difficult part was only beginning." Gurov has only learned what he knew before the story began, but he has learned it in a far deeper and more shattering fashion, and we have learned it with him. This is what the story tells us; it is Chekhov's "idea": that life is very hard, and joy unlikely. Put in those words, it is the tawdriest of commonplaces; embodied in Chekhov's story, it is a blinding revelation.

Some ambitious novels use ideas in *all* these fashions. Joyce's *Ulysses* is one such. Stephen is sometimes used to state Joyce's ideas in Joyce's own voice, as in his theory of *Hamlet*. Joyce expresses his own ideas in another character's voice when Buck Mulligan mocks Yeats for sycophantism or Synge for parochialism. Joyce lets his ideas emerge dialectically in the dialogues between Stephen and Leopold Bloom, and he develops them dramatically, with Stephen and Bloom as audience, in the Nighttown scene. He dramatizes the idea that Bloom is an embodiment of Jesus, when Bloom preaches love instead of hate in Barney Kiernan's saloon, then he states it, when Bloom is hailed as the Messiah and ascends to heaven, "like a shot off a shovel," at the end of the chapter. He dramatizes other ideas, such as having John Henry Menton parody that silence of Ajax in Hades that Longinus found "sublime," without articulating them. He expresses ideas by their opposites, as when Mulligan says that Stephen's wits were driven astray by threats of hell at school, and that consequently "He will never capture the Attic note." (How better to capture the Attic note than to rewrite *The Odyssey* for our time?) Joyce expresses complex and unparaphrasable ideas, such as the mystic consubstantiality of father and son, in symbolic form in the book, and suggests an infinitude of others in image and pun: a typical example is the "Yooka . . . Yook . . . Ook" sequence at the end of the hospital chapter, the "chap puking" that probably represents Joyce's comment on the present state of the language. And *Ulysses* contains some ideas that are, like Chekhov's, pure generalizations about life: I take Molly's Yes to be the most important of these.

Finally, there are works of fiction that do not *contain* ideas but *consist* of ideas. Laurence Sterne's *Tristram Shandy* is one such: the cascading ideas are not digressions from the story, they *are* the story. In our time, Vladimir Nabokov has published two extraordinary examples of this form. One is *The Gift*, the last of his novels written in Russian. Nabokov considerably understates the case in the foreword to the English translation:

> Its heroine is not Zina, but Russian Literature. The plot of Chapter One centers in Fyodor's poems. Chapter Two is a surge toward Pushkin in Fyodor's literary progress and contains his attempt to describe his father's zoological explorations. Chapter Three shifts to Gogol, but its real hub is the love poem dedicated to Zina. Fyodor's book on Chernyshevski, a spiral within a sonnet, takes care of Chapter Four. The last chapter combines all the preceding themes and adumbrates the book Fyodor dreams of writing some day: *The Gift*.

The Gift thus consists primarily of ideas about Russian literature, literary criticism, but it is a novel nevertheless, and an extraordinarily fine one.

Pale Fire, written in English, is even more remarkable. In appearance it is a 999-line poem by John Shade, with a foreword and extensive commentary by Charles Kinbote, who claims to be the deposed king of Zembla, and turns out to be a mad Russian faculty member named Botkin. Poem and apparatus, even the index, create Kinbote's paranoid schizophrenia, and through that distorting lens, create the reader's understanding of the true life and death of John Shade. The novel is at once the finest spoof of literary criticism that I know, a profound discourse on illusion and reality, and a moving story about people, a true novel. *The Gift* and *Pale Fire*, these fictions of literary criticism, continually threaten to shatter the novel form, but they ultimately turn out to be revolutionary enlargements of it.

Here, then, are some of the forms in which ideas appear in fiction, and some of their range of possibility: ideas about towel-racks, simple diets, learning to swim, writing a letter, committing adultery; ideas about destiny, grace, freedom, identity, and sacrifice.

Let me conclude with a word of warning, and an example. A few years ago Ignazio Silone published a short novel, *The Fox and the Camellias*, which turned out to be a rewriting of his fine short story of the 1930s, "The Trap." It was rewritten to accord with his present views, which are Christian and compassionate as they were formerly Marxist and militant, and in the process the story was hopelessly ruined. Silone has similarly rewritten such early novels as *Fontamara* and *Bread and Wine*, to bring them into line with his recent thinking, to their considerable diminishment. The work of art may express ideas, but its integrity *as* a work of art, a formal organization, is primary, and its ideas are secondary. These ideas may be true or false, significant or trivial; it is ultimately as an artifact of the imagination, a created thing, that the novel lives at all.

1964

Eight Propositions about
Literature and Society

1.   The best literature today is negative and nay-saying, whatever the mood of the times. The three finest American novels of our century, in my opinion—Fitzgerald's *The Great Gatsby*, Hemingway's *The Sun Also Rises*, and West's *Miss Lonelyhearts*—have in common a lost and victimized hero, a bitter sense of our civilization's falsity, a pervasive melancholy atmosphere of failure and defeat—although the first two were written in the booming 20s, and the third in the busted 30s. This has been no less true in the Soviet Union, where the best writers—Isaac Babel, Yuri Olyesha, Boris Pilnyak, Osip Mandelstam—have utterly neglected the glorious building of socialism, to chronicle instead the same victimization, falsity, and defeat.

2.   Our literature does not express the advanced social ethics of our time. As our ethical ideals become increasingly humanitarian, globally responsible, and equalitarian, our best poets—Yeats, Eliot, Pound, Rilke, Valery—have been aristocrats, monarchists, reactionaries, even fascists.

3.   The writer's primary interest in economics lies in finding some way to earn his living by writing. Any preoccupation with the subject beyond that will tend to encourage him to make a fool of himself, after the example of the left-wing writers of the 30s or of Ezra Pound.

4. The writer is concerned with politics only in his role as a citizen. In his role as a writer, he must subject even his own political views to the ruthless criticism inherent in a dramatic approach. Thus Leopold Bloom in *Ulysses* faithfully reflects Joyce's own political liberalism and social optimism, but in the novel these views get battered with mockery and corroded in irony, and our final impression of them is that they are admirable but absurd.

5. To the extent that the creative writer is involved with theology—and in our time this is only to a very small extent—it will not tend to be advanced or liberal theology, but radical dualism—everything not Christ's is anti-Christ's—of Dostoevsky or Flannery O'Connor, or the crabbed and sour Jansenism of Mauriac. This may result from the same sort of temperamental accident that made our best poets reactionaries, or it may be that bigoted and extreme theologies possess a built-in dramatism suitable for literature, one not possessed by an emphasis on God's grace, Christ's love, or de-mythologizing.

6. The important influence that contemporary society exercises on the writer is not to shape his approach, but to furnish his subject matter and language. The promising first novels of the 60s—Walker Percy's *The Moviegoer*, Bruce Jay Friedman's *Stern*, Thomas Pynchon's *V.*, Wallace Markfield's *To an Early Grave*—boldly confront the world of the 60s in the language of the 60s, but they see only the imagery of neurotic withdrawal, paranoid self-hatred, random yo-yoing through the world without ties or responsibilities, ludicrous pseudo-culture; in general, bad human relations on the edge of thermonuclear abyss. They do not see an American Century or a Great Society.

7. There is a sense in which all serious literature, however topical, is timeless. Stevie Smith's "Not Waving But Drowning," in its loose metrics and off-rhyming could only

have been written in our century, but its metaphor—a man in the water—is universal and timeless:

> *Nobody heard him, the dead man,*
> *But still he lay moaning:*
> *I was much further out than you thought*
> *And not waving but drowning.*
>
> *Poor chap, he always loved larking*
> *And now he's dead*
> *It must have been too cold for him his heart gave way,*
> *They said.*
>
> *Oh, no no no, it was too cold always*
> *(Still the dead one lay moaning)*
> *I was much too far out all my life*
> *And not waving but drowning.*

Here is another, "Love Song For An Avocado Plant," by the young American poet Donald Finkel. Its language is the language of 1966, but its myth is as ancient and eternal as that of Apollo and Daphne:

> *Once maybe a man could marry a plant.*
> *Nowadays, though he bow and sprinkle before one,*
> *the rites and prayers have lost their ancient sense:*
> *he goes about the business like a plumber.*
>
> *How tall she was, and fecund, how heavy with fruit,*
> *though taste of paradisal flesh is faint*
> *on a dusty tongue.*
>   *(Except for the chirimoya,*
> *which smells faintly of puke: ghost-puke: angel puke:*
> *the holy original bitch was revolted by nothing.)*
>
> *And still she deigns to blossom in this province*
> *of variable weather, fall and dust.*
> *(How pale so far from paradise, and faint!)*

I prod the soil at her feet, as if she might,
for all my shy caressing, rise with me.

In the country of the dead, the leper is queen:
I bring her drink, I brush the dust from her shoulders;
the two of us quake in the thin December sun.

8.   The only social responsibility that the writer has, as a writer, is to tell the truth.

1966

II

The Handle:
Invitation to a Beheading
and Bend Sinister

I N HIS FOREWORD to the English translation of *Invitation to a Beheading* in 1959, Vladimir Nabokov writes: "No doubt, there do exist certain stylistic links between this book and, say, my earlier stories (or my later *Bend Sinister*)." Precisely what he meant by stylistic links is puzzling, since the books are radically different in style, at least in English, but as many have noticed, they do have a theme in common, what we might call the vulgarity of power, and they make a fascinating study in conjunction.

Invitation to a Beheading was written in Russian in Berlin in 1934 and 1935, and published in Paris in 1938 as *Priglashenie na kazn'*. It is the story of Cincinnatus C., who is sentenced to beheading for "gnostical turpitude" by a comic-opera totalitarian state on the first page, and beheaded on the next to last page, after spending the intervening time in a prison that is at once horribly funny and horrible.

Cincinnatus is the weakest and most fragile of heroes, and the author properly calls him "My poor little Cincinnatus." When he hears the sentence, Nabokov writes:

> He was calm; however, he had to be supported during the journey through the long corridor, since he planted his feet unsteadily, like a child who has just learned to walk, or as if he were about to fall through like a man who has

dreamt that he is walking on water only to have a sudden doubt: but is this possible?

Cincinnatus is "light as a leaf," and so small that his wife Marthe "used to say that his shoes were too tight for her." He is illegitimate, never having known his father and scarcely knowing his mother. Cincinnatus is brave in fantasy—at one point his imaginary double steps on the jailer's face—but in reality he is a coward, dying "anew every morning" as he awaits his execution. He cries in his cell; when he is finally led to his execution his hands tremble uncontrollably, and he feels "only one thing—fear, fear, shameful, futile fear." His marriage with Marthe consisted of her tireless cuckolding of him, telling him about it "in a soft cooing voice" each time, and neither of her awful children is his. Finally, he is wishfully gullible: when his lawyer brings him a petition to obtain printed copies of the speeches made at his trial, and Cincinnatus bravely tears it up, the lawyer has only to suggest that the envelope may have contained a pardon, and Cincinnatus is down on the floor, trying to put together the scraps.

Yet with all these physical and moral weaknesses, Cincinnatus has certain strengths. When he is shorn of all other resources, like Ransom's Captain Carpenter, he still has his valiant tongue. Cincinnatus tells his jailers: "I obey you, specters, werewolves, parodies"; he announces to the prison director: "I thank you, rag doll, coachman, painted swine"; he curtly dismisses a monologue by M'sieur Pierre, his fellow inmate who turns out to be the headsman, as "Dreary, obtrusive nonsense." Beyond that, he has two further strengths: he feels "a fierce longing for freedom, the most ordinary, physical, physically feasible kind of freedom"; and he accepts the solitary human condition, so that during all the stages of the execution, Cincinnatus keeps affirming: "By myself, by myself."

The prison and the prison experience are fantastic, phantasmagoric. At one point Cincinnatus moves a table in his cell and stands on a chair on it in order to look out the window; at another point he discovers that the table has been bolted to the floor "for ages," and could never have been moved. Later the cell bulges and floods, Cincinnatus' cot becomes a boat, and he falls into the water and would have drowned except that he is fished out. Throughout the jail experience, the prison director, the doctor, the jailer, and Cincinnatus' lawyer keep turning into each other. At one point, when M'sieur Pierre is doing acrobatic tricks, the cell turns into a circus, and the prison director becomes the ringmaster. Increasingly, everything becomes a theatrical production. "A summer thunderstorm, simply and tastefully staged, was performed outside." When Cincinnatus' mother visits him, he charges that she is "a clever parody of a mother, notes that her raincoat is wet although her shoes are dry, and adds, "Tell the prop man for me." When Emmie, the prison director's young daughter, visits Cincinnatus in his cell, she whispers moistly into his ear, then flies off on a trapeze, leaving his ear wet and singing. The cell spider that had been his companion turns out to be spurious, made of plush with spring legs, and the jailer had built its webs for it.

As Cincinnatus leaves the prison for his execution, it disintegrates: first his cell disappears as he leaves it, then other cells crumble, next the whole fortress starts to come apart. The same clouds go by over and over again, clearly a stage setting. There is "something wrong with the sun, and a section of the sky was shaking," behind the first rows, the crowds at the execution are painted on the backdrop, and the poplars around the square topple one by one. By the book's last paragraph, it has all disintegrated:

> Little was left of the square. The platform had long since collapsed in a cloud of reddish dust. The last to rush past was a woman in a black shawl, carrying the tiny executioner like a larva in her arms. The fallen trees lay flat and reliefless, while those that were still standing, also two-dimensional, with a lateral shading of the trunk to suggest roundness, barely held on with their branches to

the ripping mesh of the sky. Everything was coming apart. Everything was falling. A spinning wind was picking up and whirling: dust, rags, chips of painted wood, bits of gilded plaster, pasteboard bricks, posters, an arid gloom fleeted.

The microcosm of this macrocosmic unreality is a series of cruelly funny sadistic tricks played on Cincinnatus while he is in jail. Early in the novel Cincinnatus finds everything unguarded and walks out of the jail. He walks through the town, gets to his house, runs up the stairs to his apartment, opens the door and finds himself back in his cell. The prison director promises him a visit from his wife and family, and as Cincinnatus quivers with joy and anticipation, ushers in M'sieur Pierre instead. In the cruelest of all the tricks, Cincinnatus hears another prisoner tunneling to him, he taps rhythmically to communicate with the tunneler, makes sounds to mask the sounds of digging from the guards—finally the tunnel breaks through into the wall of his cell, and M'sieur Pierre and the prisoner director climb out of the hole, shaking "with unrestrained laughter, with all the transitions from guffaw to chuckle and back again, with piteous squeals in the intervals between outbursts, all the while nudging each other, falling over each other," Cincinnatus' reaction to this kindly practical joke is "such terrible unmitigated dejection that . . . he would have lain down and died then and there." Later he escapes again and gets out on the hillside below the fortress, where he meets Emmie, who had promised to help him to freedom, and promptly leads him to her father's apartment, where the prison director and M'sieur Pierre are having tea. Just before the execution, Cincinnatus makes a list of all the things that have tricked him:

"Everything has fallen into place," he wrote, "that is, everything has duped me—all of this theatrical, pathetic stuff—the promises of a volatile maiden, a mother's moist gaze, the knocking on the wall, a neighbor's friendliness, and, finally, those hills which broke out in a deadly rash.

But Cincinnatus has one ultimate strength, which foreshadows his final triumph: his absolute isolation. He writes:

> . . . in the end the logical thing would be to give up and I would give up if I were laboring for a reader existing today, but as there is in the world not a single human who can speak my language; or, more simply, not a single human; I must think only of myself, of that force which urges me to express myself.

At the end, after he is beheaded, he stands up and walks away, as a tiny figure who is both his lawyer and the prison director reproaches him; then, "amidst the dust, and the falling things, and the flapping scenery, Cincinnatus made his way in that direction where, to judge by the voices, stood beings akin to him."

Bend Sinister was written in English and first published in the United States in 1947. It tells the story of Adam Krug, distinguished philosopher and professor in an unnamed small Slavic country, who refuses his assent to the new dictator, who was his schoolfellow, and the increasing pressures that are brought on Krug until he is finally delivered by madness and death. The title is mysterious. "Bend Sinister" is a turn to the left (in *The Real Life of Sebastian Knight*, the narrator speaks of "following the bends of his life"); it is the mark of a bastard in heraldry, and it has the dangerous suggestions of the English "sinister." I think I have some idea what the title means, but I will postpone discussion of it until later.

Krug is as visibly strong as Cincinnatus is visibly weak. He is an enormous man, confident and self-assured. When the President of his university presents a petition of support for the dictator to his faculty, only Krug refuses to sign, remarking disdainfully: "Legal documents excepted, and not all of them at that, I have never signed, nor ever shall sign, anything not written by myself." When the dictator, Paduk, whose schoolboy name was "the Toad," has Krug in for an interview, and asks rhetorically why he wanted to see Krug, Krug replies: "Because I am the only person who can stand on the other end of the seesaw and make your end rise." When he is finally brought to agree to sign a statement of support in hopes of saving his young son, the news of his son's death frees the old Krug, and he tears up the papers and tries to strangle the nearest clerk. Krug is further strengthened by his international fame: he is the only celebrity that his country has produced in modern times. He has a number of loyal and incorruptible friends, one described as "reliable as iron and oak." He is devoted to the ideal of freedom and collects inanities of the dictatorship for the "delight of free humorists" of the future. He has an exceptionally powerful brain, an unusual virility, and is so much a man of action that he not only tries to strangle the clerk, but earlier punched a government official in the mouth. Most of all, he is deeply loving, devoted to his wife, who dies early in the book following an unsuccessful kidney operation, and to his young son David.

Many of Krug's strengths turn out to be weaknesses in the morally inverted world of the dictatorship. His intellectual pride, which leads him to regard most people as "imbeciles," makes him unable to take the dictator and his popular support seriously. The philosophical complexity of his mind leads him to hesitate and delay, so that he does not escape the country when he could. His powerful imagination leads him to picture David endlessly tortured and suffering. His loyal friends are ways that pressure can be put on him, and his consuming love for David, now that his wife is dead, is his ultimate vulnerability: "And what agony, thought Krug the thinker, to love so madly a little creature."

Bend Sinister has some of the shoddy trickery of *Invitation to a Beheading*. When Ember, the first of Krug's friends to be arrested to put pressure on Krug, is seized, it is not by uniformed security police with carbines, but by "A handsome lady in a dove-gray tailor-made suit and a gentleman with a glossy red tulip in the buttonhole of his cutaway coat." The gentleman explains to Krug: "But headquarters knew that Mr. Ember was an artist, a poet, a sensitive soul, and it was thought that something a little dainty and uncommon in the way of arrests, an atmosphere of high life, flowers, the perfume of feminine beauty, might sweeten the ordeal." As M'sieur Pierre does card tricks and gymnastics, and tries to coax Cincinnatus into endless games, so Krug finds in the dictator's waiting room "various games of skill." Paduk has in fact turned the country's public ceremonials into reproductions of his school life.

A denial of reality comparable to that of *Invitation to a Beheading* runs through *Bend Sinister*. Describing Paduk, the author interrupts to say: "It is not a difficult part but still the actor must be careful not to overdo what Graaf somewhere calls 'villainous deliberation.' " As for Krug, receiving his prepared speech from Paduk: "The actor playing the recipient should be taught not to look at his hand while he takes the papers *very slowly* (keeping those lateral jaw muscles in movement, please) but to stare straight at the giver: in short, look at the giver first, *then* lower your eyes to the gift." At one point, when Krug gets home and goes into the bathroom, he finds Mariette, the maid who is a police spy and has been trying to seduce him, standing naked in the tub soaping herself. He then orders dinner from a caterer, and "She was still in the bathroom when the man from the Angliskii Club brought a meat pie, a rice pudding, and her adolescent buttocks." In Krug's notes for philosophical articles, there is "the instantaneous disintegration of stone and ivy composing the circular dungeon," as at the end of *Invitation to a Beheading*, but here it is either a metaphor for death as the instantaneous gaining of perfect knowledge, or for death as absolute nothingness.

The author is obtrusive in *Invitation to a Beheading*, calling his hero "My poor little Cincinnatus" and such, but in *Bend*

Sinister he is a godlike chess player who controls all the pieces on both sides. Krug has the selective mishearing of the preoccupied: when the President of the university makes a speech and says "when an animal has lost his feet in the aging ocean," Krug is mishearing "when an admiral has lost his fleet in the raging ocean"; when Krug reads in the speech written for him that "the State has created central organs for providing the country with all the most important products which are to be distributed at fixed prices in a playful manner," he then realizes it is a "planful" manner and corrects himself. But perhaps the original versions were right: the animal who lost his feet, or at least his toes, is Lear's Pobble, whose Aunt Jobiska could have saved Krug from a lot of his difficulty, and a "playful manner" is exactly the way the never-grown-up schoolboy Paduk would distribute goods.

The book begins with Krug seeing a curious oblong puddle on the asphalt, and ends with the author seeing it, observing that Krug had somehow perceived it earlier, and translating it into a symbol of the imprint left by a human life. Krug recalls his dead wife, as a young girl, carrying a hawk moth into the house to show to her aunt, and in his vision he directs and redirects the scene. Later, Peter Quist, a police agent who is pretending to help Krug flee the country, shows him a beautiful plate of a hawk moth. At the book's end, as Krug dies, shot by the dictator's gunmen, the author hears a hawk moth, perhaps Krug's soul, strike the netting of his window. The last words of the book are: "Twang. A good night for mothing." Earlier, when Krug's son David is seized, Krug threatens "All six of you, all six will be tortured and shot if my child gets hurt." It is the emptiest of threats, with no authority behind it but the force of rhetoric, but it has the power of fate and doom: when David is killed, all six of them are precisely tortured and shot. Finally, the author explains his direct intervention in the story as a Greek *deus ex machina*. David is dead and Krug is locked in jail, awakening from a dream. The narrator writes:

It was at that moment, just after Krug had fallen through the bottom of a confused dream and sat up on the straw with a gasp—and just before his reality, his remembered hideous misfortune could pounce upon him—it was then that I felt a pang of pity for Adam and slid towards him along an inclined beam of pale light—causing instantaneous madness, but at least saving him from the senseless agony of his logical fate.

It is thus mad that Krug attacks Paduk (heroically, insanely?) and is gunned down.

Cincinnatus and Krug, in short, have different sorts of commitment to the world. Their families are a case in point. Cincinnatus, who has no family of his own other than the mother he has seen once or twice in his life, is finally visited by Marthe's family in his cell. They arrive with all their furniture and set up domestic life there: Marthe's maternal grandfather, so old that he is transparent, exhibits a portrait of his mother as a young woman, in turn holding a portrait; Marthe's father curses Cincinnatus "in detail and with relish"; one of Marthe's brothers wears a crepe arm band and makes up word games to remind Cincinnatus of his coming fate; Marthe is accompanied by a young suitor perfumed with violet scent; Cincinnatus' subnormal non-daughter Pauline hides, and his lame non-son Diomedon strangles the cat. In contrast to this disgusting family, to whom one could feel no attachment, Krug's wife was a paragon of gaiety and charm (she once hung a Chardin in his study "to ozonize your dreadful lair") and his son is all that anyone could want in a son.

This contrast comes through most clearly in parallel images of disintegration in the books. On one occasion in his cell Cincinnatus starts to undress and comes apart:

He stood up and took off the dressing gown, the skullcap, the slippers. He took off the linen trousers and shirt. He took off his head like a toupee, took off his collarbones like shoulder straps, took off his rib cage like a hauberk. He took off his hips and his legs, he took off his arms like gauntlets and threw them in a corner. What was left of him gradually dissolved, hardly coloring the air. At first Cincinnatus simply reveled in the coolness; then, fully immersed in his secret medium, he began freely and happily to . . . The iron thunderclap of the bolt resounded, and Cincinnatus instantly grew all that he had cast off, the skullcap included.

When Krug has a comparable fantasy it is not free and joyous but a horrible nightmare about his late wife:

Olga was revealed sitting before her mirror and taking off her jewels after the ball. Still clad in cherry-red velvet, her strong gleaming elbows thrown back and lifted like wings, she had begun to unclasp at the back of her neck her dazzling dog collar. He knew it would come off together with her vertebrae—that in fact it was the crystal of her vertebrae—and he experienced an agonizing sense of impropriety at the thought that everybody in the room would observe and take down in writing her inevitable, pitiful, innocent disintegration. There was a flash, a click: with both hands she removed her beautiful head and, not looking at it, carefully, carefully, dear, smiling a dim smile of amused recollection (who could have guessed at the dance that the real jewels were pawned?), she placed the beautiful imitation upon the marble ledge of her toilet table. Then he knew that all the rest would come off too, the rings together with the fingers, the bronze slippers with the toes, the breasts with the lace that cupped them . . . his pity and shame reached their climax, and at the ultimate gesture of the tall cold strip-teaser, prowling puma-like up and down the stage, with a horrible qualm Krug awoke.

The difference, in a word, is that Cincinnatus is free because he has no hostages to fortune, and Krug, at least until David is murdered, is the prisoner of his ties to others. "Will no one save me?" Cincinnatus suddenly cries out in his cell, "opening his pauper's hands, showing that he had nothing." Since no one *will* save him, he can blithely save himself. In all his time in jail he receives only two gifts: his mother brings him a pound of candy to suck, which he ignores, and Marthe brings him a bunch of cornflowers, which she refers to as poppies. Krug, however, has real human ties: deep down inside him "a dead wife and a sleeping child," and his loyal friends who risk (and lose) their lives for him. But the key to his vulnerability is David. Near the end of his interview with Paduk, the dictator says: "All we want of you is that little part where the handle is." "There is none," Krug answers firmly, "and hit the side of the table with his fist." When the police agent Quist discovers that Krug will not leave the country without David, he realizes that *David* is the handle, and knows that the discovery will result in his promotion. "They have found the handle," the author comments when the police seize David, and in truth Krug is soon in the prison office, offering to "speak, sign, swear—anything the Government wants. But I will do all this, and more, only if my child is brought here, to this room, at once."

What the title finally means, I think, after all its obvious meanings, is the curve of that handle. "Krug" in German means some sort of liquid measure or tankard (it means "wide" in Russian), and at first it is brimming with blessings, but the bend of the handle is its dangerous vulnerability.

Beyond that, Krug is of the world, committed to its things and values, whereas Cincinnatus is in it but not of it. Cincinnatus' trade is that of a doll-maker, and the unreality (or other-reality) of his work is a further source of strength. "I am an expert in dolls," he says to M'sieur Pierre at one point, "I shall not yield." But Krug's professorship anchors him firmly to this world, in that his work relates him to real people: students, colleagues, readers. Even the tiny details of their torments by the state contrast: in his cell Cincinnatus is served toast "with tortoise shell burns," giving the simple food a kind of elegance. But when Krug looks at a railroad track and pictures escape, here is his vision: "On some bricks nearby the mournful detective assigned to his house and an organ-grinder of sorts sat playing *chemin de fer;* a soiled nine of spades lay on the ash-strewn ground at their feet, and, with a pang of impatient desire, he visualized a railway platform and glanced at a playing card and bits of orange peel enlivening the coal dust between the rails under a Pullman car which was still waiting for him."

In his foreword to the English translation of *Invitation to a Beheading*, Nabokov says that the book may have been effected by his seeing both the Bolshevist and the Nazi regimes "in terms of one dull beastly farce." Neither book is farce, but there are scenes in both which fit the "dull beastly" description very well. In *Invitation to a Beheading*, M'sieur Pierre's monologue on sex while he plays his atrocious chess with Cincinnatus, or the final public banquet for Cincinnatus on the night before his execution, where the town park is lighted by a million bulbs producing a grandiose monogram of the entwined initials of Pierre and Cincinnatus, have the proper quality; in *Bend Sinister*, they are matched by a scene in which Paduk the Toad, disguised as Mad Tom, appears at night in Krug's cell in a final effort to break him down, or by David's disgusting death, torn to pieces by hoodlums as part of a state project for their rehabilitation.

The last word on both books comes from, of all people, Cincinnatus' quasi-mother. On her visit to his cell, she inexplicably tries to explain some toys of her childhood, consisting of a "crazy mirror" and a collection of shapeless, distorted, and disgusting objects. The mirror distorted ordinary objects, but when the distorted *"nonnons"* were seen in it they "became in the mirror a wonderful, sensible, image; flowers, a ship, a person, a landscape." The world of dictatorship, of vulgar power and dull beastly farce, is those misshapen *"nonnons,"* but in the crazy mirror of Nabokov's art—and the mirror has been the most obsessive motif in his work from first to last—it takes on the shapeliness of art. Nabokov believes (or believed in the 1930s and 1940s) that in a world of tyranny, one is strongest if he has no hostages to fortune, if he neither loves nor is loved. Beyond that he is (or was) deeply Gnostic, insisting that one must be in the world but not of it. But then it is probably absurd to draw morals from his books. As the narrator says at the conclusion of *The Real Life of Sebastian Knight,* "the old conjuror waits in the wings with his hidden rabbit," and Nabokov's next rabbit may squeak "Commitment, commitment." Vladimir Nabokov is our greatest living writer, and if he has written, in the conjunction of *Invitation to a Beheading* and *Bend Sinister,* a fable about the vulnerability of having a handle, he himself seems to have no handle at all, not even a ghostly lapel by which we could seize hold of him even for a moment.

1969

Richard Wright Reappraised

I T IS CLEAR that the problem of the American Negro writer (or of the oppressed writer anywhere: Russian writers under the Czars and the Soviets make an instructive comparison) is to master (control, contain) within his art the hate and violence welling up within him. There can be no doubt that Negro hatred of whites is close to universal. We see it everywhere in Richard Wright: he says of his grandfather in *Black Boy*, "I never heard him speak of white people; I think he hated them too much to talk of them"; Gladys confesses to Cross in *The Outsider*, "I hate white people!"

It is now possible to see that Wright's literary career divided sharply into three phases. The first was the early flawed work of the 1930s, melodramatic and tractarian. This includes his poetry—a form for which Wright seems to have had little talent—on social themes, overflowing with imagery of violence and the clichés of "proletarian literature." It also includes his novel *Lawd Today*, published posthumously by Wright's widow in 1963, which is fairly described by Russell Carl Brignano, in *Richard Wright: An Introduction to the Man and His Works*, as "grim, heavy, naturalistic ploddings."

Principally, it includes his early short fiction, of which the five examples he preferred were reprinted in *Uncle Tom's Children*, along with an essay, "The Ethics of Living Jim Crow." The first three of these are medleys of racial violence in the South. The first of them, "Black Boy Leaves Home," is typical: Black Boy shoots to death a white man who has just killed two of his friends and is about to kill him, and spends the night hiding out, in a pit in the dirt, from a lynch mob, watching them burn (with rather unconvincing details) his surviving friend, beating to death a rattlesnake with "long white fangs" to start the night, and throttling to death a dog belonging to a member of the mob to end it.

The other two stories are Stalinist tracts and caricatures. In one of them, "Fire and Cloud," a moderate Negro preacher in the South is brutalized into becoming a militant leader (it is a kind of "Waiting for Blackie"). The other, "Bright and Morning Star," is based on an anecdote that Wright heard in his childhood and retells in *Black Boy*, about a Negro woman whose husband was lynched by a mob, and who came to lay out her husband's body for burial with a sheet in which she had concealed a loaded shotgun, and managed to kill four members of the mob before they got her. ("I did not know if the story was factually true or not, but it was emotionally true," Wright observes in *Black Boy*, adding, "I resolved that I would emulate the black woman if I were ever faced with a white mob.") The story is that symbolic emulation, within a frame of heroic Communist martyrdom, which very much weakens and worsens the original anecdote.

Wright's second phase was the period of his important writing, from *Native Son* in 1940 to *Black Boy* in 1945, and it includes what I believe to be his masterwork, a novella, "The Man Who Lived Underground" (it seems to have been an uncompleted novel), first published in *Cross-Section* in 1944 and reprinted in *Eight Men* in 1961. The mark of this period is Wright's break with the convention of realism. He writes in the essay "How 'Bigger' Was Born," reprinted as an introduction to *Native Son:* "what I wanted that scene to say to the readers was *more important than its surface reality or plausibility.*" *Native Son*, which Brignano properly calls "pivotal in Negro literature," is an impressive novel for all its clumsiness, didacticism, and travesty: it develops a considerable power in the reading even three decades after publication; and it seems likely to endure.

"The Man Who Lived Underground" is a radically sym-

bolist and fantasist work, finding the perfect metaphor for
Negro identity in life under the streets in a sewer that is the
foundation of *ecclesia supra cloacam*, with passageways to
other institutions of our culture. Brignano quotes the anonymous protagonist as saying, "Yes, if the world as men had made
it was right, then anything else was right, any act a man took
to satisfy himself, murder, theft, torture." Brignano identifies
this idea as an extension of Nietzsche, but it is more obviously
Ivan Karamazov's ethic for a world without God, and the
novella seems primarily indebted to the Dostoevsky of *Notes
from The Underground* and *The Brothers Karamazov*.

Black Boy is Wright's account of the first nineteen years of
his life, lived in the South. Parts of it were published from 1937
on, but the completion of the manuscript coincided roughly
with his break with the Communist Party in 1944, and thus
represented a double emancipation, with the constraints of
Negro life in the South metaphoric for Stalinist constraints.
The book is somewhat fictionalized autobiography, as we can
see by comparing some incidents with their different versions
in the earlier "The Ethics of Living Jim Crow."

The last fifteen years of Wright's work, from the publication of *Black Boy* until his death in France in 1960, were as
flawed as his early writing, now by a mild megalomania which
combined with increasingly blurred memories of the United
States to make his later work not symbolist or fantasist, but
just unconvincing. It is typified by *The Outsider*, a kind of
spurious display of French existentialism (where *Native Son*
and "The Man Who Lived Underground" have a natural,
unself-conscious and effective existentialism, derived from
Wright's reading of Dostoevsky). The *Outsider* depends on
Dostoevsky, too, but it is principally a mechanical and rigid
parallel to *Crime and Punishment*, with Damon as Raskolnikov
and Houston as Porfiry, all frozen in stiff postures by cold
drafts of theory from Wright's friend Sartre.

The recent novel which *The Outsider* most resembles is
Norman Mailer's *An American Dream:* in its preposterous plot

and events, its world of grandiose fantasy, its endless hokum (the protagonist assures us that "being a Negro was the least important thing in his life"), and its cancerous and pointless violence.

We can see this same violence and failure to convince in other examples of the late fiction: the hackwork of *Savage Holiday* culminates in the brutal butchering of a woman; *The Long Dream* represents a melodramatic South which never existed; and the later stories in *Eight Men* include one in which a Negro kills and mutilates a white librarian, and a comic radio script about an African who beheads his white benefactor.

James Baldwin, in the days before his voice had become shrill and hysterical, wrote in *Notes of a Native Son:* "There is . . . no Negro living in America who has not felt, briefly or for long periods, with anguish sharp or dull . . . simple, naked and unanswerable hatred; who has not wanted to smash any white face he may encounter"; Baldwin's own recent fiction has as its one authentic motif this intense bitterness and race hate. Those whites with a commitment to integration and interracial fraternity, who find the open hostility of present-day black militants so distressing, can be cheered (or at least reconciled) by the realization that if one grants the universality of that hatred—and, if not its legitimacy, at least its inevitability—it is probably healthier for everyone concerned to have it openly expressed than to have it bottled up and seething.

What Wright did with this hatred and inner violence in the period of his important work was what every serious writer must do, which is to find what Eliot called an "objective correlative" for his emotions. We can see models of this process in such a masterly short story as Isaac Babel's "History of My Dovecote," where the 1905 pogrom in Russia is rendered in two delicate and precise images: the boy's beloved pigeon crushed against his face so that the warm guts trickle down his cheek, and his granduncle Shoyl, a fish peddler, lying murdered with a live pikeperch flapping in a rip in his trousers. Picasso's painting *Guernica* shows comparable mastery in rendering the violence and horror of the bombing of the defense-less Spanish city by the Fascists in the objective imagery of the knifelike bull, the torn horse, the soundlessly screaming woman.

If Wright never attained the classic control of these works, his best books show comparable objective correlatives; the terror-inspired muscle tension that unwittingly smothers Mary Dalton in *Native Son;* the dirt floor of the sewer cavern studded with useless diamonds (Burke would call this a "perspective by incongruity") in "The Man Who Lived Underground"; Shorty allowing himself to be kicked sprawling by whites for a quarter in *Black Boy;* and so on. For this brief period of four or five years, Wright had an aesthetic mastery over his passions. Earlier, he had not yet attained that control, and later he lost it. If a Negro writer never strives for this sort of control, or rejects it as not worth having, he may end as an artless racist demagogue on the order of LeRoi Jones; if he overcontains his emotions, he becomes a white Negro writer, in the long gray line from Phyllis Wheatley to Frank Yerby.

The second problem that Wright faced, and briefly resolved, was the development beyond the confines of realism and naturalism. Here it is important to see *Native Son* as deliberately modeled on *An American Tragedy.* The account of young Wright's first reading of Dreiser in Memphis in his late teens given in *Black Boy* is quite revealing: from reading Dreiser, Wright says, he derived "nothing less than a sense of life itself. All my life had shaped me for the realism, the naturalism of the modern novel." "The Man Who Lived Underground" is a pioneering work in going beyond realism and naturalism to symbolism and fantasy, and is thus perhaps the single most revolutionary work in American Negro literature. Along with the short fiction of Ralph Ellison, Wright's younger protégé, in the 1940s, and then *Invisible Man* in 1952, it made a later serious Negro imaginative literature possible. For James Baldwin, according to his testimony in *Nobody Knows My Name*, it was *Black Boy* a year later, not "The Man Who Lived

Underground," which proved "an immense liberation and revelation"; in fact, which enabled Baldwin to write his two fine early novels, *Go Tell It On The Mountain* and *Giovanni's Room;* but *Black Boy* only continues, less surrealistically, the escape from the fetters of naturalism that the earlier novella began.

The final problem that Wright confronted, and inadvertently solved for at least a brief period, was how to be a novelist in a post-Freudian world. Wright attempted to make deliberate fictional use of the unconscious imagery charted by Freud, to add an unconscious dimension to the power of his effects, from at least the stories in *Uncle Tom's Children* in 1938, which deliberately utilize castration imagery in the lynching scenes and elsewhere, to the contrived Freudian dream in *Savage Holiday* in 1954. This worked, but not in the simple fashion that Wright anticipated. As Freud pointed out, when the lairs of the unconscious are known, the unconscious simply goes elsewhere. What happened in Wright's case, I believe, is that the tensions and guilts connected with sexuality, openly recognized and deliberately manipulated in the fiction, fled into the color imagery, and gave it a sexual resonance and ambiguity *not* consciously contrived, which powerfully reflected the racial undercurrents of American life and *did* increase the power of Wright's work. We can see it in Sarah's nightmare of "a wide black hole" in the aptly titled "Long Black Song" in *Uncle Tom's Children;* in the white cat which perches on Bigger's shoulder in *Native Son;* in the imagery of school as white chalk on a blackboard in *Black Boy;* in Cross's image in *The Outsider* of Eva looking "into the black depths of his heart."

Rereading early Wright after a third of a century makes some things clear which were formerly obscure. One, for example, is that the charge made in 1940, in reviews of *Native Son* in the *American Mercury* by Burton Rascoe and in the *Atlantic Monthly* by David L. Cohn, that the book would encourage and increase Negro hatred of whites, is absurd. If hatred of oppressive and colonialist masters were learned from novels, the masters would find life a great deal simpler. Minority race hate, in fact, arises out of the daily conditions of minority life, and books which express it can be cathartic and curative, the doctor rather than the disease.

Another thing much clearer than it was in 1940 is that Bigger Thomas in *Native Son* is a direct, even a deliberate, challenge to white liberalism. Mrs. Dalton talks of Bigger in a jargon ("I think it's important emotionally that he feels free to trust his environment. . . . Using the analysis contained in the case record the relief sent us, I think we should evoke an immediate feeling of confidence") that is ultimately dehumanizing and offensive, as blind as her sightless eyes. "Bigger" is "Nigger" and "Booger" and he demands acceptance as a representative figure who is neither Ralph Bunche nor the women's magazine paragon of *Guess Who's Coming to Dinner?* Furthermore, in his hatreds and fears, his grandiose fantasies and mindless violences, Bigger is not simply a slum hoodlum; he is a part of Richard Wright and of every other Negro intellectual, and perhaps of everybody.

In "How 'Bigger' Was Born," Wright denies that he "agreed with Bigger's wild and intense hatred of white people," but it is clear from *Black Boy* and other of his writings that he did, to some degree, share it. Bigger for the first time became fully human, acquired a sense of identity and manhood, "pride," "a new life," even a sense of "elation," from his murders, precisely as Wright did from the symbolic murders of his fiction. "He was more alive than he could ever remember having been," Bigger thinks, and "In all of his life these two murders were the most meaningful things that had ever happened to him." In the novel's key explanation, Bigger understands his sacrificial, even redemptive, role: "Had he not taken fully upon himself the crime of being black?" In *Black Boy*, Wright talks of his childhood passion for novels "to feed that thirst for violence that was in me." Bigger and Wright share in the same redemptive criminality (as do at least some readers), but

Wright and the readers share in it symbolically, using Bigger as their symbolic vessel.

Another thing clearly visible now but difficult to see then is that Wright was never a very convincing Marxist or Stalinist, and that the end of *Native Son* is certainly not the Communist tract it has been taken to be. There is a kind of humanist early Marxism, anticipating the Marx of the *1844 Manuscripts*, in Max's conversation with Bigger in his cell, and there are tags of Communist slogans in Max's long speech in court, but the speech itself is clearly, to a reader now, not Communist but Negro nationalist in tendency, the defense of Bigger as a uniquely oppressed and deprived black. There is an unbroken line from the Reverend Taylor's preachment at the end of "Fire and Cloud," "Freedom belongs to the strong!", to Max's defense of Negro life "expressing itself not in terms of our good and bad, but in terms of its own fulfillment," to Cross Damon lengthily orating his neo-Sorelian or Burnhamite theory of history. These are transient forms taken by a kind of permanent vulgar Nietzscheanism in Wright, which began with his reading of Mencken in his teens; when the Communist Party leaders and followers in *The Outsider* find Cross's oration impressive Marxist analysis or observe that he "ought to be on the Central Committee," Wright only reveals his own incomprehension of (or lack of sympathy for) Marxist thought.

Wright was rare among those of his generation and social origins (he was born in 1908 and grew up in rural Mississippi) in his total insensitivity to the blues. Anyone who believes that Negroes have some sort of innate or gut sense of the blues has only to hear the record of *King Joe*, a "blues" about Joe Louis, sung by Paul Robeson, with words written by Wright, or to read Wright's fulsome introductory tribute to Paul Oliver's *Blues Fell This Morning*, surely the most ludicrous and inadequate book ever written on the blues, to learn better.

Wright makes a few references to the blues in his books ("The strains of blue and sensual notes," "blues or jazz records whose wild rhythms wailed up to him," and such), but they only reveal his tin ear for the form. Ralph Ellison's *Antioch Review* article on *Black Boy* in 1945, "Richard Wright's Blues" (later reprinted in *Shadow and Act*), is less a description of Wright's book than a manifesto for Ellison's own novel-in-progress, *Invisible Man*. If, as the new black militants never tire of telling us, the Negro personality is more spontaneous and creative than the white, we can only answer that there are a variety of Negro personalities, including some such as Wright's, which are doggedly and painfully creative, not spontaneous or "swinging" at all.

In noting the violence and race hatred which Wright had to master, and did successfully master in his best work, we must not neglect the self-hatred and contempt for other Negroes which so often accompany this. A much quoted passage in *Black Boy* (amusingly reminiscent of Henry James's list of all the cultural features necessary for literature which were lacking in America) lists the defects Wright found in American Negro life:

> I used to mull over the strange absence of real kindness in Negroes, how unstable was our tenderness, how lacking in genuine passion we were, how void of great hope, how timid our joy, how bare our traditions, how hollow our memories, how lacking we were in those intangible sentiments that bind man to man, and how shallow was even our despair.

(A related passage in the book analyzes "the cultural barrenness of black life.") Baldwin knew Wright in his last years in Paris, and he became for Baldwin (as influence and father-symbol) an obsessive figure Baldwin had to get off his back, so that he devotes three of the fifteen essays in *Nobody Knows My Name* to Wright. These memoirs, among other "revelations," identify Wright's "real" impulse toward American Negroes as "to despise them."

To the extent that this was true, it is a displacement of self-hatred, and is imposed on Negroes and members of other minorities by the dominant American culture. However, being a writer alienated from white America by a black skin, and being doubly alienated by despising one's fellow blacks, is not so unpromising a stance from which to observe American culture as it might seem (Nathanael West had a similar doubly alienated perspective as an anti-Semitic Jew, and Flannery O'Connor wrote from a triply alienated perspective as a Southern Catholic woman, and in the Gnostic or Jansenist tendency in her Catholicism, even teetered toward a fourth alienation.) The overwhelming violence of Wright's fiction arises out of this racial hatred turned outward toward whites and inward toward other Negroes and the self, but it can be cathartic and therapeutic when it is rigorously disciplined by criteria of economy which are ultimately aesthetic.

If the black militants today have taken a number of foolish and self-defeating positions tending toward apartheid and racist hostility, they have taken at least one life-giving position, the "Black is beautiful" emphasis on pride in Negro identity. In Wright's time this was not possible, and all that he could do, in such later work as *The Outsider*, was to affirm a self which transcended Negro identity. But in other respects Wright's work shows a remarkable anticipation of some of the current lines of black militancy (Wright's books may in fact have influenced such of their ideologists as Frantz Fanon, Malcolm X, Stokely Carmichael, and others).

Max's speech to the court in *Native Son* talks of a Negro embodiment of white guilt which has "made itself a home in the wild forest of our great cities, amidst the rank and choking vegetation of slums!" He goes on to make the current use (or misuse) of the term "ghetto-areas" for these slums, and to threaten the day when "*millions* rise" and "another civil war in these states" comes (when the book appeared in 1940, these references seemed to refer to class struggle, but they are deliberately vague, and it is now obvious that they envisage race struggle instead). On the last page of the novel, Bigger ends by

67

affirming violence, while "Max pleaded despairingly against it." *The Outsider* speaks of political parties "denying the humanity of the Negro, excluding his unique and historic position in American life." In his 1953 book of that title, about the transition from the Gold Coast to independent Ghana, Wright first named "Black Power." Brignano's conclusion, quite properly, is that present black militants may scorn Wright, but that they nevertheless descend from him.

In a final evaluation of Richard Wright, we would have to say that however ill-written, flawed, and limited his work is, at least that part of it from *Native Son* to *Black Boy*, particularly "The Man Who Lived Underground," seems likely to survive. The wintry cage-pacing of his best writing speaks to our condition; as Baldwin says, "Wright's unrelentingly bleak landscape was not merely that of the Deep South, or of Chicago, but that of the World, of the human heart." And this brings us to Brignano's *Richard Wright: An Introduction to the Man and His Works*. Brignano writes awkwardly and even ungrammatically; he does not understand Marxism very well; and he sometimes misreads even the simple events of a novel. But he understands many things well, particularly that Wright's "almost compulsive drive to create scenes of violence and destruction in his fiction" should not make us forget "the rational idealist behind them." Brignano's book is not the last word, but it is a useful word.

One hopes that the current revival of Wright will result not only in a better general understanding of his significance, but in some young Negro writers (who live among black militant slogans rather like the Stalinist slogans he heard in the thirties, exalting message over craft) who can learn from Wright's successes as well as from his failures.

1970

Kenneth Burke
at Seventy

Language as Symbolic Action displays the vast range of Kenneth Burke's operations at present. In one of his aspects (not the one most congenial to me) he is a kind of philosopher, an original thinker and system-builder. He is a philosopher of language, a study he calls "logology" (words about words), and of human motivation. Burke calls his whole system "Dramatism," having taken "Ritual Drama as Hub" as far back as 1941, and defines Dramatism: "A theory of language, a philosophy of language based on that theory, and methods of analysis developed in accordance with the theory and the philosophy." Dramatism relies heavily on Aristotle's "entelechial principle," the principle of perfection, in taking things to the end of the line.

In this, as in other respects, Burke is a quirky and characteristically American original thinker or philosopher, on the order of Thoreau or Veblen (or, as R. P. Blackmur once suggested, Charles S. Peirce). Burke is scornful of the "technological psychosis" of present-day science, he regards the products touted over our air waves as "the damnedest batch of poisons and quack drugs," and he is preoccupied to the point of obsession with the excretory processes (or, as he might say, he has a "cloacal psychosis").

Burke is self-taught (more even than the rest of us, since he never finished college) and he is formidably self-taught: French, German, Latin, Greek, Hebrew; just about any branch of knowledge you can name, even, warily and to his own purposes, a little science (he uses "nova" to mean "the sudden flaring forth of a term"). As a critic of other thinkers he is shrewd and perceptive, showing how Marshall McLuhan throws out "content" and then smuggles it back in as "information," or how Cleanth Brooks practices sociology "in the name of No Sociology." In his own spinnings Burke is endlessly fertile and resourceful.

Of Burke's political concerns of the '30s, little is visible in this book except an overwhelming detestation (which I share) of our presence in Vietnam. In Burke's curious reversal of Freud, sexual fantasies "are a displacement of political motives," or can be (perhaps his own political motives have been displaced similarly). Burke's tone is now stoic rather than optimistic, as when he subscribes to Freud's "ultimate qualified resignation" rather than Norman O. Brown's heady Utopianism. "Mankind's only hope is a cult of comedy," Burke writes, since "the cult of tragedy is too eager to help out with the holocaust." He defines the "comic mood" as "essentially humane," and says of such comedy, "for these mean days, it is good medicine."

It is in his aspect as a literary critic that I find Burke most congenial. He is simply the finest literary critic in the world, and perhaps the finest since Coleridge. Burke calls this activity "Poetics," as Aristotle did, and defines it in Aristotelian fashion as "an approach in terms of the poem's nature as a kind," in which "each species has aims intrinsic to itself." Like the only living critic comparable, I. A. Richards, Burke manages to combine his Aristotelian concern for structure with a Coleridgean concern for texture: the imaginative process, the tension of opposites, the language of poetry. In defining the poem as *"instructions* for performing," like a musical score, Burke goes to the same Coleridgean extreme that Richards reached in his famous "Definition of a Poem" in *Principles of Literary Criticism*, while making it compatible with an equally extreme Aristotelian emphasis on "the dynamics of form."

Half the essays in *Language as Symbolic Action* deal with specific works, and Burke's practical criticism is a marvel. The essay on "Kubla Khan" is masterly, and its pursuit of the poem's connections with other writing by Coleridge makes the perfect complement to John Livingston Lowes' pursuit, in *The Road to Xanadu*, of the poem's sources in Coleridge's reading. In an essay on Djuna Barnes' *Nightwood*, Burke finds the book coming "to stylistic fulfillment in the accents of lamentation," with its perverse actions as secular forms of religious themes, so that, for example, "The motives of Christian vigil become transformed into the 'night watch' of women like Nora in love or like Robin prowling."

The essay that I think the best of all, "The Vegetal Radicalism of Theodore Roethke," demonstrates Roethke's poetic vocabulary of "drip" and "root" by contrasting it with such diction in Eliot's "Burnt Norton" as "inoperancy" and "abstention"; relates Roethke's theories of poetic language to those of Dante, Wordsworth, and Lawrence; shows how Roethke's "communicative verbs" work; identifies his technique for "leaving implicit the kind of tonal transformation that Hopkins makes explicit"; differentiates among the terms "intuitions," "concepts," and "ideas" in Kant's *Critique of Pure Reason;* and somehow brings all this to a focus in beautiful textual analysis of "The Lost Son" and other poems. The piece is the best imaginable refutation, even to its title, of the statement John Crowe Ransom made in "An Address to Kenneth Burke" in 1942: "There are two kinds of poetry (or at least of 'literature') and Burke analyzes one kind with great nicety, and honors it, but shows too little interest in the other. The one he honors is the dialectical or critical kind, and the one he neglects is the lyrical or radical kind."

Burke's thoroughness is fantastic, whether he is indexing all the key words in the three plays of Aeschylus' *Oresteia* (Burke's special form of critical indexing is explained and illustrated in "Fact, Inference, and Proof in the Analysis of Literary Symbolism" in *Terms for Order*), or chasing what he calls "the Demonic Trinity" (the burlesque analogue of the Trinity in the interrelationship of the fecal, the urinary, and the genital) through *Alice in Wonderland*, Wagner's *Ring Cycle*, Flaubert's *Temptation of St. Anthony*, Aeschylus' *Prometheus Bound*, Mallarmé's "Pure" Poetry, and some of Burke's own works.

Language as Symbolic Action gives the reader a sense of sitting beside Burke as he works. "How closely dare we tie in things here?" he will write, or, "And now I am already in a bit of trouble," or, "this would put us wholly to rout." "One need not be in the literary business long," Burke remarks, "to detect a considerable amount of whistling in the dark here." He has been in the literary business for half a century, but he has never lost the quality of wonder: "Almost breathtaking in their implications," he exclaims, of a set of terminological transformations in Flaubert.

This same freshness gets into his style—not always, but often. "Burns, who fraternized with dispossessed field mice," he writes, or a word "stirs up a belfry of bat thoughts." At times he produces a tiny lyric ("a guarded and guardian garden") or a simile that is a thumbnail ballad ("like outlaws in the antique woods converging upon the place where a horn has sounded"). He is sometimes quite eloquent, particularly in endings.

Of course the book has flaws, some of them the defects of Burke's qualities. It is wordy, repetitious, sometimes arid, carelessly edited, and with far too much self-quotation and self-citation. Burke is at times owlish, as when he follows Bergson in denying the existence of negatives in nature (such examples of "Thou shalt not" as thorns and the rattlesnake's rattle, such examples of "it is not" as protective coloration and mimicry), then smuggles them in as pre-linguistic "primitive negatives"; or arguing that Freud's Love and Death principles "are not directly antithetical," although he surely knows that "Love" is Freud's "Life" term. Burke occasionally falls into tautology, as when he says that "The negative as such offers a basis for a tendency to think in antitheses," which is only an elaborate way of saying "The negative offers a basis for negating."

The worst fault of the book is a confusion of function or entelechial end with origin, and the consequent assumption that Burke is qualified to pronounce on origins in technical areas. He shows how certain dreams function to wake the sleeper when his bladder is full, and from this presumes to correct Freud on dream origins; he shows how myths function for such purposes as "governance" or attain entelechial perfection in their development, and from this presumes to decide how they originate. (Freud, here the victim, was a comparable sinner: he announced that the Earl of Oxford wrote the plays of William Shakespeare.)

Kenneth Burke has been my master and friend for 30 years. He taught me to think, and when I disagree with him, which is often, I wield weapons that he has forged. He is a liberator, a comic humanist, and a great man.

1967

A Multitude
of Lieblings

With Liebling's death last month, *The Most of A. J. Liebling*, edited by William Cole, suddenly became a memorial. It is not the best selection possible—it contains nothing from that brilliant book *The Telephone Booth Indian*—but it is a good sampling of Liebling's amazing variety of specializations.

There were, in fact, a multitude of Lieblings. My favorite is Liebling the reporter of the raffish and the larcenous. In this he was simply the best in the world, the finest scoundrelologist since Mark Twain. These pieces are so funny that one tends not to notice the perfection of anthropological observation. *Back Where I Came From* (1938), Liebling's first book, is a collection of *World-Telegram* and early *New Yorker* pieces. *The Most* reprints several gems from it.

"Tummler" (Yiddish for "bustler") is about Hymie Katz, who opens fraudulent and evanescent nightclubs. In a few pages that are marvels of economy, Liebling gives Hymie's inspiring story, and describes the processes of parlaying a borrowed $50 into a (briefly) going nightclub. The piece concludes with a tribute from Izzy Yereshevsky, the owner of the I. & Y. (for "Izzy" and "Yereshevsky") cigar store that is Hymie's club. Izzy says: "He's a real tummler, that Hymie. He knows to get a dollar."

Another marvelous piece from *Back Where I Came From* is " 'What Do You Expect for Two Dollars?' " It is about a run-down old restaurant at a New York beach, a restaurant that combines superb food with cranky old waiters who try to drive customers away, and a cranky old owner who sits by the bar all day to see that no waiter gets away with a glass of beer. Here is a waiter talking: " 'The cook is forty-nine million years old,' he said. 'Some day he'll fall into the clam chowder. At the end of every season the old man says to him, "I never want to see you no more. You're as dead as a doornail." And at the beginning of the next season he sends a taxicab for him.' " The mystic affinity between mean old people and fine food has not yet been explored psychoanalytically; Liebling explored it comically, but it is a Chekhovian comedy tinged with melancholy.

The best of all of Liebling's books, to my taste, is *The Honest Rainmaker* (1953), in which the perfect scoundrelologist found the perfect subject, the elderly promoter and publicist whose pen name is "Col. John R. Stingo." *The Most* is dedicated to the Colonel (using his real name, James A. Macdonald) at the age of 90, and it reprints two chapters and three fragments from his saga. These are matchless. The Colonel is a masterly reshaper of the language: freely transposing parts of speech ("the old doctor overweened himself") or creating superior back-formations ("they would become reconciliated"). The Colonel may be a scoundrel, but he is a highly moral scoundrel, as when he boasts of taking in a prominent oyster grower: "We beat that squarehead for forty grand, and he had starved hundreds of oyster shuckers to death."

Hearing the Colonel explain that the brand of ale he favors, Black Wolf, "is brewed in the Yellowknife country, two hundred miles within the Arctic Circle, the home of the world's richest unexploited gold deposits. I have frequently seen a bottle sold for one ounce of gold dust," or seeing him drive his way through a crowd of school-children, "making effective though surreptitious use of his pointy shoes," one realizes that with life's usual capacity for imitating art, it has finally thrown up in reality the character that W. C. Fields played in illusion.

The Most has two chapters and a note from *The Earl of Louisiana* (1961), a less successful recreation of a colorful figure, Governor Earl Long. Earl is terribly funny, wearing a tie that is "perhaps a souvenir Rorschach test," or announcing that he is in favor of every religion "with the possible exception of snake-chunking" (Liebling explains: "The snake-chunkers, a small, fanatic cult, do not believe in voting"). The problem is that all this, unlike the Colonel's adventures, is a little too close to the real world. When Earl passes out coins, "a quarter to the white kids and a nickel to the niggers," the joke sours.

The finest of all of Liebling's raffish pieces, "The Jollity Building" from *The Telephone Booth Indian*, is not in *The Most*, perhaps because it has been so much anthologized. To make room for this classic ethnography and for more about Colonel Stingo, to my taste the editor could have dispensed with anything else in the book. But the other Lieblings too show great distinction, and each has his devoted following. One is Liebling the war reporter. *The Most* includes material from *The Road Back to Paris* (1944), *Normandy Revisited* (1958) and a 1956 piece from Algeria. As a war reporter Liebling is sometimes quite funny (he explains the secret of successful cursing as "cadence, emphasis, and antiphony") but more often respectful and a little awed (he writes, of the dead cows on the Normandy battlefield, "we lived in the stench of innocent death").

Another Liebling is the critic of the press, and *The Most* includes a dozen pieces and fragments on that subject. As critic of the press Liebling stalked through the jungle, armed with blowgun and poisoned darts. When a *Herald Tribune* obituary observed that Patton had more flair than any other general since Custer, Liebling commented: "Though what poor Custer had a flair for I wouldn't know—certainly not Indians." All Liebling's criticism is informed by his vision of "a great, free, living stream of information, and equal access to it for all." In one of the pieces Liebling describes himself as "a chronic, incurable, recidivist reporter." He was that, but he was also the best thing that happened to American journalism since John Peter Zenger.

Then there is Liebling the boxing expert. *The Most* includes one piece from *The Sweet Science* (1956) along with a later article on Liston, but the most interesting use Liebling makes of boxing is to quote gnomic wisdom from the trainer Whitey Bimstein or the old fighter Sam Langford as metaphors in remote contexts.

Far from Eighth Avenue and Stillman's Gym, there is Liebling the Francophile. The war pieces are full of his love for France and the French, and his literal translations of French idiom are masterly. "A chagrin of love never forgets itself," a waitress will tell him; "You must not make bile about it." There is a fine comic piece, "French Without Scars," about Liebling getting beat up on his first stay in France in 1926, and learning idiom and argot from the comments on his appearance made by French acquaintances.

One of the things Liebling liked best about France was its food. This introduces Liebling the gourmet, or, in his own description, Liebling the glutton. *The Most* contains excerpts from *Between Meals* (1962), including Liebling's menu for "the ideal light lunch" in Normandy: "a dozen *huîtres de Courseulles*, an *araignée de mer* (spider crab) with a half pint of mayonnaise on the side, a dish of *tripes à la mode de Caen*, a partridge Olivier Basselin, poached in cream and cider and singed in old Calvadoes, *a gigot de présalé*, a couple of *bifteks*, and a good Pont l'Evêque." There is also some praise for what Liebling calls "the glorious diversion," sex, but not in the same generous proportions.

There are traces in the book of still other Lieblings: the medievalist and scholar (he calls Earl Long "the old vavasor," which means "feudal lord"); the political commentator (Liebling could be withering: he remarks of Alva Johnston, who believed "that stupid Presidents were best," "It is a pity he did not live to see Eisenhower"); the Philistine who made fun of the literary quarterlies and of such words as "dichotomy."

Liebling's mind was naturally comparative, perceiving similarity in dissimilars, which Aristotle called the sign of genius. A tribute to Harold Ross has paragraphs of comparisons of Ross to everyone from Beatrice Lillie to Eddie Arcaro. Liebling's natural trope was the simile. Opening a nightclub, Hymie Katz "is under a compulsion as strong as the drive of a spawning salmon to swim upstream." The moon goes into a cloud abruptly, "like a watch going into a fat man's vest pocket."

Around Liebling, Colonel Stingo adopted his sort of simile ("a steak with a coverture of mushrooms like the blanket of roses they put on the winner of the Kentucky Derby") as did Earl Long ("A four-hundred-dollar suit on old Uncle Earl would look like socks on a rooster"). Lest this fact cast doubt on their existence, let me say that I once dined with Liebling and the Colonel, and that for all I know the Governor may have been a real person too.

In recent years these figures of speech thickened, and Liebling's style became baroque. In the 1950s a sentence might combine a metaphor and a simile, as: "The Norman carp is a conservative investor, not to be taken in, like a trout, by the flash of an obviously spurious insect flourished under his nose like a prospectus for Montenegran carbuncle mines." By the 1960s Liebling was apt to pile four similes on two metaphors.

In these same years, Liebling's articles became complex in structure, shifting back and forth in time: the *Normandy Revisited* pieces interweave strata from Liebling's experiences in France in 1926, 1944, and 1955. Like the comparisons and the boxing wisdom, the strata introduce perspectives by incongruity (to borrow a term from Kenneth Burke). Hymie Katz and a Norman carp do after all inhabit the same world. *The Most of A. J. Liebling* contains multitudes, but one man embodied them all. We have lost a lot.

1964

The Art of
Joseph Mitchell

HE GENERAL AGREEMENT that Joseph Mitchell is the paragon of reporters seems to be so complete that his importance as a writer, a unique figure in our literature, has been generally overlooked. The publication of Mitchell's longest and most ambitious piece to date, *Joe Gould's Secret*, invites a general assessment of his work and offers an opportunity to correct the misemphasis. Mitchell is a formidable prose stylist and a master rhetorician; he is a reporter only in the sense that Defoe is a reporter, a humorist only in the sense that Faulkner is a humorist.

The history of Mitchell's writing is a remarkable example of the development of a formal convention to fullest effectiveness, then of breaking through it. Mitchell's first publications were two short stories, "Cool Swamp and Field Woman" in *The New American Caravan* in 1929 (published while he was still an undergraduate at the University of North Carolina), and "The Brewers" in *American Caravan IV* in 1931. Both stories are misty, heavily symbolic, "poetic" in the dubious sense of that word, moody atmospheric sketches.

Mitchell left college in the summer of 1929 and came to New York to work as a reporter, on the staff of the *Herald Tribune* and then of the *World-Telegram*. His first book, *My Ears Are Bent* (1938), reprints some of his newspaper feature stories. These are as far as can be from the dreamlike fiction. They are hard-edged, factual and objective interviews with strippers,

79

athletes, small-time criminals, and such. The tone is sometimes flip, the style is at times mannered, the humor is occasionally forced. At its best *My Ears Are Bent* gives a sense of the tropical-rain-forest luxuriance of New York life; it everywhere demonstrates Mitchell's gift of perfect pitch for human speech; and in a few places (particularly a moving tragic study of Billy Sunday, done entirely by understatement and implication, called "Old Ball-Player in Winter Underwear") it shows the complex richness of Mitchell's mature work.

Late in the 1930s, Mitchell became a staff writer for the *New Yorker* (to which he had earlier contributed), and in a few years there he reshaped the magazine's traditional reportorial forms, the "Profile" and "A Reporter at Large," into supple and resourceful instruments for his own special purposes, blending the symbolic and poetic elements of his early fiction with the objectivity and detail of his newspaper reporting. A selection of these pieces, along with some fiction, was published as *McSorley's Wonderful Saloon* (1943). *McSorley's* was enthusiastically reviewed and had a considerable sale, but no one seemed to notice that the forms of reporting were being used to express the archetypal and the mythic: that Mazie might run a Bowery movie house but is an Earth Mother nevertheless; that Cockeye Johnny Nikanov, the king of 38 families of slum gypsies, is simultaneously a Winter King; that McSorley's looks very like an ale-house but is in fact a Temple.

Old Mr. Flood (1948) took the next step, into fiction: its protagonist, Hugh G. Flood, the retired 95-year-old "Mayor of Fish Market," is an invented composite figure. The preoccupations of *Old Mr. Flood* are those of the later Yeats: the lust and rage of the old, the terrors of death, the joyous hopes of resurrection and rejuvenation. The language is a torrent of rhetoric and eloquence. Here is Mrs. Birdy Treppel, a fishwife, on the harbor breezes:

" 'Well, son, I tell you,' she said, hopping up and down as she talked,' if you went up to the North Pole in the dead of December and stripped to the drawers and picked out the biggest iceberg up there and dug a hole right down to the heart of it and crawled in that hole and put a handful of snow under each arm and sat on a block of ice and et a dish of ice cream, why, you wouldn't be nowhere near as cold as you'd be in Peck Slip in a sheepskin coat with a box fire in the gutter.' "

Since *Old Mr. Flood*, Mitchell's *New Yorker* pieces have returned to dealing with actual people, but with an imaginative breadth and a symbolic depth that makes them quite unique. One of them, "The Mohawks in High Steel," originally printed in 1949, was reprinted in Edmund Wilson's book *Apologies to the Iroquois* (1960), and six of them with the waterfront as their scene were published as *The Bottom of the Harbor* (1960). "The Mohawks in High Steel," about a colony of Canadian Mohawks settled in Brooklyn, has already become a classic of imaginative ethnography, as, among other things, one of the few successful capturings of traditional Indian eloquence. *The Bottom of the Harbor* pieces make bold metaphors out of the river and harbor life of the New York area: a dragger captain who collaborates with oceanographers becomes an allegory of nature and culture in harmony; the shad running up the Hudson become an affirmation of rebirth; and so on.

Mitchell's major themes are the familiar themes of tragedy and epic. One is human dignity; thus his subjects, particularly in *McSorley's Wonderful Saloon*, have been mostly the insulted and injured: bums and gypsies, freaks and buffoons, cracked old men and drunken old women. "They are as big as you are, whoever you are," he writes truculently, and their most admirable affirmation of human dignity is often biting the hand that feeds them. (Symbolically, these outcasts are Southern Negroes, and such figures as Mazie—"No matter how filthy or drunk or evil-smelling a bum may be, she treats him as an equal"—and old Mr. Flood—the originator of the Human Race Parade—are ideal images of interracial fraternity.)

As the theme of human dignity comes out of Mitchell's experience as a Southerner, so another important theme, the Edenic image of the good old days, is indebted to the tent revivalist sermons he heard in his youth. Cockeye Johnny preaches a magnificent sermon on the text "When I was a little knee-high boy the U.S. was gypsy heaven." (This is the idyllic pastoral vision of the American Eden on which *The Great Gatsby* ends: "the old island here that flowered once for Dutch sailors' eyes—a fresh, green breast of the new world.") Mr. Flood summons up a lost world in which simple food—an egg, an apple, a loaf of bread—had flavor and gave delight, until progress improved them all into nullity. "The Mohawks in High Steel" similarly ends with Mr. Diabo's beautiful evocation of "old red-Indian times."

Another important theme in Mitchell's work is fertility and resurrection, expressed in an unbroken chain of images from the bursting watermelon in "The Brewers" to the teeming pomegranate in the sermon that concludes the unwritten novel in the new book. Oysters in *Old Mr. Flood* are the resurrection and the life: eating a few dozen oysters can rejuvenate an old man as it can make a 22-year-old truck horse scamper after a mare down an icy street. Here is Mr. Flood's account of the process: " 'Damn your doctor! I tell you what to do. You get right out of here and go over to Libby's oyster house and tell the man you want to eat some of his big oysters. Don't sit down. Stand up at that fine marble bar they got over there, where you can watch the man knife them open. And tell him you intend to drink the oyster liquor; he'll knife them on the cup shell, so the liquor won't spill. And be sure you get the big ones. Get them so big you'll have to rear back to swallow, the size that most restaurants use for fries and stews; God forgive them, they don't know any better. Ask for Robbins Islands, Mattitucks, Cape Cods, or Saddle Rocks. And don't put any of that red sauce on them, that cocktail sauce, that mess, that gurry. Ask the man for half a lemon, poke it a time or two to free the juice, and squeeze it over the oysters. And the first one he knifes, pick it up and smell it, the way you'd smell a rose, or a shot of brandy. That briny, seaweedy fragrance will clear your head; it'll make your blood run faster. And don't eat six; take your time and eat a dozen, eat two dozen, eat three dozen, eat four dozen. And then tip the man a quarter and buy yourself a fifty-cent cigar and put your hat on the side of your head and walk down to Bowling Green. Look at the sky! Isn't it blue? And look at the girls a-tap-tap-tapping past on their pretty little feet! Aren't they just the finest little girls you ever saw, the bounciest, the rumpiest, the laughingest? Aren't you ashamed of yourself for even thinking about spending good money on a damned doctor? And along about here, you better be careful. You're apt to feel so bucked-up you'll slap strangers on the back, or kick a window in, or fight a cop, or jump on the tailboard of a truck and steal a ride.' "

A woman chaser in "The Rivermen," the final chapter in *The Bottom of the Harbor*, picks up young widows visiting their husbands' graves in the cemetery on Sunday, thus providing a kind of rebirth after death (the Widow of Ephesus motif), and the piece ends with an old shad fisherman affirming that "the purpose of life is to stay alive."

Mitchell's other major theme, most boldly imaged in *The Bottom of the Harbor*, is the depths of the unconscious. Dusty hotel rooms shut up for decades and now reluctantly explored are infantile experience; the wrecks on the bottom of the harbor, teeming with marine life, are festering failures and guilts; the rats that come boldly out of their holes in the dark before dawn are Id wishes; Mr. Poole's dream of the draining of New York harbor by earthquake is a paradigm of psychoanalysis; Mr. Hunter's grave is at once tomb and womb and marriage bed.

Joe Gould's Secret, Mitchell's fullest study of a single subject to date, consists of a Profile of a Greenwich Village bohemian published in the *New Yorker* in 1942, and a sizable amplification of it in the light of later knowledge, published in the magazine in 1964. On its surface, the book is a comic portrait of an eccentric, a Harvard-educated bum who recites what he claims is "Hiawatha" translated into the language of sea gulls. As do Mitchell's other outcasts in *McSorley's Wonderful*

Saloon, Gould affirms human dignity: he may beg, but "He doesn't fawn, and he is never grateful." Gould even has some of the grace of a more famous comic tramp: he smokes his cigarette butts picked up out of the gutter in a long black holder, and he lights them "with an arch-elegant, Chaplinlike flourish."

Read less superficially, the book is a pathetic and moving account of a "lost soul" who had been an unloved boy. In Mitchell's first sight of Gould, Gould "had something childlike and lost about him." Gould tells Mitchell of his childhood: he was undersized, inept, and runny-nosed; his teachers despised him as "a disgusting little bastard"; his surgeon father mocked him as incompetent to be a surgeon or anything else; his mother could offer him only tears of pity.

In literary terms, *Joe Gould's Secret* is a Jamesian story of life's necessary illusion (the secret is that the nine-million-word Oral History of Our Time that Gould had spent his lifetime producing did not exist). The book is written, however, not in intricate Jamesian prose, but in the bubbling, overflowing manner of James Joyce. Mitchell sees Gould "sitting among the young mothers and the old alcoholics in the sooty, pigeony, crumb-besprinkled, newspaper-bestrewn, privet-choked, coffin-shaped little park at Sheridan Square." When he meets Gould in a Sixth Avenue saloon, it is "long and narrow and murky, a blind tunnel of a place, a burrow, a bat's cave, a bear's den."

In deeper terms, Gould is a masking (and finally an unmasking) for Mitchell himself. In *Joe Gould's Secret* Mitchell seems freer than ever before to talk about himself, his resolutions and intentions, his methods of reporting and writing, even his life: "I was still under the illusion that I had plenty of time," Mitchell says, to explain his listening to Gould hour after hour, until "my eyes would glaze over and my blood would turn to water and a kind of paralysis would set in." Eventually the situation becomes comparable to that of Bellow's *The Victim,* and Mitchell writes: "I set out deliberately to get him off my back." By the end of the book, when he discovers Gould's secret, Mitchell becomes, not Gould's bearer or Gould's victim, but Gould himself, and the unwritten Oral History merges with Mitchell's own unwritten novel, a New York *Ulysses* (which Blooms magnificently even in four-page synopsis). Then we realize that Gould has been Mitchell all along, a misfit in a community of traditional occupations, statuses, and roles, come to New York to express his special identity; finally we realize that the body of Mitchell's work is precisely that Oral History of Our Time that Gould himself could not write.

In the book's universal meaning, Gould is an archetype of Ishmael. "In my eyes," Mitchell writes, "he was an ancient, enigmatic, spectral figure, a banished man. I never saw him without thinking of the Ancient Mariner or of the Wandering Jew or of the Flying Dutchman, or of a silent old man called Swamp Jackson who lived alone in a shack on the edge of a swamp near the small farming town in the South that I come from." Gould is a paradigm of alienated man, of what he himself once called "the tragic isolation of humanity." Mitchell writes of his look: "I have seen the same deceptively blank expression on the faces of old freaks sitting on platforms in freak shows and on the faces of old apes in zoos on Sunday afternoons." Ultimately Gould becomes metaphoric for all mankind. Mitchell decides not to expose him in an image that merges Gould with the faceless masses of Asia: "I didn't want to tear up his meal ticket, so to speak, or break his rice bowl." "God pity him," Mitchell concludes, "and pity us all." Joe Gould's secret, which is the burden of Joseph Mitchell's powerful art, is ultimately the secret of our brief lonely existence on a disinterested planet.

1965

Mark Twain, Half Twain

THE BEST AMERICAN WRITER? Mark Twain, of course. And the worst? Mark Twain, drat it. I am driven to this far-from-helpful conclusion by the reissue of Twain's first novel, *The Gilded Age*, written in collaboration with Charles Dudley Warner. No book is at once so delightful and so awful, and in that respect, I am sorry to say, it does typify the body of Twain's work.

"Awful" in this case refers primarily to tearjerking sentimentality. Here is Clay's reaction to the death of his mother:

"He leaned upon the open coffin and let his tears course silently. Then he put out his small hand and soothed the hair and stroked the dead face lovingly. After a bit he brought his other hand up from behind him and laid three or four fresh wild flowers upon the breast, bent over and kissed the unresponsive lips time and time again, and then turned away and went out of the house without looking at any of the company."

Here is his adoption after the funeral by kind Mrs. Hawkins:

"And after breakfast they two went alone to the grave, and his heart went out to his new friend and his untaught eloquence poured the praises of his buried idol into her ears without let or hindrance. Together they planted roses by the headboard and strewed wild flowers upon the grave; and then together they went away, hand in hand, and left the dead to the long sleep that heals all heart-aches and ends all sorrows."

"Delightful" refers primarily to the re-creation of American speech, which Twain brought to a height of comic perfection not attained before or since. Here is one of Col. Sellers' twins talking:

86

"It's our clock, now—and it's got wheels inside of it, and a thing that flutters every time she strikes—don't it, father! Great-grandmother died before hardly any of us was born—she was an Old-School Baptist and had warts all over her—you ask father if she didn't. She had an uncle once that was bald-headed and used to have fits; he wasn't *our* uncle, I don't know what he was to us—some kin or another I reckon—father's seen him a thousand times—hain't you, father! We used to have a calf that et apples and just chawed up dishrags like nothing, and if you stay here you'll see lots of funerals—won't he, Sis! Did you ever see a house afire? *I* have! Once me and Jim Terry—"

By 1873, when *The Gilded Age* was published, Twain had already shown the world his command of oral narrative in "The Celebrated Jumping Frog of Calaveras County" and the wonderful Old Ram story in *Roughing It*. In later years these powers would produce Twain's triumphs: the comic mastery of his lectures (lecturing in Vienna in 1898, Twain reduced Sigmund Freud to paroxysms of helpless laughter by announcing the title of his lecture, "The First Watermelon I Ever Stole," pausing for a moment, then muttering: "*Was* it the first?"); the formidable vocal range of *Life on the Mississippi*; and that ultimate masterpiece of oral narrative, *Adventures of Huckleberry Finn*.

Twain had similarly shown his defects to the world before *The Gilded Age*, in the philistinism and flogged wit of *The Innocents Abroad*. If folk speech freed him, culture and history constrained him, and in the future this inability to breathe in the realm of ideas would produce the vulgarity of *A Connecticut Yankee in King Arthur's Court*, the pretentiousness of *Personal Recollections of Joan of Arc*, and the utter tedium of *Christian Science*.

In Philip Rahv's useful if oversimple distinction of American writers into Palefaces and Redskins, Twain is taken as pure-blood Redskin. More accurately, he was a Redskin who simultaneously aspired to Paleface and mocked that aspiration. (Van Wyck Brooks' efforts to credit Twain's Paleface aspirations to his wife produced one of the monumental travesties of biography, *The Ordeal of Mark Twain*.)

The plot of *The Gilded Age* is a crazy jumble. Twain contributed two main strands: the fortunes of the Hawkins family, who own 75,000 acres of worthless Tennessee land, and the related adventures of their friend Col. Beriah Sellers, the most glib and optimistic of promoters. Warner contributed other strands: the wooing of the Philadelphia Quaker Ruth Bolton by an ungilded graduate of Yale named Philip *Sterling*, with subplots involving Ruth's family, Philip's irresponsible friend Harry Brierly, and poor Alice Montague, who also loves Philip. Twain and Warner worked together on the showiest strand, the rise and fall of the beauteous Laura Hawkins.

What most of these characters have in common is their vision of an effortless fortune, to be made by one or another speculative and unscrupulous promotion. No one achieves a fortune, however, except Philip, who discovers a coal mine for himself and Ruth's father by pick-and-shovel labor with his own soft Yale hands. An early work of socialist realism, in short.

Warner was a popular essayist who lived near Twain in Hartford, and it is hard to imagine what besides propinquity could have made Twain decide to collaborate with him. Warner's parts of the novel are uniformly terrible. Here is a Homeric simile: "as a brook breaks into ripples and eddies and dances and sports by the way, and yet keeps on to the sea, it was in Ruth's nature to give cheerful answer to the solicitations of friendliness and pleasure, to appear idly delaying even, and sporting in the sunshine, while the current of her resolution flowed steadily on." Warner writes so carelessly that he contradicts himself on adjacent pages, and he will never say "house" when he can say "home," or "women" when he can say "the gentle sex."

Twain shares in the responsibility for the silliest part of the book, the sad story of Laura. After a scoundrel robs her of her virtue by means of a false bigamous marriage, she becomes a Washington adventuress, breaking hearts and blackmailing politicians with equal ruthlessness. What does Laura think of her life? "But this is a desperate game I am playing in these days —a wearing, sordid, heartless game." The scene in which we see her at blackmail is preposterous from start to finish. Eventually Laura shoots her seducer dead, is acquitted by a jury, takes to the lecture platform, and dies of disappointment at the turnout. Honest.

The book's theme, its satire of the Gilded Age of Grant, is mostly heavy-handed and unsuccessful. Washington landladies will not rent rooms to Congressmen unless they pay in advance. The votes of "high moral" Senators cost more than the votes of ordinary Senators, "because they give tone to a measure." The leaders of the "Weed" Ring are not convicted because "our admirable jury system" enables them "to secure a jury of nine gentlemen from a neighboring asylum and three graduates from Sing-Sing." Congress is so jealous of its honor that if a member "had been proven guilty of theft, arson, licentiousness, infanticide, and defiling graves, I believe they would have suspended him for two days." And so on.

Twain's unforced humor, on the other hand, is thoroughly successful. I have space for only one example. When the Colonel and Harry bribe the surveyors of a railroad to route it through their property at Stone's Landing, this has one important effect: "There was such a panic among the turtles that at the end of six hours there was not one to be found within three miles of Stone's Landing." When the bypassed town on Hawkeye outbids Stone's Landing in bribery, and the route is changed back, what happens? The turtles return.

Most of the humor surrounds Col. Sellers, who is one of Twain's finest comic creations, and the only solid gold in this gilt book. His conversation is a marvel of visionary pyrotechnics. When Washington Hawkins catches the Sellers family dining on cold water and raw turnips, the Colonel explains that the turnips are Early Malcolms, the finest and costliest variety in the land. When a mob bilked in one speculation decides to hang the Colonel, he gives them choice suburban lots in the next speculation. When we last see Col. Sellers, he is on his way to begin a new career in the law, with his sights set at Chief Justice of the Supreme Court of the United States, and we have no doubt that he will make it.

This reissue of *The Gilded Age* comes with a long and, for the most part, quite helpful introduction by Justin D. Kaplan. Kaplan is sometimes extremely perceptive, as when he writes: "By the process of displacement money plays the role of sex in Mark Twain's work. He was notoriously reticent about dealing with mature sexual and emotional relationships, but he did write a kind of pornography of the dollar." My only disagreement is with Kaplan's tendency to take the book too seriously, to see it as "a novel of reaction and despair," "the most savage satire on democracy that American literature has to offer." Far from being savage, Twain's satire is affectionate and often runny. Like the late A. J. Liebling, one of his most gifted heirs, Twain was drawn to every scoundrel in the world, if the fellow was not sanctimonious in addition.

There is only one truly sanctimonious scoundrel in *The Gilded Age*, Senator Dilworthy, who masks his corruption with Christian piety; in the course of the action he is exposed and disgraced. Even here we can feel Twain's sneaking fondness for him: he is hypocritical with a certain sniveling style. And it is almost complete extenuation that he is a Senator. In *The Gilded Age*, when a newspaper reports of a burglar that he served one term in the penitentiary and one term in the United States Senate, the burglar writes in: "The latter statement is untrue and does me great injustice."

1964

Truths
from the Grave

BACK IN THE DAYS when poets had three names, in 1916, Edgar Lee Masters' *Spoon River Anthology* appeared, and scandalized the nation. I doubt that after almost half a century it will scandalize anyone. Yet it retains an odd sort of power despite its quaintness, like grandmother's pearl-handled revolver.

Spoon River Anthology consists of almost 250 epitaphs, all but two or three of them spoken by the deceased. Their composite picture of the Illinois town of Spoon River is thoroughly repulsive. Julia Miller married an old man to legitimize her unborn child, then took a fatal dose of morphine anyway. Nellie Clark, at eight, was raped by a 15-year-old boy, and the disgrace pursued her ever after and wrecked her life. Yee Bow was killed by a sneak punch from the minister's son. Oscar Hummel, drunk, was beaten to death by a fanatic prohibitionist. The amount of hidden crime would shame Singapore, and its quantity is equalled only by its nastiness.

The town's pervasive hyprocrisy is worse than its crimes. From the epitaph of Daisy Fraser, the town whore, we learn that only she is honest in her whoredom: the newspaper editor takes bribes to suppress the instability of the bank; the judge is on the payroll of the railroad; the clergymen speak or keep silent as their masters command. Deacon Taylor is a prohibitionist and secret drinker who confesses that the true cause of his death was cirrhosis of the liver; and one after another all the hyprocrites and whited sepulchres confess.

91

The Critic's Credentials

Unhappiness is endemic in Spoon River. "A bitter wind . . . stunted my petals," cries Serepta Mason. "Sex is the curse of life," says Margaret Fuller Slack, who might have been a great novelist if she had not had eight children. The cemetery is strewn with the wreckage of dreams and hopes. Only a handful of the dead are happy: a dedicated old maid schoolteacher, a blind mother of sighted children, a fiddler who had no worldly ambition, a loving old couple, a dancer whose final placid years were spent living in sin in Spoon River, a reader of Proudhon who murdered his rich aunt and got away with it, a man whose wife loves him and mourns him, several people who were inspired by knowing Lincoln, and a few others.

As poetry, *Spoon River Anthology* is wonderfully old-fashioned now and was wonderfully old-fashioned when it appeared. By 1916 Pound had published eight volumes of poems and translations, and Eliot had published most of the poems in *Prufrock and Other Observations*, but Masters was writing in an older tradition. He took that tradition to be that of the Greek Anthology, and his poems are full of references to Hades, Furies, Fates and other Grecian properties, but his true tradition is Browning, Whitman and the native ironies of Yankee gravestones.

The world of the poems is more remote from us than Mycenae. Wickedness is summed up by "I was drinking wine with a black-eyed cocotte" in Paris, or "I killed the son/Of the merchant prince, in Madam Lou's." A nickel then bought a supply of bacon, or was a proper tip for a waiter.

The style is fittingly archaic. "But thou grievest," Masters writes, or "Thou wert wise." Many of the poems end with exclamation points, and one ends with a little thicket of them:

> *The loom stops short! The pattern's out!*
> *You're alone in the room! You have woven a shroud!*
> *And hate of it lays you in it!*

The form is free verse. Sometimes it becomes almost metrical, falling into lines mostly anapaestic ("I know that he told that

I snared his soul/With a snare which bled him to death") or mostly iambic (" 'O, son who died in a cause unjust!/In the strife of freedom slain!' "); and sometimes it approximates rhyme ("Go out on Broadway and be run over,/They'll ship you back to Spoon River").

Masters' figures of speech are ponderous: labored similes ("She drained me like a fevered moon/That saps the spinning world") or interminable metaphors (Dippold the optician sees the afterlife as an eye examination, Joseph Dixon the tuner will be retuned by the great Tuner). In the much-anthologized "Petit, the Poet," Masters mocks the ticking of Petit's little iambics "While Homer and Whitman roared in the pines." There are several Homeric similes in the book, but I am afraid that despite his self-identification, Masters ticks irregularly more than he roars.

The touch is very unsure, and *Spoon River Anthology* is full of failures, many of them in endings. One poem ends with a true whimper: "Refusing medical aid." A good poem in which a tethered cow is a metaphor for the limited freedom of the will is ruined when the metaphoric cow pulls up its stake and gores the homespun philosopher to death. Masters overdoes everything. In a typical poem, he is not content with blind Justice; her eyes must suppurate under the bandages. The mock epic and play with which the book concludes are worse than the worst of the lyrics.

To balance these there are considerable successes. We encounter fine single lines ("Toothless, discarded, rural Don Juan") and fine similes ("While he wept like a freezing steer"). There is an eloquent impression of a rattlesnake ("A circle of filth, the color of ashes,/Or oak leaves bleached under layers of leaves") and a vivid mean description of a woman:

> *She was some kind of a crying thing*
> *One takes in one's arms, and all at once*
> *It slimes your face with its running nose,*

The Critic's Credentials

And voids its essence all over you;
Then bites your hand and springs away.
And there you stand bleeding and smelling to heaven!

Two of the poems seem to me, in their different fashions, completely successful. One is "Roscoe Purkapile," a slight comic poem about the ironies of marriage. The other is Masters' most famous poem, "Anne Rutledge," where his Lincoln worship somehow found its proper voice, the eloquence of understatement, and something that really does rival the spare beauty of the poems in the Greek Anthology was achieved.

The enormous popularity of *Spoon River Anthology* on its appearance warrants some discussion. One obvious explanation is *succès de scandale*—it was the sex-shocker, the *Peyton Place*, of its day. Knowing that childbirth would kill his wife, Henry Barker impregnated her out of hatred. The only feeling Benjamin Pantier inspired in his wife was sexual disgust. Old Henry Bennett died of overexertion in the bed of his young wife. Hamilton Greene is really his father's child by the German maid, as her epitaph confesses, although his own epitaph blindly boasts his "valiant and honorable blood." There is even a touch of sodomy. We have not advanced that much further in half a century.

Another feature that would have attracted readers in 1916 is the book's sour socialism. Its pervasive fable is the easy fable of Populism: that the pioneers built the land by their labor and endurance but that it was all stolen from them by "the bank and the courthouse ring." "English Thornton" appeals to the descendants of the veterans of the Revolution and the Indian wars to rise up and battle the descendants of the profiteers and the thieves, to recover their inheritance. After Lincoln, Masters' heroes idolize Altgeld, Bryan and Henry George. Matching this Populist politics is the religious iconoclasm of the village atheist. "The reason I believe God crucified His Own Son," Wendell P. Bloyd explains, "is, because it sounds just like

94

Him." Another hero is "Foe of the church with its charnel dankness."

The total effect of bitterness and frustration that *Spoon River Anthology* gives is greater than the sum of its poems. The dead really seem to be trying to tell us something about the quality of American life, something ugly yet essential to our knowledge. These are truths from the grave, thus *grave* truths. In his epitaph, the Town Marshall exults that Jack McGuire was not hanged for killing him, since he had first attacked McGuire. "In a dream," he says triumphantly, "I appeared to one of the twelve jurymen/And told him the whole secret story." But McGuire's epitaph on the next page explodes that inspirational account. McGuire really escaped hanging, he explains, because his lawyer made a crooked deal with the judge.

The most important factor in the appeal of the book, I believe, is that, as in *Winesburg, Ohio*, some larger vision of life shines through all the pettiness. The terms in which this is put are mostly inadequate. "I thirsted so for love!/I hungered so for life!" says the shade of the poetess Minerva Jones, raped by a bully and dead of an illegal abortion. Frank Drummer tried to memorize the Encyclopaedia Britannica. Mrs. Williams doesn't think Spoon River would have been any worse had its people "been given their freedom/To live and enjoy, change mates if they wished." Mrs. Charles Bliss pleads from her experience that divorce is far better for the children than a bad marriage. "Love of women," Ezra Bartlett argues, may lead one to the divine. Harmon Whitney has been wounded by his wife's "cold white bosom, treasonous, pure and hard." Edmund Pollard pleads boldly for hedonism and joy.

It is almost inarticulate, and much of it is silly, yet some suggestion of the good life, a richer and fuller life than Americans knew in 1916, is there. Masters never understood the reasons for his success in *Spoon River Anthology*, and he never attained it again. He is not a great writer, nor even a good one. But he confronted the spiritual poverty of his America—which is still

The Critic's Credentials

our America—without blinking, whereas Sinclair Lewis in *Main Street* ultimately turned away, and Thornton Wilder in *Our Town* never looked at America at all, merely sat down to copy *Spoon River Anthology* in a sculpture of fudge.

1963

Anthropologist of
Gopher Prairie

FOR A NUMBER of reasons, one of them the thorough tarnishing of Sinclair Lewis' reputation by the 1930s, I never read *Main Street* or *Babbitt* in my youth. However, *Arrowsmith* was for a time in high school my favorite book, and it was *Arrowsmith* that determined me to become a microbiologist. I forget now why I never did become a microbiologist, and perhaps I will yet. The current attempt to revive interest in Lewis, gives me an opportunity to end my long neglect of the first two, and to take a fresh look at the third.

Read now, more than forty years after its publication, *Main Street* is still an important book. Although its answers are contradictory and evasive, it raises all the basic questions about American life. In Carol Kennicott's revolts against the provincial meanness of Midwest village life in Gopher Prairie, we see the competing claims of the one and the many, art and life, beauty and utility, spirit and nature. Carol's frigidity fortunately keeps these problems from being dissipated in adultery. We recognize, when Carol sees through Guy Pollock, the village esthete, that the novel is determined not to be *Madame Bovary;* when she transfers Miles Bjornstam, the working-class radical, to her Swedish maid, we note that it is equally determined not to be *Lady Chatterley's Lover.*

Carol's frigidity is essentially right for the book; the combination of warm heart and cold groin makes her properly archetypal. Lewis insistently universalizes her. "A rebellious girl is the spirit of that bewildered empire called the American Midwest," he writes early in the book. Later he suggests that the reader probably has "within his circle at least one inarticulate rebel with aspirations as wayward as Carol's"; that there are "hundreds of thousands" like her in American small towns. It is *Main Street's* triumph (amid its many failures) to have revealed the immortal longings in all of us. So many later American novels are implicit in the book. The Carol who finally accepts Gopher Prairie becomes a line from *Alice Adams* to *Marjorie Morningstar*; the Carol who rejects and denies is the mother of Miss Lonelyhearts and the grandmother of Holden Caulfield.

Babbitt somewhat muffles the cry from the heart. George F. Babbitt suffers from a diffuseness of the author's intention, and he is really two inconsistent characters—a ludicrous buffoon who mouths peppy slogans, and a sensitive and rather decent fellow who sees through them. Sometimes the book becomes the purest comic strip, as when Sir Gerald Doak reveals himself to be the British counterpart of the Zenith businessman, as he might to Jiggs. If the point of *Main Street* is that Americans seethe with longings for beauty, culture and the good life, *Babbitt* substitutes the diminished observation that they are often lonely and unhappy. "A longing which was indistinguishable from loneliness enfeebled him," we are told of Babbitt. Where Carol suffers from the malady of the ideal, George seems to suffer mainly from gas.

Arrowsmith is a better novel than its predecessors, with a plot involving real action rather than nervous twitching, and a sense of pace they lack. Its vision is romantic pastoral: the pure dedicated life of scientific investigation (producing such embarrassing puerilities, dear to my high school days, as Max Gottlieb's Creed of the Scientist and Martin Arrowsmith's Prayer of the Scientist); Leora the fantasy wife, with her casual "Anglo-Saxon monosyllables" and her perfect devotion; Terry Wickett and the riches of poverty in a Vermont shack.

Arrowsmith makes painfully clear what is deeply concealed

in *Main Street* and half-concealed in *Babbitt*, that the protagonist's deepest vision of happiness is homosexual. In isolation, Carol's crush on the effeminate Erik Valborg would be very hard to recognize for what it is. George's feeling for Paul Riesling, "admiring him with a proud and credulous love passing the love of women," smiling at him with "the rare shy radiance he kept for Paul Riesling," are more immediately recognizable. But Martin's deserting his wife's bountiful bed and board to live in the woods with Terry is the purest homosexual "Wraggle-Taggle Gypsies, O." The book's picture of the two men, on the edge of tears at being reunited, pawing each other and growling, can be matched in any locker room in the nation.

Reading Lewis now, it is not hard to see what is wrong. He had superb material, all the richness of American life, and impressive power in rendering it. It results only in a series of static tableaus, however, since he cannot organize his material, manipulate it imaginatively, or even get it moving. The plot of *Babbitt* begins in the last 50 pages, and a most perfunctory plot it is. Whenever Lewis senses that he is neglecting the writer's craft, he turns out a "literary" sentence ("As the vast girdle of crimson darkened, the fulfilled land became autumnal in deep reds and browns"), or inserts a pat symbol (Carol returns to her violin and finds that "since she had last touched it the dried strings had snapped, and upon it lay a gold and crimson cigar-band").

If Lewis is not much of a novelist, he is a first-rate anthropologist. Those prodigies of research into the professions, those careful catalogues of the contents of suitcases or of the addled minds of Rotarians, are not accumulations of pointless detail but the very texture of observed life, keys to the tribal ways he is charting. Lewis once wrote of his "sociological itch," his novels are frequently identified as journalism, and E. M. Forster called him a photographer; yet more than any of these his field is anthropology. His picture of Midwest culture is oversimplified, his descriptions of Midwest personality are somewhat caricatured, but they are no more so than comparable studies of the Baganda or the Dobuans. Lewis' famous remark, in a review of Willa Cather, that to a writer of a certain sort a Sears, Roebuck catalogue is "a more valuable reference book than a library of economics, poetry and the lives of the saints," becomes less infuriating when we recognize it as an assertion of the importance of material culture to a field ethnologist.

Lewis was full of pieties: to his father's practice of medicine, to Sauk Centre and Minnesota, to the good old USA. His defenses against them often took the form of satire and cynicism, but he readily recognized and admitted (as in a shrewd self-obituary he wrote in 1941) his underlying sentimentality. The problem is that in more important respects he never recognized his own nature. In this he very much resembles Carol Kennicott, George F. Babbitt and Martin Arrowsmith. His bad marriages and unhappy life make it clear that he never understood his sexual nature. His bitter resentment of critics who praised him for his "good ear" rather than his art shows that he never understood the nature of his gift, either.

Lewis has one fable which he tells over and over again. It is the Return of the Prodigal: Carol to Will's arms, Babbitt to the Zenith boosters, Arrowsmith to pure research. The prodigal is always finer than the pack, and rejoins it with regrets; when the character is idealized enough, like Arrowsmith, there are two packs, and the false one is repudiated in the act of rejoining the true one. It was Lewis' inner war, as it is our own inner war, but in him it was so dimly apprehended that the antagonists struggle in darkness.

Mark Schorer has created the revival of interest in Lewis, and thus occasioned these reflections, with a whopping biography, *Sinclair Lewis: An American Life*. This book, a monument of research, will surely be the definitive biography for a long time, perhaps for all time. Schorer details the life, sometimes day by day, and succeeds in explaining as well as documenting its failures: Lewis' rootlessness, alcoholism and ingenuity in self-destruction. He is equally successful in defining Lewis' literary powers and limitations, and in explaining his extraordinary success as well as his ultimate failure. Schorer devotes many pages to characterizing Lewis' novels and placing them in the world of art, and he concludes, I think justly: "He was one of the worst writers in modern American literature, but without his writing one cannot imagine modern American literature."

Schorer demonstrates that Lewis' novels incarnate the ideas of H. L. Mencken, but he is much less convincing, to my mind, in his contention that they similarly dramatize or popularize the ideas of Thorstein Veblen. Schorer's prose is sometimes as fancy or heavily ironic or corny as his subject's; he is sometimes relentless in exploring the utterly inconsequential; an occasional reference, like an identification of John Donne, suggests that he is writing down to a wide popular audience. *Sinclair Lewis: An American Life* is nevertheless an important, even an invaluable, book, and anyone writing about Lewis from now on must be hopelessly in its debt.

The most powerful image in the Schorer book is of Sinclair Lewis as a tireless and compulsive mimic, parlor entertainer, monologist and dialect comedian. In this he may remind us of Joyce's father, John Stanislaus Joyce, as we see him caricatured in his son's *Portrait of the Artist as a Young Man*. Joyce caricatures himself in the book as Stephen Dedalus, a development beyond these folk arts to the sophisticated art of literature. In a sense, Lewis never developed beyond the pre-literary stage of mimicry. It is interesting to learn from Schorer that the one time Lewis and Joyce met, in Paris, Joyce did not get a chance to say a word.

1961

Prince Myshkin
in Hollywood

NATHANAEL WEST had, supremely, what Fitzgerald in *The Crack-Up* called "the authority of failure" (a term popularized in the title of William Troy's excellent article on Fitzgerald). He despised and rejected his family's (pre-Depression) business success, and if he wanted large sales for his novels or commercial success in the theater, he developed the melancholy authority which comes from not getting those things. West was probably the most hard-luck writer of our time. When *Miss Lonelyhearts* received excellent reviews, financial chicanery in the Liveright office got most copies of the book attached by creditors until public demand no longer existed. West's application for a Guggenheim grant was rejected (although his sponsors were Fitzgerald, Cowley, Wilson, and George S. Kaufman); his nearest approach to a theatrical hit ran for two nights on Broadway (with West's last thousand dollars invested in it); at his nadir in Hollywood he was even swindled out of his shoes; his four novels brought him a total income of $1,280; when, near the end of his life, he tried to get an advance of $1,000, and thus a little freedom, from Bennett Cerf, Cerf told him not to be unreasonable and gave him $250; for the last eight months of his life West was happy for the first time, married to Eileen McKenney and finally succeeding in Hollywood, then he and Eileen, at 37 and 27, were killed in an auto accident.

This driven figure fought the world by cheating: he forged

a transcript from Clinton High School to get into Tufts; he used the transcript of a more scholarly Nathan Weinstein (West's born name) to transfer to Brown; he copied his roommate's exam and induced his roommate to confess to the act. West fought similarly by endless lying, although Jay Martin, in his *Nathanael West: The Art of His Life*, obscures the record by calling West's lies "a heroic tale of a mythical, epic sort," "free fantasy," "constructing a myth," and so on.

West did not marry until his last year because of a bad case of what Freud calls "the degradation of the erotic principle." He idealized his mother and sisters, especially Laura, and, as Martin says, was always "more at ease with prostitutes than with those girls he regarded as 'nice.'" Finally, West's books were (and still are) greatly misunderstood, even by those close to him. For example, William Carlos Williams, West's discoverer, saw the theme of *Miss Lonelyhearts* as "the terrible moral impoverishment of our youth in the cities," and West's friend Edmund Wilson blurbed the book as "a miniature comic epic."

At the same time, while West failed and suffered, in more important terms he was a figure of success and good fortune. He was a profound self-analyst and self-critic, as Martin shows, and not only understood his worldly failure but used his peculiar gifts to their utmost. As a Communist fellow traveler in Hollywood in the 1930s, he tried to write positive and didactic fiction, but proved unable to do so: a meeting of the Hollywood Anti-Nazi League had to be cut out of *The Day of the Locust* because "it didn't fit." West's personality was richly complex and ambivalent, even somewhat schizoid: Shrike in *Miss Lonelyhearts*, the mocker, is as much an aspect of West as is the title figure, the idealist. "He could be his own Shrike," Martin says somewhat patly, later explaining that West had "a particularly intense hatred" of shrikes.

At least in *Miss Lonelyhearts*, West was the closest thing we have had to Dostoevsky (as in the same analogy with Flannery O'Connor's radical Christian dualism, this is a matter of kind, not of scale). West found Dostoevsky's novels overupholstered compared to his model, *Madame Bovary*, but he was fascinated by the figure of Myshkin, and briefly called himself "Prince Myshkin" in 1930. He told a newspaper interviewer the following year that "the next two thousand years belong to Dostoevsky's Christianity." Perhaps the fairest judgment is that of Boris Ingster, West's collaborator in Hollywood and a literate man by local standards, who said that *Miss Lonelyhearts* might have been another *Idiot* "if West had not committed himself to understatement." West shared with Dostoevsky the curious trait that his early drafts for novels (which Martin prints and synopsizes in profusion) invariably seem hopeless, yet his "almost faultless skill in revision" invariably succeeded in quarrying out the pure marble. In my opinion (already stated in my pamphlet *Nathanael West*) West was the finest American writer of the 1930s, and *Miss Lonelyhearts* is one of the three best American novels of the first half of our century (with *The Sun Also Rises* and *The Great Gatsby*).

Nathanael West: The Art of His Life, in one of its aspects, is like lifting up flat rocks and watching the little creatures, Hollywood writers and 1930s "progressives," scurry for cover. The book has a number of impressive virtues. First, Martin is a demon researcher: he fully documents West's "murderous" absent-minded driving, the cause of the Wests' death; he goes into extensive detail on all the classes West cut and all the courses West failed; he reports at least three occasions when his hero had gonorrhea; he reveals the names of the originals of the brothels in *A Cool Million* and *The Day of the Locust;* he finds the real-life source for the dwarf Abe Kusich in the latter novel; he even details a sad "intense" adultery which West had with a married neighbor in Erwinna, Pa., in 1934 and 1935.

Along with his bales of documentation, Martin contributes a number of genuine insights. He reveals the previously unknown cause (a rather shoddy betrayal by West) of the break between West and his fiancée Alice Shepard, and adds perceptively that West "had at last (however unconsciously) forced a separation rather than face real involvement." He shrewdly observes that "Shrike shows a wit so devastating that it is close to hysteria and implies, what Miss Lonelyhearts never sees, that Shrike himself is undergoing torments similar to his own." Martin properly praises the various speech patterns in *The Day of the Locust* as "vivid and alive, evocative and complexly symbolic of the characters." Sometimes Martin shows a tentativeness, a humility, which is engaging in contrast to all this bold assertion: "West's own surrealist fiction—if it can be called that"; "But this wound, if it was such."

Alongside these virtues there are, alas, some faults (I have space for only a single example of each). Like Richard Ellmann and certain other of his illustrious predecessors, Martin is a better biographer than critic. When West takes an authentic letter from a girl who has no dates because of a slight limp, and turns it into the famous letter in *Miss Lonelyhearts*, from the girl with no nose, Martin says that West has made the original "seem more 'real' "—surely "real" here means "fantastic." Martin is somewhat casual about his sources, chary with credits, so that I recognize far more ideas, published by myself among others, than he acknowledges. He is often inelegant ("These groups sponsored ideals importantly dissimilar"); owlish (when West autographs copies of *Balso Snell*, "From one horse's ass to another," Martin translates, "All men are deceitful, base Trojan horses"); pretentious (Abe Kusich and Homer Simpson in *The Day of the Locust* are interpreted as Abraham and Homer, "the fountainheads of Hebrew and Greek culture"); a laborer at the obvious ("West tended to fantasize in compensation for unsatisfactory reality"); and melodramatically ironic (his first and last chapters, on the fatal accident, are awash in irony). Beyond all this, Martin's worst fault is quite simply that he presumes. He refers infuriatingly to "several other writers from *The New Yorker*, as well as journalists like A. J. Liebling"; he even dares put on divine authority and tell his readers why West fell in love with Eileen McKenney: it was "a love whose source was compassion."

For all its virtues and faults, Jay Martin's book leaves us ultimately, as does West's work except at its very best, with Westian images. When West was at a low ebb in Hollywood in 1935, alone and sick, he was cared for by a midget and a part-time hooker, who alternately brought him chicken soup. Earlier, when he felt most lonely at his farmhouse, he used to dance with his dogs. Had he lived, West might have written *The Insulted and Injured*, with both those scenes in it.

1970

Couplings

WHAT IS WRONG with John Updike's novel, *Couples?* Just about everything. It is a strong contender in the most-ill-advised-work-by-a-writer-of-great-talent sweepstakes. For reasons that are difficult to imagine Updike has elected to raid the fictional territories occupied by John O'Hara, Peter De Vries, and Mary McCarthy (not to say Grace Metalious). As a most enthusiastic admirer of Updike's, standing in a rubble of dashed expectations, I can only try to isolate some of the causes of the disaster.

First, and very much in *Couples'* foreground, is an endless sexual explicitness that succeeds quickly in making sex revolting and succeeds ultimately in making it boring. One of the ingredients of this appears to be a revulsion with the body sometimes expressed by Piet Hanema, the most active adulterer among the ten couples in Tarbox, Massachusetts, whose doings, mainly sexual, we follow for a year. "Why all this fuss about bodies?" Piet asks plaintively at one point. In this perspective we learn that his plump wife Angela has "thick-thighed legs" with varicose veins, "surprisingly luxuriant pudenda," and that she is addicted to Lesbian fancies and masturbation. Piet's first mistress, Georgene the dentist's wife, is a vision of "kitten-chin glutinous with jism," her "strangely prominent coccyx" is "the good start of a tail"; when Piet stands up to dress, he observes, "Like butter on a bright sill her nakedness was going rancid." His third mistress, Bea the rich man's wife, is somewhat passive, and Piet stirs her up in classic fashion: "He spat between her breasts and lifted his arm as if to club her."

Piet's one-night-stand, Carol, the wife of the jet pilot, paints her nipples orange, and her feet "stank like razor clams." His first girl, Annabel, remains a lovely memory of a "rank elastic crotch," or "How Annabel would spread her legs as if imperiously to seize his entire face in the lips of her young swamp." Nor is this repulsive imagery confined to Piet. Harold Smith the broker, walking down a Boston street with his best friend's wife, Janet, wonders "what it would be like to suck each dirty one of ten toes clean." Shortly after, they pop into bed together and Harold's dream comes true: "Trembling as if whipped, he licked her eyelids and sucked her toes, one by one."

Worse in a way than the revolting is its opposite, what Yeats called in regard to his own early verse a "disagreeable sentimental sensuality." This is usually confined to Piet's second mistress and true love, Foxy Whitman, the wife of a college teacher. I am wary of reprinting these gooey ecstasies lest my typewriter keys get stuck together, but a small nonsentence should suffice to convey the tone: "Foxy's powdery armpits and petaled cleft simpler than a rose." The sexual practices of Piet and Foxy include some that the *Kama Sutra* assures us can only be performed by specially-trained hummingbirds.

Another basic mistake of the book is gigantism. We get a packed year of the elaborate couplings and recouplings of ten marriages, with adulterous affairs involving six of the men and either eight or nine of the women (depending on whether the reader decides that Terry, Piet's partner's wife, seen cavorting in the ocean with her lute teacher's husband, is Up To No Good). The material of a real novel, the story of Piet's affair with Foxy and its consequence in the collapse of both of their marriages, has been inflated until it becomes grotesque, two worms lost in a tangle of other worms in a bait can. Updike's slice of life, to vary the figure once more, is so large that the reader chokes on it.

A related failing is portentousness. The novel has epigraphs from Tillich and Blok that would not disgrace a treatise on Pre-

Lapsarian Predestination. To give the story a spurious seriousness, at various times the book's couples are described as a
"church," "a subversive cell. . . . Like in the catacombs," and
"a conspiracy to protect each other from death"; we are told
that the collapse of Piet's marriage has been "sacrificial" to
them (which seems to mean that they switch to playing bridge
in the evenings). There is an effort to make Piet, whose work is
building and restoring houses, into an avatar of old-fashioned
ethics and handicraft against present-day fraud and shoddy.
Nothing is too insignificant for this sort of inflation: a slice of
lemon in a bowl of consomme is "an embryo"; an olive in a
martini is a "tame green egg"; a salami sandwich is "minced
death."

The symbolism is similarly ham-handed and grandiose. The
weathercock on the Congregational church that Piet and Foxy
attend has a bright copper eye, which may be the eye of God,
watching their sins. Foxy is Sleeping Beauty, and Piet has
awakened her from a bad marriage that was "seven years'
sleep." At the end of the novel the Congregational church
burns down as some sort of moral lesson to Piet and Foxy, and
Piet feels a "lightness in his own heart, gratitude for having
been shown something beyond him, beyond all blaming."
What he was shown is beyond all knowing, too, so far as I
am concerned, since everything is made pointless at the end:
Piet and Foxy marry, move to a nearby town, and are "accepted as another couple." Perhaps the wages of sin is more
jerry-building, since "The carpentry in there [the church]
can never be duplicated."

Most unusual for Updike is the bad prose of *Couples*. Some
sentences would be at home in the Rover Boys series ("She
handed her can to—Ken!"), or late Steinbeck ("Amid laughter
and beer and white wine, through the odors of brine and tennis
sweat, the play was passed around"), or any woman's magazine ("Yet he had lifted and hurled thousands of lives safely
across the continent"). Many of the tropes are far-fetched and
strained: "Carrying within her like a contraceptive loop her

knowledge of her lover"; "Adultery lit her from within, like the ashen mantle of a lamp, or as if an entire house of gauzy hangings and partitions were ignited but refused to be consumed and, rather, billowed and glowed, its structure incandescent."

Finally, parts of the book seem derivative and secondhand. If the sex scenes suggest everybody from Walter Benton to Henry Miller, other scenes raise other ghosts. A long list of death images beginning "The Chinese knife across the eye. The electric chair dustless in the tiled room," could have been lifted from early Auden. There are several fleeting reminiscences of *The Great Gatsby:* a scene in which Georgene judges Piet and Foxy ("Having coaxed the abortion from their inferiors, they were quite safe") reminds the reader of Nick's description of Tom and Daisy after Daisy has killed Myrtle; a later confrontation of the Hanemas and the Whitmans is dully reminiscent of the confrontation of Gatsby and the Buchanans at the Plaza, and Piet displays a trace of Gatsby's quixotism. Even an occasional Malamud touch is apparent, as when Piet says winningly to Angela, "My stomach is a ball of acid."

No book by a gifted writer could be wholly bad, and *Couples* is not. Updike has a redeeming sense of comedy that saves him from his worst excesses. In the most blatant of melodramatic touches, he has Freddy Thorne the dentist, Georgene's husband, insist on a night with Angela as his price for getting an abortion for Foxy, pregnant with Piet's child. "One night with Angela. Work it out, fella," he says, "his face very ugly, the underside of some soft eyeless sea creature whose mouth doubles as an anus." But the actual night, Angela fortified by her copy of *Beyond the Pleasure Principle* ("It's very severe and elegant"), Freddy terrified, pudgy, and impotent, is wonderfully funny and successful. A similar thing happens at the climax of the leaden Hanema-Whitman confrontation when the Whitman baby burps.

Other achievements in the novel come from Updike's habitual perspectives by incongruity. They range from a tiny scenic effect (the high dunes on the beach littered with abandoned underpants), to a brilliant account of the Kennedy assassination as Foxy hears the news in Freddy Thorne's dentist chair. What can only be called Updike's wit produces a few modest and perfect touches. He shows passion in a Boston broker in a masterly image: "Ringlets of vibration, fine as watch springs, oscillated on the surface of his Gibson." Piet talks to Georgene on the phone in his office in a scene of wonderful comic double talk: Georgene tells him her sexual miseries, and Piet, for his partner's ear, translates his end of the conversation into details of home restoration.

To compensate for the bad prose there are some triumphs of style, with gigantism this time used comically. Here is Piet's view of a small bug: "a citizen out late, seen from a steeple." And here is the life and death of a hamster, seen in hamster consciousness:

"Several times the hamster had nosed his way out and gone exploring in her room. Last night he had made it downstairs, discovering in the moon-soaked darkness undreamed-of continents, forests of furniture legs, vast rugs heaving with oceanic odors; toward morning an innocent giant in a nightgown had admitted a lion with a mildewed eye. The hamster had never been given cause for fear and must have felt none until claws sprang from a sudden heaven fragrant with the just-discovered odors of cat and cow and dew."

None of John Updike's novels has been entirely satisfactory. *Rabbit, Run* is a fine book despite weak spots. The first chapter of *The Centaur*, is an immortal masterpiece on the order of the Circe chapter of *Ulysses*. This novel, Updike's fifth, is his most ambitious and worst. All that this enthusiast and fan can do is insist again on the formidable range of his gifts, and hope that for his next novel he will return to his normal scope and to the true country of his imagination.

1968

The Book of the Year?

I WAS ABROAD when Philip Roth's *Portnoy's Complaint* came out, and I am still abroad, but I have been following the American reviews like a breath of stale air from home.

The panegyrics are of the sort that might embarrass the author of the Pentateuch. Christopher Lehmann-Haupt in the *Times* described the book as "a technical masterpiece." Paul Carroll in *Book Week* called it "simply one of the two or three funniest works in American fiction" (he is the chairman of literature at Columbia College, as one could tell by his misusing the adverb "hopefully," and his true vocation seems to be that of a professor of marketing, judging by his "hunch" that *Portnoy's Complaint* is "the book of the year," as *The Armies of the Night* was of last year, *In Cold Blood* of 1966, and *Franny and Zooey* of 1961). Clifford A. Ridley in the *National Observer* compared Roth to a range of authors from Kafka to Cozzens, assigned the book as "required reading for anyone seriously interested in what fiction is saying about the personal themes of our time," and concluded that if it "is not the novel of the decade, it very possibly is the novel of the year."

Granville Hicks in the *Saturday Review* called it "something very much like a masterpiece." Josh Greenfield in the *New York Times Book Review* gave it an encomium so powerful— "the story finally ties together with the epiphanous neatness of any patient's last gestalt"—that I have not the slightest idea what it means, and he added that it is "the very novel that every American-Jewish writer has been trying to write" (Lionel Trilling?). Raymond A. Sokolov in *Newsweek* described Roth as "a serious writer of the first rank and no sales-hungry smut peddler." The reviewer in *Playboy* said that the book has "the exuberance and gusto of Eddie Cantor singing *Whoopee*," and concluded, for those born too late for that magical moment, that "he has produced a small masterpiece, a comic gem." Isa Kapp, in *The New Leader*, said: *"Portnoy's Complaint* may become the Book of the Year because Roth is so electrifyingly tuned in." Brendan Gill in the *New Yorker* listed "the company of the great pornographers and scatologists," including Rabelais, Shakespeare, and Joyce, and added, "Roth has edged into the outskirts of that company"—into their petticoats or bloomers, that old reprobate Leopold Bloom would have said.

The worst of all the puffballs was Geoffrey Wolff in the *Washington Post* (reprinted in the international *Herald Tribune*). He called the book "a classic," announced "we will judge our friends by what they say about this novel," defined its form, "confessional monologue," as "the dominant expressive form of our time," and concluded, "Roth has composed what for me is the most important book of my generation."

The denunciations of *Portnoy's Complaint* were much more moderate than the panegyrics (where they were not, they tended to dynamite all the fish). *Time* announced: "It is a work of farce that exaggerates and then destroys its content, leaving a gaping emptiness." Edmund Fuller in the *Wall Street Journal* said "Sometimes it is nasty." Alfred Kazin in the *New York Review of Books* observed that Roth, unlike Bellow, "writes without the aid of general ideas." Miss Kapp concluded: "We nevertheless are only too eager to escape from this airless place." Gill noted that the convention of narrating to a psychoanalyst, as well as "the pretense" that Portnoy is the Assistant Commissioner of Human Opportunity in the Lindsay Administration (rather than a successful writer) "are both archaic nuisances."

The two all-out attacks were by Marya Mannes, in a dissent from Hicks in the *Saturday Review*, and Kingsley Amis in the *Atlantic*. Miss Mannes charged the book with generating revulsion, being "hard-core pornography" on the order of Gore

Vidal's *Myra Breckenridge* (a particularly low blow), called Portnoy "the most disagreeable bastard who ever lived," and concluded that the book is a "mixture of bile, sperm, and self-indulgence." She accused Portnoy (and by implication, Roth) of being "without compassion," but herself showed about as much compassion as Judith of Bethulia. Amis' tone was more melancholy. He simply said that he did not find Jewish jokes funny and thus "I did not find Mr. Roth's book funny" (he and Miss Mannes were the only American reviewers I read who didn't), described the book as "a heavily orchestrated yell of rage . . . and rage wears one down," and noted that at the spurious epigraph "my spirits fell a little," and that as he read on, "my spirits fell a little further."

The best of the reviews I saw, and the one that seemed to me most nearly adequate to the book, was by Charles Thomas Samuels in *Book World*. It was sharply critical, while conceding the book's delights as comedy and satire. The effects "lost force through repetition," Samuels noted; "Everything is underlined." The work is "limited in insight," it uses a narrative device "that enables Roth to make his points without having to construct a story" (Gill said essentially the same thing), and Portnoy exploits "the pathetic woman he derisively calls Monkey." Samuels concluded by praising Roth's daring, adding: "But the Muses have left out of him a crucial courage that distinguishes entertainment from art."

There were a number of curiosities among the reviews. Scarcely anyone paid much attention to Portnoy's girls, as though like him they saw them simply as concave or convex, remarkably easy to clean, and no one even mentioned that The Monkey was a human being named Mary Jane Reed. There were a number of efforts, just this side the actionable, to equate Roth and Portnoy: *Time* went into some detail about how "Roth's past life resembles Alex Portnoy's"; Gill called Portnoy Roth's "hero and counterpart"; Amis talked of Roth's "unconcern to invent." Here Roth himself was most cooperative in an interview with George Plimpton in the *New York Times*

Book Review, admitting "There is certainly a personal element in the novel."

In regard to the stylistic comparison most frequently made, with the comedy of Lenny Bruce, Roth was considerably less cooperative, telling Plimpton sharply: "I would say I was somewhat more strongly influenced in this book by a sit-down comic named Franz Kafka and a very funny bit he does called 'The Metamorphosis.' " Among other oddities in the reviews were a curious hedging by the enthusiastic Greenfield ("it may very well be what is called a masterpiece—but so what? It could still also be nothing more than a cul-de-sac"); an odd feminist ambivalence by Miss Kapp (she "read it full of mixed feelings," and complained that the girls Portnoy used orogenitally should have been rewarded by "gratitude"); and a brave effort by Gill to clear the turgid Jewish atmosphere by generous quotations from William Butler Yeats and Patrick Kavanagh.

The few English reviews I have managed to see (the book was only published here last week) have been both calmer and shorter. Panegyrics included a comparison in the *Times Literary Supplement* with the work of Chaplin and Svevo (Julian Mitchell in the *New Statesman* also said "fit to stand beside Svevo's Zeno"); John Moynihan in the *Sunday Telegraph* called the book "a distinguished piece of literature, finely written, and often funny"; and Anthony Burgess in the *Sunday Times*, as might be expected, hailed it as "the first great novel of masturbation," and listed a variety of sordid details that add up to make it "a great joy and indicate a large verbal talent." The only two denunciations I have so far seen were both ambivalent. Elizabeth Berridge in the *Telegraph*, reviewing it with four other books, found it "nauseating . . . for a woman, at any rate," but conceded "such integrity in the writing, such forcefulness and witty conviction." Richard Jones in the *Times* attacked it from his first sentence ("this overlong sickroom document disguised as a comic novel") to his last ("about as funny as a cry for help"), with such endearments along the way as "banal," "cheap," "smart-alick," and "trivial," but somewhere in the middle his conviction faltered, and he exclaimed: "all this is brilliantly done."

The English reviewers, if they knew much less about New Jersey Jewry, were much less squeamish than their American counterparts in describing the book's gamy sexuality. (In the American reviews I saw, only *Time* had noted that Portnoy and Miss Reed go to bed with a Roman whore, *Newsweek* had bravely said "oral" and "cunnilingus," and Miss Kapp had referred somewhat coyly to "the oral ministrations of lovers"). Moynihan called The Monkey "superb," clearly not in reference to her literacy, Burgess went into the sexual variations in considerable detail, and A. Alvarez in the *Sunday Observer* noted objectively, of Alex and Miss Reed, "He has a passion, which she happily shares, for oral coition." Finally, there were two ideas odder than anything I saw in the American reviews. One was a trope by Mitchell announcing that the book "arrives here flaunting its reputation ahead of it like the bloated phallus of a Greek comedian," and the other was Miss Berridge's lovely idea that what Dr. Jekyll was afraid of about Mr. Hyde "could be identified with Portnoy."

What, then, is my own view? I think *Portnoy's Complaint* is a slight book, written with the left hand. It has far too many faults to list, so that the only one I will mention is that what Roth takes to be unique to the Jewish family is actually universal lower middle class (as both Fuller and Amis come close to saying). Beyond that, the book has virtues that the most flatulent panegyrists missed. Again, I will note only one, that Roth is *not* Portnoy, and that Roth *has* compassion. The high school yearbook description of Alex's mother ("*Sophie Ginsky the boys call 'Red,'/She'll go far with her big brown eyes and her clever head*") is heartbreaking in its suggestion of all that was stunted by her marriage; and if Alex sees Miss Reed only as a dumb sexual acrobat, Roth sees her as a person, and her plea for help "to be grown up," to "be an adult," is valid and moving. Roth has a matchless eye and ear and a superb talent for wild comic exaggeration, but he has not yet mastered the novel as a form, and this is scarcely a novel. As for the reviewers, with one or two honorable exceptions, you might better read fortune cookies.

1969

Fun and Love

I F JOHN BARTH is a major novelist, as I believe him to be, he is surely the most disputed major novelist we have. Each of his four novels has had, among those qualified to judge, its passionate enthusiasts and its passionate detractors. *The Sot-Weed Factor,* which I, among many, consider an immortal comic masterpiece, seems to others, whose judgment cannot readily be dismissed, a worthless and boring pastiche. The case of his *Giles Goat-Boy,* is even more extraordinary. Those reviews that did not call it a work of monumental tedium tended to propose it as the ultimate work of genius for which the writings of Proust, Joyce, and Mann had prepared us. The charges against Barth are principally three. One is that he is fundamentally not serious, that his work is all fluff, on the order of cotton candy. A second is that however serious and important he may be, he is coldhearted, sour, and without compassion, and that this makes his comedy always schizoid and ultimately unsatisfactory. The third charge accepts Barth's seriousness, but adds that it is hopelessly flawed by his over-ingenuity and delight in his deft jugglery of language; that his fiction suffers because its author is a ham.

These charges are best refuted by Barth's book of short fictions, *Lost in the Funhouse.* The two best pieces, the title story and "Menelaiad," make it clear that Barth is both serious and compassionate and that his ingenuity is properly harnessed to the traditional tasks of fiction, however novel his techniques. The title story is about Ambrose, the perhaps autobiographical boy who is the protagonist of several other stories in the book. He is spending a Fourth of July with his family in Ocean

City, in Maryland, during the Second World War. As Barth begins the story, he begins simultaneously to lecture the reader on the techniques of fiction: He explains why he italicizes certain phrases, in a lofty note on the literary use of italics; he reduces names to initials and blanks, and explains why the nineteenth century believed that this practice enhanced reality; he discourses on the problems of beginning a story, of narrative viewpoint, and so forth. This is at first simply amusing as a somewhat pedantic mockery of the authorial voice in fiction, but then it becomes significant as the story starts to veer out of the author's control: "We should be much farther along than we are; something has gone wrong; not much of this preliminary rambling seems relevant," the author suddenly confesses. He tries to recover his assurance, but it is too late; the story has run wild ("No reader would put up with so much with such *prolixity*," he declares), and it will all have to be rewritten to make Ambrose "eighteen at least" instead of thirteen.

By the time this authorial collapse is complete, the story has brilliantly and compassionately taken us inside Ambrose's tormented adolescence: his doubts and terrible fears, his lust for Magda (the fourteen-year-old neighbor his family has taken along), his complex feelings toward his parents and his less sensitive older brother Peter. Peter and Magda desert Ambrose in the funhouse, where he is lost for a brief time, or a long time, or forever, or perhaps they all went on the merry-go-round and never got to the funhouse at all. The story is a triumph, but Barth's joke is that it is the triumph of its own vital force over the author's difficulties. He cannot finish his sentences ("The fellow's hands had been tattooed; the woman's legs, the woman's fat white legs had," "And it's all too long and rambling, as if the author") and there are odd repetitions ("Where she had written in shorthand *Where she had written in shorthand* Where she had written in shorthand *Where she* et cetera").

Eventually, with Ambrose, we come to understand that the funhouse symbolizes sex, that "the whole point of Ocean City" is sex. Beyond that, the funhouse stands for life or the world ("His father should have taken him aside and said, 'There is a simple secret to getting through the funhouse' "). But most insistently the funhouse is art, the art of fiction, the art of *this* fiction. In one of the endings Barth offers us, Ambrose "took a wrong turn, strayed into the pass *wherein he lingers yet.*" In another, Ambrose "died of starvation telling himself stories in the dark," but, "unbeknownst to him," the funhouse operator's exquisite, unusually well-developed daughter took them all down and preserved them for posterity. In the story's final ending, however, we have a wry acceptance of vocation (echoing Dylan Thomas's "In My Craft or Sullen Art"):

> He wishes he had never entered the funhouse. But he has. Then he wishes he were dead. But he's not. Therefore he will construct funhouses for others and be their secret operator—though he would rather be among the lovers for whom funhouses are designed.

The story is moving and beautiful, not in spite of its critical self consciousness but by means of it, as Nabokov's *Pale Fire* and *The Gift* are true novels, although built out of literary criticism and the spoof of literary criticism. Ambrose, wise beyond his years, raw with sensibility, prescient, paralyzed by self-doubt and multiple possibility, is absurd, yet marvellous and deeply true to our experience. Our final vision of Ambrose is:

> He wonders: will he become a regular person? Something has gone wrong; his vaccination didn't take; at the Boy Scout initiation campfire he only pretended to be deeply moved, as he pretends to this hour that it is not so bad after all in the funhouse, and that he has a little limp.

The author, a middle-aged Ambrose type, similarly comes to life for us. "I'll never be an author," he cries out. "It's been forever already, everybody's gone home, Ocean City's deserted, the ghost crabs are tickling across the beach and down the littered cold streets." He is his own stern critic, a Jamesian voice saying "There is no *texture of rendered sensory detail*, for one thing." Ambrose makes a speech to Magda that turns into technical advice about how to do such a speech in a work of fiction. Eventually, the author dissolves into ghostly voices, and we hear wishful statement followed by harsh rejoinder: "This can't go on much longer; it can go on forever." Barth's comic mastery enables him to reveal to us all the weaknesses and self-doubts of the artist, the sensitive adolescent still within each middle-aged frame, but to reveal them to us within a story of consummate craft and absolute success.

"Menelaiad," in its different way, is just as wonderful—a set of variations on "The Odyssey," a monologue by Menelaus, addressing visiting Telemachus and Peisistratus about his life and difficulties with Helen. At first it looks like the modish vulgarizing of Greek myth that French writers from Gide to Giraudoux seem to specialize in, as when Menelaus remarks, "Better open your palace to every kid in the countryside than not know whose your own are in, Mother and I always thought." The comic technical device of "Menelaiad" is story-within-story-within-story, so that the strings of quotation-marks-within-quotation-marks lengthen to the ridiculous. This device serves to telescope time and create polyphony, and it justifies itself as fully as do Sterne's stylistic vagaries in *Tristram Shandy*. There are wild, comic pages of Rabelaisian exaggeration, as in an astonishingly funny account of Menelaus taking out on his ship and crew his sexual frustration by Helen. The voices of Proteus, of his daughter Eidothea, and of Helen rise periodically to become a mad cacophony. As Proteus narrates Menelaus's imaginings, Helen's infidelities become so prodigious in number and variety that they overflow onto faithful Penelope, and we learn "how faithless Penelope, hearing Odysseus had slept a year with Circe, seven with Calypso, dishonored him by giving herself to all one hundred eight of her suitors, plus nine house servants, Phemius the bard, and Melanthius the goatherd."

The Critic's Credentials

For all its style and wit, "Menelaiad" shares with "Lost in the Funhouse" the serious purpose of fiction: to move us by re-creating the actions and passions of human beings. Helen insists that she has been a paragon of marital fidelity and did not go to Troy at all (Aphrodite sent an ethereal Helen in her place, as Euripides proposed); Menelaus believes her to be so adulterous that she has popped into bed with Telemachus while Menelaus is telling his story in the darkened hall. Both are right, in a sense. Helen's infidelities are like Molly Bloom's: in the flesh, human weaknesses to forgive; in the spirit, divine rites of fertility. Menelaus's obsessive question in "Menelaiad" is why Helen chose *him*, the least of her suitors, and the curious Christian answer is finally supplied by Proteus: "Helen chose you without reason because she loves you without cause." (This is not unlike the answer Molly Bloom's final soliloquy gives to a similar question: Why, of all people, she chose Leopold.) The last words of "Menelaiad" affirm "the absurd, unending possibility of love."

The dozen other pieces in the book are, if lesser, equally dazzling in their range and variety, from the first, which is literally, and physically, a Möbius strip (that is, the reader is asked to do some paste-and-scissors work), to one called "Glossolalia" (the gift of tongues), which goes into what appears to be an Africanlike language of Barth's invention. "Night-Sea Journey" is a serious working of Kafka's vein; other stories echo Beckett and Borges. "Petition" is a passionate plaint of the spirit against the flesh; "Anonymiad" is the chronicle of a Bronze Age bard who fails to become Homer. "Title" is a dialogue, about writing, between husband and wife, or author and critic, or writer and muse. Barth remarks in his Author's Note: " 'Title' makes somewhat separate but equally valid senses in several media: print, monophonic recorded authorial voice, stereophonic ditto in dialogue with itself, live authorial voice, live ditto in dialogue with monophonic ditto aforementioned, and live ditto interlocutory with stereophonic et cetera, my own preference; it's been 'done' in all six." For all of these glittering show-biz possibilities (chiefly resembling a *Sot-Weed Factor* list), the story nevertheless affirms that "What goes on between [people] is still not only the most interesting but the most important thing in the bloody murderous world, pardon the adjectives." "Life-Story," a dazzling display of virtuosity about fiction versus reality, asks, "Who doesn't prefer art that at least overtly imitates something other than its own processes?" These affirmations and questions are part of the joke, but they are part of the seriousness, too. " 'Love it is that drives and sustains us!' " Barth writes in "Night-Sea Journey," and then, "I translate: we don't know *what* drives and sustains us, only that we are most miserably driven and, imperfectly, sustained."

John Barth is fiendishly clever, or, if you prefer, angelically brilliant. I believe his only peers in our time are Joyce and Nabokov. Like them, he is a comic humanist, so his giant funhouse at first bewilders, then delights, and finally returns us to the world saner and wiser. I take the "lost" in his title in a good sense—that he is in there for life, abandoned and shameless in his labyrinthine art.

1968

Germ's Choice, Shame's Voice

"The only arms I allow myself to use—silence, exile, and cunning," Stephen Dedalus proclaims proudly near the end of *A Portrait of the Artist as a Young Man*. His creator and prototype, James Joyce, used a lifetime of exile, certainly, but not much silence or cunning. The large volume of his letters edited by Stuart Gilbert in 1957 has now been reissued with corrections, and supplemented with two additional volumes edited by Richard Ellmann. In these 1,600-odd letters we have, instead of silence, endless whining and recrimination; instead of cunning, all too often, Joyce making a fool of himself.

Ellmann has performed another of his prodigies of scholarship: footnotes translate all the letters not in English, identifying every indelicate pun in, say, an imitation of a Slovene speaking Triestine Italian; some of Joyce's acquaintances were so fleeting that he never learned the man's name, but Ellmann knows it and tells it.

The new biographical facts that emerge are of interest only to specialists, since, for the common reader, Ellmann's *James Joyce* (1959) is quite enough biography. Joyce's correspondence with other writers is of more general interest, and is a remarkable record (writers being what they are) of the esteem for him among his compatriots: William Butler Yeats writes to him, of *Portrait*, "I think it is a very great book—I am absorbed in it"; Sean O'Casey writes to him, calling *Ulysses* "that great and amazing work"; Yeats writes, when the Irish Academy is being founded, "Of course the first name that seemed essential both to Shaw and myself was your own."

Of most value to the reader, perhaps, are the letters that furnish sources or offer clues to the books. Much of the material in these volumes, however, is of little or no interest on any basis. Ellmann says in his preface that about 100 "trivial communications" have been omitted, but they could not have been more trivial than some of what is gravely printed: a postcard from Nora Joyce to Frank Budgen saying "Sorry you cant come for Jim's birthday"; a card to Ettore Schmitz ("Italo Svevo") and his family, wishing them "Buon Natale"; a postcard to Joyce's son George and his wife, reading, in its entirety, "Here's my hotel and my news is coming"; a postcard to two of the English Players from Elsinore, reading "Greetings to the English Players from here in Elsinore."

Other letters will be boring to everyone but card-carrying Joyceans (Father Conmee said that Joyce's letters home from Clongowes were "like grocer's lists"): "Today for dejeuner I had some cold ham, bread and butter, Swiss cream with sugar; for dinner I had two poached eggs and Vienna bread, macaroni and milk, a cup of cocoa and a few figs"; "Georgie's cold seems to be better. He can walk across the room by himself now and he has two new teeth."

The letters are primarily important as a portrait of a man, and it is an unlovely portrait. Joyce was, as we all are, a flawed human being, but his marks of weakness, marks of woe, stand out quite vividly. These letters show Joyce as, among other things, a sponge and toady to the rich, an unloving brother, an unsympathetic son, a perverse husband, a hater of his native land, and a repulsive self-publicist. We see him, as sponge and toady, begging support from Lady Gregory while despising her, or allowing Harriet Shaw Weaver to commission an episode in *Finnegans Wake*, or buttering-up any reviewer who mentions his name.

As unloving brother Joyce writes incessant begging letters to Stanislaus, and eventually observes, "I daresay you are tired of these letters. I am too." Early in his courtship, he writes to Nora, "My brothers and sisters are nothing to me." When

The Critic's Credentials

Herbert Gorman was writing Joyce's biography, Joyce told him that he didn't know where his sisters lived.

As unsympathetic son, Joyce wrote so offensively to his father that John Joyce broke off the correspondence for several years. (It is true that John himself is no prize. Sometimes he postures as King Lear: "Perhaps in years to come, long after my release from this world, you may learn to feel some of the pangs I have endured, and then you will appreciate the feelings of a Father who loved his children and had high ambitions for them, and spared no money when he could afford it, to educate them and make them what they should be, but who when adversity came and he could no longer gratify all those wants, was despised disrespected, jeered at, scoffed at and set at defiance." Worse, we see him at the age of 82, posturing as the first page of *Portrait:* he reminds his 49-year-old son that James used to be "Babie Tuckoo" and that John used to tell him "all about the moo-cow.")

A series of intimate letters to Nora in 1909 (the only sensational material in the new volumes) is disconcerting less for its revelation of Joyce's broad streak of the perverse than for the infantile nature of his thought and language. A letter accusing Nora of adultery and questioning his paternity of George asks melodramatically, "How am I to drive away the face which will come now between our lips?" Or Joyce writes, with horrid coyness, "There is a place I would like to kiss you now, a strange place, Nora. *Not* on the lips, Nora. Do you know where?" Here is a swatch of deathless prose (the dots mark a censorship by Ellmann):

"I am your child as I told you and you must be severe with me, my little mother. Punish me as you like. I would be delighted to feel my flesh tingling under your hand. Do you know what I mean, Nora dear? I wish you would smack me or flog me even. Not in play, dear, in earnest and on my naked flesh. I wish you were strong, *strong*, dear, and had a big full proud bosom and big fat thighs. I would love to be whipped by you, Nora love! . . . Pardon me, dear, if this is silly. I began this letter so quietly and yet I must end it in my own mad fashion.

"Are you offended by my horrible shameless writing, dear? I expect some of the filthy things I wrote made you blush. Are you offended because I said I loved to look at the brown stain that comes behind on your girlish white drawers? I suppose you think me a filthy wretch. How will you answer these letters? I hope and hope you too will write me letters even madder and dirtier than mine to you."

As a hater of Ireland, Joyce writes Miss Weaver that his father cursed "his native country and all in it," as does his father's son. Home on a visit in 1909, Joyce writes to Nora, "I loathe Ireland and the Irish." (In other moods, it must be said, he thought Dublin beautiful and hospitable, and wished there were an Irish Club in Rome.)

Joyce's letters relentlessly promoting and publicizing his work are the most repulsive of all in their cold and mechanical conniving ("It would be very useful to me if your correspondence with the writer did not cease"). Joyce had more than a touch of paranoia. We see him writing to Stanislaus that he is registering his entry to a newspaper puzzle contest so that he cannot be cheated out of the prize, or writing to Nora, "Are you with me, Nora, or are you secretly against me?" He explains to Ezra Pound that he did not go back to Ireland to see his father before his death because "I never dared to trust myself into the power of my enemies."

"I propose to mark firmly what is ridiculous and odious in the Shelley brought to our knowledge by the new materials," Matthew Arnold writes in a review of Dowden's *Life of Shelley*, "and then to show that our former beautiful and lovable Shelley nevertheless survives." My task is similar in regard to Joyce. Our beautiful and lovable Joyce survives in his books, where all that is ridiculous and odious is transmuted into magnificent comic and tragic art. The ungrateful supplicant to

The Critic's Credentials

Lady Gregory becomes the parodist author of *Ulysses* who has Buck Mulligan reprove Stephen for his treatment of "that old hake Gregory": "She gets you a job on the paper and then you go and slate her drivel to Jaysus. Couldn't you do the Yeats touch? . . . 'The most beautiful book that has come out of our country in my time. One thinks of Homer.'"

The unloving brother creates the Stephen in *Ulysses* who sees his sister Dilly buying a French primer for a penny, realizes that she shares his aspirations, and understands tragically that he dare not help her: "She is drowning. Agenbite. Save her. Agenbite. All against us. She will drown me with her, eyes and hair." ("Agenbite of inwit," a motif in the book, is "remorse of conscience.")

The unsympathetic son turns into the author of the Cork episode in *Portrait*, that moving and perfect dramatization of the inability of like father and like son to break down the barriers of misunderstanding between them, then into the author of *Finnegans Wake*, that 628-page anecdote about an encounter John Joyce once had with a tramp in Phoenix Park.

The infantile perverse husband is transformed into Leopold Bloom, the magnificent comic hero of our time, and all his infantile perversities are apotheosized into the "Circe" chapter of *Ulysses*, one of the peaks of the world's literature. The embarrassing language of the letters to Nora is broadened comically into the style of the "Nausicaa" chapter, accurately characterized by Joyce in a letter to Budgen as "a namby-pamby jammy marmalady, drawersy (alto là!) style with effects of incense, mariolatry, masturbation, stewed cockles," and so forth.

The hater of Dublin and Ireland becomes the author of *Finnegans Wake*, that Joyous love letter to "Dear Dirty Dumpling" and "the matter of Erryn." The repulsive self-publicist with streaks of paranoia becomes Bloom the lion-hearted, standing up to the Cyclops on behalf of justice, love, and the truth that "Christ was a jew like me"; his reward is transformation into "ben Bloom Elijah" and immediate ascent to heaven "like a shot off a shovel."

Yeats said, in another connection, that we must choose perfection of the life or of the work. James Joyce chose perfection of the work, and it is the glory of our century. We can forget those deformations, Germ's Choice and Shame's Voice.

1966

The Lawrence Mob

M ANY WRITERS bore and repel me, but there are only two important ones whom I detest. They are Edgar Allan Poe and D. H. Lawrence: Poe for his cold mechanical hand; Lawrence for his shrill hysterical voice. Lawrence is worse, because of the cultists. If I had the humorless fanaticism of Maxwell Geismar, I would write a book against Lawrence and the Lawrentians. Instead, considering in the bowels of Geismar that I might be wrong, I have just read through the new two-volume *The Complete Poems of D. H. Lawrence*, edited by Vivian de Sola Pinto and F. Warren Roberts. The scholarly labors of the editors deserve the highest praise. I cannot say as much for their critical opinions (what could Pinto mean by "poetic" in his statement in the introduction that "Lawrence's poetic genius finds its fullest expression in prose works"?).

At least seven different Lawrences wrote verse, six of them in various degrees objectionable. It might be useful to disentangle the mob. The first is the Young Lady. I did not name her, Lawrence did. He says in the preface to *Collected Poems* (1928), of the first two poems he wrote: "Any young lady might have written them and been pleased with them." The Young Lady did not immediately disappear, as Lawrence thought; she stayed around to write verse all his life, as his friend Anais Nin recognizes, in *D. H. Lawrence: An Unprofessional Study*, when she talks of the "androgynous" quality of his writing. The Young Lady is a constant female voice in the poetry: speaking as the bride in "Wedding Morn"; speaking as the rejected girl in "Forecast"; speaking as a bereft girl in "Ballad of Another Ophelia"; speaking as the dancing girl in

"Tarantella"; speaking as a mother rejoicing in her baby in "Baby Songs" and "Baby-Movements."

After a while, one is no longer disconcerted when a poem begins, as the effective "Casualty" does: "As I went down the street in my rose-red pelerine." Where the Young Lady does not write openly as a woman, she is a remarkably girlish male voice. She begins "Mystery," ludicrously, "Now I am all/One bowl of kisses," and continues in the same vein: "And down my slim/White body drips/The moving hymn." It is she who addresses the rabbit as "bunny" in "Rabbit Snared in the Night," or writes in "Little Fish" that "their little lives are fun to them."

The second voice is obviously what the Freudians call a "reaction-formation" against the Young Lady. I name him "Tarzan" because he writes in "Scent of Irises": "you, woman, and me, man." His specialty is a monotonous and boring affirmation of the male self. Tarzan rewrote the Young Lady's "Virgin Youth," a girlish poem about Lawrence's "beautiful, lonely body," to be the "Virgin Youth" of *Collected Poems*, an amazing cultic hymn in the worship of Lawrence's penis. It is Tarzan, somewhat soured, who asks "why am I in hell?" in "Next Morning," or prays "Oh God, to be mutilated!" in "Mutilation." He is entirely preoccupied with his physical and emotional self, and when he considers another person, as in "Wedlock," it is in purely selfish terms: "Suppose you didn't want me!" In the later poetry Tarzan inflates the self to monstrous proportions, and eventually he writes with absolute seriousness in "Auto-Da-Fé": "But the day they burn my pictures they burn the rose of England."

The most vulgar of the Lawrences, who develops out of young Tarzan, is the Peepshow Barker, who wants to show us his wife's bellybutton or tell us how great the Lawrences are in bed together. The Peepshow Barker wrote most of *Look! We Have Come Through!*, but his voice is heard in every volume. It is the Barker who complains in "Last Words to Miriam" that her frigidity "broke/My craftsman's nerve," and who wrote, even more disgustingly, in an earlier draft of the poem that her failure to respond darkened his "eternal fame." The Peepshow Barker exhibits himself nuzzling Frieda's great breasts in "Song of a Man Who Is Loved," or kissing her invaluable orifices in "Seven Seals"; he compares amorous bruises with Frieda in the morning in "A Bad Beginning," and boasts of how vigorously she responds to his lovemaking in "One Woman to All Women."

With the announcement, in "Man Reaches a Point–," that "desire has died in me," the Hedge Preacher takes over. The Hedge Preacher speaks in weak prose rhetorical questions and exclamations, which he prints as verse. He is a master of the ruinous ending. The Hedge Preacher concludes "Shades": "For I have told you plainly how it is." He ends "Frost Flowers": "for what kind of ice-rotten, hot-aching heart must they need to root in!" He concludes "Figs": "What then, when women the world over have all bursten into self-assertion? / And bursten figs won't keep?"

The Hedge Preacher proclaims that "philanthropy and benevolence" are "Just a bad smell," and calls down malediction on "foul equality" and "still more foul human perfection." He writes most of *Pansies* (Lawrence's odd version of *Pensées*): asking, "why have a financial system to strangle us all in its octopus arms?"; warning, "Beware, O my dear young men, of going rotten"; complaining, "Why don't you know what's what, young people?"; proclaiming, "And we've made a great mess of love, mind-perverted, will-perverted, ego-perverted love." He preaches against lesbians, against money, against flat-chested women, against "our brightest young intellectuals," against Chekhov's "wimbly-wambly wet-legs," against police spies, against anything in fact that displeases him. Nor is the Hedge Preacher's verse any less prosy when he is in favor of something. "O! Americans," which is a long awful poem in defense of the American Indian, says lyrically: "He is far too few to cause any apprehension in any direction."

Several more Lawrences remain to be noticed. One is Mard-

Arsed Bertie, the son of a Nottingham coal miner, who rose in the world. ("Mard-arsed" is from "The Collier's Wife," and "Mardy" seems to have been Lawrence's childhood nickname —"mard" being Nottinghamshire for "*petted.*") It was Mard-Arsed Bertie who used to write Lawrence's friends on crested notepaper, explaining: "My wife's father was a baron, and we're just using up old note paper." Bertie is the author of a series of pansies which, in the guise of warning the working class of all they lose by rising out of their class, actually boast of Lawrence's climb to social eminence. The Lawrentians proclaim that Lawrence is the most ruthlessly honest of writers, but Mard-Arsed Bertie is sly and dishonest in just this have-it-both-ways fashion. It is Bertie who rewrote the honest "The Piano," in which the trained singer drowns out the memory of Lawrence's mother singing, into the dishonest "Piano," in which, much more conventionally, the reverse happens.

The worst of all Lawrences is Spiteful Ted, the surly and mindless streetcorner tough. Ted is the author of the shrill *Nettles,* properly called by Richard Aldington "about the worst and most trivial thing he ever published." Spiteful Ted is not limited to the *Nettles* volume. He contributes all the sadistic violence that led Cecil Gray to call Lawrence "a potential Hitler." Ted wants to blind clever women, to crush the bourgeoisie "like sickening toadstools" ("Kick them over, the toadstools,/Smash them up"), "to pee in the eye of a police-man," and so on.

But there is one more Lawrence. Amazingly, he is a poet, a true poet. Furthermore, he appears in the verse from first to last, although he is the author of no more than perhaps 20 of the 1,000-or-so poems and drafts in *The Complete Poems.* There are lines of real poetry even in the juvenilia, written before Lawrence was 26, notably in "Reading in the Evening." In *Rhyming Poems,* the end of the revised "Wild Common" is beautiful, as is the reference to "the ermine moth's/Twitching remark" in "The Yew-Tree on the Downs." "The Enkindled Spring" and "Firelight and Nightfall" are fine poems. "Snap-

Dragon" has great power and tension, and had them even in first draft. "Reading a Letter" shows masterful economy.

In the fleshy wastes of *Look! We Have Come Through!* there is one real poem, "The Song of a Man Who Has Come Through." *Birds, Beasts and Flowers* displays Lawrence's sharp eye in "Bat" ("Wings like bits of umbrella"), and a rare, delightful humor in "Purple Anemones" and "Man and Bat." "Snake" is a powerful and impressive poem, and "Turkey-Cock" shows the sort of craftsman's skill that rarely interested Lawrence, introducing the colors of steel-slag in describing the cock's wattles, then using them to produce a strong phoenix image at the end.

Amid all the hysteria of *Pansies* there is one superb poem, "Swan," and some of its quality carries over into two sequels, "Leda" and the final stanzas of "Give Us Gods." It is hard to imagine Lawrence being funny and engaging on the woman question, but a little pansy called "It's No Good!," imaging women as volcanoes, miraculously is both. The collection published posthumously as *More Pansies*, in the midst of all the nonsense, has one poem of the greatest beauty, "Andraitx—Pomegranate Flowers"; another, "Name the Gods!," rises to magical eloquence in its final lines.

Last Poems has its share of triumphs. "The Greeks Are Coming!" is effective and lovely until the last stanza, when it turns into Masefield's "Cargoes." "The Body of God" is masterful in its bold pun on incarnation in the line, "And becomes at last a clove carnation: lo! that is god!" Best of all is the deservedly famous "Bavarian Gentians," which Pinto's introduction accurately calls "the greatest of his mythological poems." I think that it and the less ambitious "Swan" and "Andraitx—Pomegranate Flowers" are deathless masterpieces. How to explain the fact that Lawrence could write magnificent poetry but so rarely did? The rest of the mob were using the pen.

1965

Playing Doctor,
Playing War

Negatives, by Peter Everett, winner of the Somerset Maugham prize, is a most unusual novel. To get the worst said immediately, it is psychologically shallow and has a streak of hokum running through it. Nevertheless, it is a real novel, however slight, on a serious subject; as cannot be said of all real novels on serious subjects, it is economical, well-paced, and continuously interesting, what the English call a "good read."

The setting is a run-down curio shop, now mostly trading in second-hand furniture, in an unattractive section of an English city. A man named Theo and a woman named Vivien run the shop and live in the squalid rooms above it. The plot, however bizarre, can be simply synopsized. Theo and Vivien have a sex game that they play, in which he dresses up as Dr. Crippen, complete with gold-rimmed spectacles, glued-on mustache, and celluloid collar, and she disguises herself variously as Belle Elmore, the wife Crippen poisoned, and Ethel Le Neve, the mistress who replaced her. In the course of the novel, a German girl named Reingard spoils the Crippen game, with unfortunate results for both Theo and Vivien, by encouraging Theo into a more consuming identification with Baron von Richthofen, the German flying ace of the First World War.

In his various roles as Crippen, Theo is sometimes a meek and submissive husband, polishing the shoes of imaginary boarders at Belle's orders; sometimes the infatuate lover of Ethel, showering her with his wife's furs and jewels; sometimes the guilty criminal who panics and flees England with Ethel disguised as his nephew.

As von Richthofen, Theo has only one part to play, the solitary king of the air who slew the slayer and shall himself be slain, but he comes to play it more and more exclusively. First he takes to wearing a leather flying jacket in the shop, and his posture becomes "militarily casual." Then Reingard gives him a von Richthofen haircut, and he takes to clicking his heels and addressing the cat as though it were a German dog. Finally he acquires a wrecked British training plane, and, with the help of the shop's upholsterer, reconstructs it to resemble a Fokker. Sitting in its cockpit dressed in a copy of von Richthofen's uniform, wearing duplicates of his decorations, squeezing the buttons of wooden models of his machine guns, Theo *becomes* von Richthofen, and in that role he symbolically kills and is killed.

The power of the novel lies in the creation of these atmospheres: the dust and clutter of the shop and the peeling decay of the apartment; the overdressed and sweaty sensuality of the Crippen game; the hysteria and eventual despair of the von Richthofen game. Everett is less successful in the creation of character, or, rather, I do not think that he has tried very hard.

Theo is a man in his early 30s with little education or ambition. He has a good mind that he uses only for chess problems, and good looks that he is letting run to fat. When he was a child, he imagined romantic crimes; as a young man, he sneaked upstairs with a different woman every night; now, when his libido is not being released in a fantasy game, it turns reflexively on himself: he is always scratching his groin or picking at sunburnt skin on his shoulders or studying his own body in the bath.

Vivien is probably older than Theo. She was once an actress and a beauty, or says that she was; she is now an alcoholic and a despiser of men in general and of Theo in particular. While Theo does chess problems she plays the piano, badly. Vivien has a history of emotional disturbance and disorientation, she is given to acting out fantasies (the Crippen game, we discover, was her idea), she is simultaneously domineering and masochistic.

Reingard is younger but more dramatically perverse than either. She is a photographer and voyeur, fascinated by abnormality and violence: she gets sexually aroused by bloodshed, war, deformity, and disease. Reingard is an active trisexual (men, women, and herself); she smokes hashish and washes down contraceptive pills with cognac. Most of the book's hokum is associated with Reingard. She is always on the edge of being the Charles Addams witch, passionately crushing a puff-ball in her strong fingers or trembling excitedly as she photographs an idiot child. Sometimes she slides over the edge and becomes comic: when she reads up on ant-killing insects, or shows Theo the worms in her urine, or identifies herself with the goddess Kali, or observes "In this outfit I've been mistaken for Garbo," or sends a discarded lover a parcel of obscenities designed to make him vomit at breakfast.

The Crippen game is socially harmless deviant behavior, like many other forms of sex perversion. Its identification is not primarily with Crippen's murderousness (he was the meekest and most unlikely of poisoners) but with the possibilities of sexual variety in his career: as the invalid Belle, Vivien comes to Theo padded and veiled, imperious and insatiable; as the typist Ethel, naked in Belle's furs, she is at once demure and randy; as Ethel on shipboard, disguised as a boy, she is a vision of ambiguous delights, pastel blue underwear showing through open trousers. (These costumed conjunctions, incidentally, are described with great sensuality and power.)

"It gave copulation a flavor," Theo later explains to Reingard, in a masterly English understatement. He is a classic example of English marginal sexuality, bored and kinky. The Crippen game is absurd, perhaps even disgusting (to my mind it is far less disgusting, being at least adult, than the bear-and-squirrel game with which Jimmy Porter and his wife work themselves up to heterosexuality in *Look Back in Anger*). Nevertheless, the game indulges Theo's fetishism, his sadomasochistic impulses, his latent homosexuality, his compulsive promiscuity, all within a stable heterosexual relationship. It is life-giving, in short. The eroticism of "a pale-green Edwardian corset" or "the black garters with the scarlet frills" in its deepest meaning is the eroticism of Theo's dead mother, an Oedipal gratification, and Vivien is really Jocasta in furs. As Crippen, Theo can symbolically indulge his forbidden wishes, and symbolically punish himself for them. He does not have to commit real adultery or incest, kill or be killed; as a result of the Crippen game he may even be a better man.

The von Richthofen game is socially harmless deviant behavior too, in that Theo does not actually shoot any planes down in flames with his wooden machine guns. But it has far more dangerous implications. Its identification *is* with von Richthofen's murderousness: he is the killer given social approval instead of punishment, the killer seen as hero rather than as criminal. The identification with von Richthofen turns Theo away from Vivien, as she recognizes from the first, but more than that it exchanges Vivien, and all women, for a mechanical cockpit, remarkably easy to clean. When Vivien kicks the plane, Theo hits her; when Vivien and Reingard quarrel, Theo retreats into the cockpit; when Vivien attacks him and tries to smash the plane, Theo kicks her in the breast; when finally she is carried off deranged and screaming, Theo climbs back into the cockpit, and there "huddles down, staring at the instrument panel and holding his knees."

The roots of the von Richthofen game are military homosexuality and sadism, not unique to the Germans but peculiarly identified with them by recent history. Von Richthofen seems to have been a talented man with the odd quirk of liking "to show friends the photographs of charred corpses of the men he had shot down." These men are not only his rivals and his victims, they are ultimately his symbolic mates, and their bodies have his bullets in them. In the last analysis the von Richthofen game indulges Theo's perversities in the service of sterility and the death wish. It is purely masturbatory: its climax is Theo alone in the cockpit, trembling. When Theo tells Vivien that he has discovered his true game, she cries out: "It has no sex in it!" Actually, it has lots of sex in it, but it is the sex of death. Its consequences for society are the extinction of life by catatonic withdrawal, suicide, genocide, or thermonuclear war.

Negatives, in short, is a fable of seduction and corruption, perhaps an allegory of modern history (The names have the patness of allegory: Theo is "God," Vivien is "Life," Reingard is "Guardian of Purity.") Everett is not fully in control of his medium, particularly of the resources of symbolism and fore-shadowing. The anticipation that Theo will murder Vivien is continually built up, to no purpose. A number of details seem symbolic but eventually turn out to have no significance: the morning glory has seven flowers one morning, and twelve an-other, but that is the nature of morning glories; a moth gets into the hospital ward where Theo's father is dying, and a moth similarly gets into a bedroom briefly shared by Theo and Rein-gard, but such is the habit of moths.

I would say that the writer who has most influenced Everett is Alain Robbe-Grillet. Many of the effects in *Negatives* are strikingly reminiscent of those in *Jealousy*, even to the present tense and other cinematic devices. But Everett is a popularizer rather than a revolutionary: instead of taking Robbe-Grillet's principles to the end of the line, which is the non-novel or the anti-novel, he uses them within traditional narrative conven-tions. The result is small-scale success rather than monumental failure. Occasionally Everett shows more than that, in some truly imaginative touch. For example: lying in the hospital, Theo's father dreams of an old woman with 15 cancers, one of them called Tono Bungay. A young writer who can invent a cancer named Tono Bungay has a bright future.

1965

The Bulging Pockets
of Anthony Carson

Anthony Carson is the funniest travel writer since Mark Twain. He is the perfect travel writer for sedentary types like myself, who have never been anywhere. Carson claims to have been everywhere, but the places he describes—Seville, St. Tropez, Palermo—clearly do not exist, and I incline to believe that *he* has never left his study armchair either. One piece in the book, "Off the Map," describes a swindle Carson helped perpetrate, taking a party of tourists on a Mystery Trip "behind the Iron Curtain"—actually to Wales. I doubt that Carson ever really got as far as Wales.

"Are all the books being published as full of sex and violence as the ones you review?" a nice old gentleman asked me the other day. "Yes, alas," was my answer. Now I can modify it: a true humorist sometimes makes sex and violence gentle, funny and palatable. Carson's "The Man with the Gun" is a case in point. For peculiar reasons he sets out to hitchhike across Australia. After two days on the road he is invited to settle at a farmhouse, to protect the women against the boss, an old man who has been shooting at them, and whom they have locked in the woodshed.

The women turn out to be the housekeeper and her two daughters. The bad daughter, her mother says, led the old man "a hell of a dance and promised to marry him, and now she owns half the farm, two tractors, two automobiles, a pearl necklace and all the dogs. When she turned him down he ran for his gun and began shooting." Carson goes to visit the boss in the woodshed, finds him gentle and frail, talks to him about Naples and Vesuvius, then locks him up again. The piece concludes:

"I stayed in the house four more days. They had let the old man out and he seemed quite peaceful. I left for the north and Moon Daisy. Lily had given me a little white dog called Spin. As I got back on to the road I thought I heard two shots ring out."

As he tells it, Carson has an extraordinary capacity for misadventures with animals. In the Hamburg Zoo, he is bitten by a parrot. On a train through Switzerland to Austria, a live white rabbit, heavily dutiable, its nose trembling "like a tuning fork," pops into his suitcase. In Morocco, he finds himself on a parapet in the hot sun, deticking tortoises with a forceps. In Galicia he buys a bagless bagpipe, learns to play a tune on it, and all the local sheep follow him.

The human world Carson encounters has the same outrageous quality. A Maori princess in New Zealand tells him that a tourist fed her a peanut. A young Spanish bullfighter, "just beginning to fight terrible old bulls in obscure villages," describes the bulls to Carson: "They know Latin and Greek, and are as big as cathedrals." A friend in London gives him checks drawn, not on banks, but on the trees in Kensington Gardens.

Carson successfully resists the temptation to glamorize himself in these pieces. He describes his appearance: "I can only wear any suit for about twenty-four hours, and after that I should throw it away. It crumbles, shrinks, and gets covered with soup, wine and olive oil. Dogs bite it, cats scratch it, and moths eat it. The pockets bulge with cigarette butts and handbills." Although Carson continually chases girls, he rarely catches one, and he admits ruefully that he is well past his prime and a bit too old for the pursuit. The photograph on the back of the jacket, showing Carson looking like a seamier Robert Graves, does not give the lie to any of his statements.

Unlike those ragged bootblacks who die and leave three million dollars to the Public Library, Carson's shabbiness accurately reflects his means. He never has a penny, or never for long, and everywhere he travels functionaries can smell out the emptiness of his pockets. All Carson is rich in is *joie de vivre*. He loves to eat, to drink, to go to bed with Spanish girls who are "tender, insinuating and as sharp as a diamond," or to try to do the same with American girls who glow "like petunias." Carson's preferred drinking companions are liars and boasters, prodigious jokers; his favorite is a "fat lord of misrule," redolent of "the winy belch of Bacchus." Carson's spiritual home is "Drift" in Morocco, where "Complete liberty prevails. There are vice, drugs, cheap alcohol and constant sunshine."

The Enemy, to use Auden's youthful category, are the respectable people everywhere. They include: "The English, coshed, influenza-ridden and stoically guilty"; Switzerland, "a country of exactitude, of perfect prose, where poets die"; "the long savers" of the world; the Germans with their "marzipan music, the mock Gothic sob at the heart of things"; all "grocers and limp traditionalists." Carson is at war with the Enemy, but he has been subverted, infected with their guilt and unhappiness. Beneath his joy there is a deep melancholy, as in the great clowns (Carson writes of "a clown's planet of despair"), and his comedy is often wry, poignant and heartbreaking.

Carson's prose, at its best, has the vigor and tension of good poetry. A lion cage is "sly with the fug of dens." "Van Gogh had not only painted this landscape," Carson writes at Arles, "he had planted the corn and bled the poppies and wept the cypresses." At night on the Riviera, "an owl pierced the dark of sleep with love and terror."

The book displays a mastery of imagery. Provence in the rain looks "like a beaten woman," fish leap "like knives in the river," a girl is "dry and brittle as an unwatered flower bed," a man looks "like a cardboard hangman," the people of Naples "shine like butter," the Galician sun is "as soft as the tongue of a calf," lobsters glow "like rubies," back in London Carson coughs "like an old dispersed lion."

In his company our senses are invigorated. We hear "the rasp of rooks," see a performing tiger "put on a popular face," hear a German talk "excellent iced-water English," see farmland "pricked to blood by the hoe," hear a quarrel in which "the ohms crackled in recriminations and private lightning filled the room," see a millionairess "covered with old gold," hear a ring-dove's "woodcry of drowned bells."

Carson combines the bold imagery of poetry with the economy and understatement of modern fiction. One of his masters is Hemingway. Here is the ending of a poignant love story, "The Girl from Barcelona":

"I never saw her again. A man I knew in Paris called Faraday gave me a return ticket to London (which somebody didn't want because of a horizon of life); and there I was, standing in Newhaven harbour.

" 'British?' said a huge policeman.

" 'Yes,' I said.

" 'On the right,' said the policeman."

Another piece, the one about the fellow who wrote checks on trees, ends: "I turned to Sandiman but he had gone and all I could hear was the mournful hoot of a polar bird." Carson can do quite a lot in a sentence. He meets a French widow on a train and, in response to a question, tells her that he has been living with gypsies in the Camargue. " 'The gypsies?' she said. 'I envy you; I am such a gypsy myself.' She looked neat, clean, alert and business-like." Finding himself on a cyclist's path in Hamburg, Carson wonders: "Was there also a children's path, a dogs' path, and a thin meandering track for cats?"

The distinction of Carson's style can best be conveyed by quoting a whole paragraph. He writes:

"In Vence you drink wine slowly, without the *coitus inter-ruptus* of the English licensing laws, and listen to gossip. You stroll, time slows down, you stand and stare at the street corner, in the grey, rainy square and the buildings compose themselves to a gradual innate satisfaction of the spirit. The people then merge into these still, weathered shapes, the women at the doors of their magic groceries, which are crammed with flowers, sausages, milk, wine, soap, tins of sardines and postcards, and where you can never quite get the object you want, the card-players shouting at the table, jerseyed like macaws, surrounded by old men recalling epics and disasters, a popinjay policeman twirling his cape, the village madman, the randy drunk. The mountain behind, as clean as a scrubbed step."

Like any humorist, Carson is sometimes unable to bring it off. Occasionally he falls into monotonous formulas, or repeats sequences of funny names beyond the point of diminishing returns. If the two shots at the end of "The Man with the Gun" are delicate and funny, the two Poles shot at the end of "The Duce at Home" are less delicate and funny. The irony is at times heavy, as when Carson shows his fellow tourists at Arles a Van Gogh scene, and one of them pulls out a camera with the remark: "It would look fine in colour." Several of the pieces end with corny O. Henry snappers or joke punchlines.

For the most part, though, Carson is brilliantly successful. On second thought I do not really doubt that he has been to all those places, or that all those things did happen to him. If they did not they should have. In *Travels: Near and Far Out* Carson writes of "England, where the puritanical addiction to 'truth' is more important than fulfillment by fantasy, or style, or super-realism. In my own way, I know and have suffered from this, since my writing is composed of exact truths and formalistic lies, like a mosaic, and through this medium I intend a general light of life to filter through." Anthony Carson's truth is that man is inextricably both flesh and spirit, and the lies he tells on its behalf are no more reprehensible than the lies making the same affirmation that that other old reprobate, William Butler Yeats, published as poems.

1963

III

The Blues

How can one write about the blues, when less is known about them than about the Abominable Snowman? The blues are a folk song that seems to come, not from a Negro "folk" in any of the traditional senses of the word, not from solid citizens, as do the work songs and the spirituals, but from a declassed semi-underworld, a world of brothels and honky-tonks, or, at best, of failed farmers and blind beggars. Yet they are a high art, perhaps with the skyscraper the only high art of American origin, and they are or should be our pride.

Technically—and as a musical illiterate I simply parrot my betters—the blues is usually a song in twelve bars: melodically peculiar in that the third and seventh intervals, and sometimes the fifth, are flatted; harmonically restricted to a simple progression of the tonic, subdominant, and dominant seventh, the old hymn chords; rhythmically 4/4 with offbeat phrasing. The lyrics are a rhyming couplet with the first line repeated, AAB, each line in four bars, with the words characteristically ending in the middle of the third bar, leaving the accompaniment to fill out the remaining bar and a half. That is the standard form, but there are many variants: eight-bar blues that are a simple AB; sixteen-bar blues often AAAB; even a twelve-bar form that the performers call "fast blues," in which one of the lines breaks into two rhyming lines of two bars each, filling most of the space usually taken by the accompaniment and others. Despite the variations, the melodic line is always immediately recognizable, the harmonies are always the same fixed sequence, and all of the thousands of blues that have been sung fit into a form as tight and perfect as the Petrarchan sonnet.

Unfortunately, the blues have no prehistory. There is no clear written evidence of such songs before the 1890s, and no one recorded any lyrics until the first decade of this century. Most white authorities believe that the blues arose around 1890 or even later, out of some other kind of Negro folk song (generally the field holler), but there is a stubborn Negro belief that they are much older. In the 1940s, "Big Eye" Louis Nelson, a New Orleans clarinettist, told Alan Lomax:

> The blues? Ain't no first blues. The blues always been.
> Blues is what cause the fellows to start jazzing.

A few motifs in blues lyrics clearly go back to slavery (although that is not evidence that any song itself does) like the commonplace that Bessie Smith sings in Ted Wallace's "Work House Blues":

> *Cause I'm goin' to the Nation, goin' to the Territor'*

The "Nation" and "Territor' " here is the Cherokee Nation in Oklahoma, a refuge for escaped slaves, and except as a folk memory it makes no sense after Emancipation. The first blues with music, "Baby Seals Blues," by Baby F. Seals, was published in 1912; and the first blues recorded, Perry Bradford's "Crazy Blues," was cut by Mamie Smith in 1916. In the half century since, a few hundred blues have been published and many thousands recorded, but the first books on the blues are only beginning to appear, and their prehistory is skimpy or non-existent.

The way to learn about the blues is to hear them sung, most easily done these days from records, and hear enough to get a sense of the infinite possibilities inherent in the tight form, of the sophisticated emotional ambivalence, the complex combination of misery and high spirits, that characterizes them. But even a few bars will do. "Ma" Rainey singing the last stanza of "Big Feelin' Papa,"

> *There's a whole lot left, what's left is good,*
> *Gimme a chance, honey, I'll make you change your*
>   *neighborhood.*

148

tells more about the blues than one could ever get down on paper. Nevertheless, it should be possible to make useful background remarks, and on behalf of that modest ambition it is most convenient to divide the subject into the artificial categories of folk study: origin, structure, and function.

The origin of the blues is of course unknown. The likeliest theory is that the form represents a marriage of vocal song from Africa, ceremonial plaint or abuse, with European harmony; the rhythm also a compromise, African offbeat phrasing on European march rhythm. It has been much easier to believe in the survival of African song among American Negroes since the demonstration, by Melville Herskovits and others in the last quarter of a century, of West Africa as a unified culture area, and the vigorous survival in the Americas of many traits of its language and custom. Herskovits' *The Myth of the Negro Past* in 1941 gave the cultural isolationists in the study of Negro folksong a jolt from which they have never recovered. As early as 1914, H. E. Krehbiel in *Afro-American Folksongs* had argued the African origin of some features of American Negro music, but too far in advance of the anthropological evidence that has since confirmed his brilliant conjecture.

Walter Lehrman, in an unpublished work on the blues he has kindly made available to me, has gone furthest in tracing specific West African origins. In Captain R. S. Rattray's books *Ashanti* (1923) and *Religion and Art in Ashanti* (1927) Lehrman finds a number of specific features of the blues. In the Apo ceremony, a quest for fertility through ritual obscenity and abuse, he finds the ritual origins of the fast blues. In funeral ceremonies he similarly finds the ritual origin of the slow or mournful blues, in such lyrics as:

> *Always I think of the day of death.*
> *I cannot eat.*
> *I walk in sadness, and I die.*

The Critic's Credentials

Even the AAB form of the blues can be found in Ashanti "drum sayings," as in:

If you will play with me, I shall play with you.
If you will not play with me, I shall not play with you.
What play is it to be?

In his New Orleans researches, Lomax identified jazz with the African concept of music "as a *source* of energy, rather than a *demand* for it." Since then, one of Herskovits' former students, Richard Alan Waterman, has published a comprehensive account, "African Influence on the Music of the Americas," in the Proceedings of the 29th International Congress of Americanists in 1952. Waterman showed that such characteristic features of American blues as the offbeat phrasing (a term he proposes in place of the misleading "syncopation"), the flattened blue scale, and falsetto style, are all African, as are the melodies of at least two American Negro folk songs, "Run Old Jeremiah" and "Long John."

The European elements in the origin of the blues, the hymn chords and the basic rhythm, need no explanation. If the melodies and their burdens are originally African, they have adapted so thoroughly to the western musical tradition, to the American experience with its problems, imagery, and style, as to become a new American product. As Bronislaw Malinowksi showed in the symposium *Culture* in 1927, the adaptation of a diffused culture trait to the context and functions of a new environment is so radical that neither term of the old controversy, "diffusion" or "independent origin," makes sense, and we might best speak of an American "creation" of the blues from derived materials. In this view, other forms of American Negro folk music—field hollers, work songs, spirituals, and gospel hymns—are not sources of the blues but analogues, with their own putative African and European prehistories. One of the most curious origin theories of the blues, the suggestion of Abbe Niles in W. C. Handy's *Treasury of the Blues* that all blues derive from one prototype, "Joe Turner," has this much truth in it: that the melodies of all blues are remarkably akin (Niles says that any folk blues and "Joe Turner" "may actually be played or sung together without any serious difficulties being encountered").

I will confine my remarks on the structure and dynamics (the dynamics being the alteration of the structure in time) of the blues almost entirely to the lyrics. The terms "slow blues" and "fast blues" are inadequate, since the plaintive blues are not always slow, the abusive or gay blues not always fast, and some blues do not fit readily into either type. However, the distinction is a real one, and until better terms are produced we may as well use the traditional terms of the performers. Whatever the origin of the blues, one must assume a parallel development of slow blues and fast blues from similar origins, as the Cambridge ritual school has shown to be the case with Greek tragedy and comedy.

The basic unit or building-block of the blues seems to be not the song but the stanza. On the analogy of stock units in the ballads, we may call these "commonplaces." It is they that are folk-transmitted, and the singer (or composer if he is not the singer) stitches them together into a song, rearranging them and adding his own material. (Perhaps if our knowledge were greater we would find that no original material is added, that all blues stanzas are commonplaces.) These proverbial commonplaces are familiar to anyone who has ever heard the blues. I quote a few (in each case, assuming the repetition of the first line):

Love is like a faucet, it turns off and on,
But when you think it is on, baby, it has turned off and gone.

Big fat mamma with the meat shakin' on her bones,
Every time she shakes it makes a skinny woman leave her home.

Sittin' here wonderin' would a matchbox hold my clothes,
I ain't got so many, and I got a long long way to go.

The Critic's Credentials

You don't miss the water, till the well runs dry,
You don't miss your woman, till she tells you goodbye.

I'm goin' away just to wear you off my mind,
I got the blues and I just can't keep from cryin'.

My mama told me, my papa told me too,
Everybody grins in your face, son, ain't no friend to you.

The organization of the blues, the relationship of one stanza to another, is lyric and thematic, like that of modern poetry, rather than narrative or dramatic. This is quite remarkable, since all other true folk song seems to preserve a dramatic form, however attenuated, from its ritual origins. The blues stanzas may be lyric fragments broken off from a dramatic whole and taking on independent life (as have lyric fragments of certain ballads, outstandingly the "Who will shoe my little foot?" stanza from Child 76, "The Lass of Roch Royal"). Unfortunately, this seems unlikely, and the dramatic wholes are difficult to imagine. What internal development the blues song has is generally to some resolution in action, real or fantasied, often leaving or sending away.

Whatever the general or social problem with which the blues begins, the development is always toward personalization, making the events metaphoric for the human condition (not the singer's autobiographical condition, as one realizes hearing some of a singer's repertoire, but that of his or her *persona*). Thus "Ma" Rainey's "Backwater Blues" begins describing the events of the 1927 flood, but ends with an ultimate alienation that far transcends the flood:

Uh-um, I can't move no mo',
There ain't no place for a poor old girl to go.

Scrapper Blackwell's "Hard Time Blues" starts with the details of unemployment, homelessness and poverty in the Depression, but ends with a deeper meaning of the events in a timeless misery:

Soon as hard times strikes me, my baby puts me out,
Now, guess you know what these hard times is all about.

A few overwhelming themes dominate the blues. One is travel, journey, leaving. Sociologically, it reflects the relatively aimless Negro horizontal mobility because of limitations on Negro vertical mobility. Events are resolved, conditions remedied, by going to another place, adjusting matters in space rather than in time, which in the blues quickly becomes a fantasy dream time. Thus Jim Jackson sings a "Kansas City Blues" in which each stanza has the refrain:

I'm gonna move to Kansas City, I'm gonna move to Kansas City,
I'm gonna move, baby, honey, where they don't 'low you.

Robert Johnson concludes his ironic "Kind Hearted Woman Blues" with the powerful understatement so characteristic of blues language:

Some day, some day, I'll shake your hand goodbye,
I can't give you any more of my lovin' cause I just ain't satisfied.

If it is not leaving, the solution is sending away, as when Bessie Smith sings in "Worn Out Papa Blues":

Your use done fail, all your pep done gone.
Pick up that suitcase, man, and travel on.

Obviously related to the power to break away or dismiss is a theme of grandiose fantasy. Bessie Smith sings in "Work House Blues" (on the record, the trombonist punctuates it by turning his chords into a hymn tune):

Say, I wisht I had me a heaven of my own,
I'd give all those poor girls a long lost (?) happy home.

"Ma" Rainey sings in "Downhearted Blues":

I got the world in a jug, the stopper in my hand,
I'm gonna hold it until you come under my command.

The underside of this bravado is the theme of self-pity, the familiar lament or plaint of the blues. The persona of the blues singer is a motherless boy a long long way from home, like Josh White singing "Hard Time Blues":

> *My mama's away and my daddy's dead,*
> *I ain't got nobody, and I'm seldom fed.*

Otherwise the singer is a poor old mistreated girl, like Billie Holiday beginning "Fine and Mellow":

> *My man don't love me, treats me awful mean,*
> *He's the lowest man that I've ever seen.*

Matching these themes of the slow blues are the interwoven themes of obscenity and abuse in the fast blues. As F. M. Cornford showed in *The Origin of Attic Comedy*, obscenity and abuse are the positive and negative of one life-giving act, the obscenity promoting fertility and the abuse exorcising evil spirits. We can see their interrelationship in Jabo Williams' "Fat Mama Blues," which alternates,

> *She's got great big legs, she's got whoppin' thighs,*
> *And every time she shakes she makes my courage (?) rise.*

with

> *I said oh, fat mama, keep them great big legs off of me,*

and

> *Said I'm goin' away mama, and I'm goin' to stay,*
> *Them big legs, baby, gonna keep me away.*

The classic fast blues, raising obscenity and abuse to a considerable comic height, is the "Dirty Dozen" recorded by "Speckled Red."

The custom of the "dozens" is even more mysterious than the origin of the blues. As most of us encounter it, it is an abuse game played by Negro children in the school yard, in which rhyming slurs are made on the legitimacy, fidelity, heterosexuality, attractiveness and cleanliness of the opponent's family. It seems obviously of African origin, but scholarship has been wary of or oblivious to it, and I know of no scholarly treatment except for a rather owlish learned article by John Dollard, defining the custom as "a pattern of interactive insult" and relating it to joking relationships among the Manus, Tikopia, Aleuts, and so forth, but giving no texts. Buster Bailey reports, in *Hear Me Talkin' To Ya*, the jazz documentary by Nat Shapiro and Nat Hentoff, that "King" Oliver was addicted to playing the dozens on his friends, as were many other jazz musicians. The history of the fast blues is clearly related to the dozens, and the subject awaits a bold researcher.

All of these themes, travel and leaving, grandiose fantasy and self-pity, obscenity and abuse, are African as well as American, in fact are universal. The emphasis on traveling on is reinforced by the American limits on Negro vertical mobility, but it need not arise from them; it has many African and Afro-American analogues. "Ajo Ajo," a Shango cult song recorded by Herskovits in Trinidad, endlessly repeats the simple lyric:

> *Journey, journey,*
> *This is my journey.*
> *What are we?*
> *Journey, journey.*

The useful concept here is Freud's "overdetermination." Thus the understated and allusive nature of the blues lyric might go back to an African tradition of indirection and hermeticism, but if so it would be reinforced by a need for just that tactic under slavery and under the conditions of Negro life after Emancipation, and by the further need for an in-group private language and the evasion of the censorship in performance and recording. Since any of these is strong enough to produce the tradition independently, African origins really tell us nothing, although the concept of overdetermination allows us to find all later conditions reinforcing prehistoric ones.

The final point that needs making about the structure of

blues lyrics is their remarkable power of language and poetic metaphor. The simplest of means conveys enormous complexity of meaning. We see it when Georgia White sings Sox Wilson's "Married Woman Blues":

When we married, we promised to stick through thick and thin,
But the way you thinnin' out is a lowdown dirty sin.

We see it in the superb single line of Robert Johnson's "Kind Hearted Woman Blues":

She's a kind-hearted mama, studies evil all the time.

Langston Hughes and Arna Bontemps, in *The Book of Negro Folklore*, report a blues commonplace I have never heard, of frightening metaphoric power:

Did you ever see a one-eyed woman cry?
She can cry so good out of that one old eye.

The characteristic mode is irony, Empsonian ambiguity. Bessie Smith sings in "Gulf Coast Blues":

Some of you men sure do make me tired,
You got a mouthful of gimme, a handful of much obliged.

Georgia White sings of sexual passion in "Fire in the Mountain":

Fire in the mountain, there ain't no water round,
My smokestack is blazin', and the firemen's all drunk in town.

Even where the words seem only plaintive, the accompaniment undercuts and mocks their lament, producing the complex tension of the blues. "Pine Top" Smith sings in "Pine Top's Blues":

Now my woman's got a heart like a rock cast down in the sea,
Seems like she can love everybody and mistreat poor me.

As he goes through the series of pitiful charges—that he brought her breakfast in bed but she threw a teacup at his head, that every time he gets in trouble she lets him go to jail, that she evicted him when he ran out of money, that she will not help him rob and steal, as a consequence of which he never gets a decent breakfast—his boogie-woogie piano accompaniment races on with arrogant joy. It is a convincing example of the impossibility of understanding the blues from the lyrics alone.

The function of the blues is actually a great many functions. On the simplest level, there is the sociological function for the group as Malinowski showed in *Myth in Primitive Psychology*, oral lore performs many of the functions of an educational and legal system, teaching and encouraging proper behavior, warning against and punishing improper behavior. We can see that most clearly in our own culture in children's lore, when a kid chants:

> *Tattle tale tit*
> *Your tongue will be slit*
> *And all the dogs in our town*
> *Will have a little bit.*

The blues perform similarly in a Negro folk community: warning, sanctioning, mocking, threatening. If this sociological functionalism seems too simple, we can translate it into the more sophisticated configurational functionalism of later anthropology, and see the blues as a chart for distinguishing approved personality patterns and cultural ways. If we turn from the vocabulary of cultural anthropology to that of social psychology, the blues channel and provide proper and socially-sanctioned cathartic outlets for all sorts of dangerous and anti-social impulses.

For the individual, the function is psychological. In Kenneth Burke's terminology, the blues are symbolic actions, strategies for encompassing a wide variety of situations, the sort of all-purpose "medicine" he finds proverbs to be. In Freudian terms, the blues function like dreams, furnishing a disguised fulfillment of repressed wishes (sometimes very little disguised and repressed indeed). If the gloomy choice Freud offers us in *Beyond the Pleasure Principle,* turn the aggression inward or outward, is really the only human alternative, then the slow blues choose the first alternative, masochism, and the fast blues the second, sadism. In a fuller account, the blues warns against a forbidden impulse, gratifies it in fantasy, and symbolically punishes for it.

We can even distinguish, in real people, something we might call the "blues personality." The best example I know is the enormously talented jazz pianist and composer "Jelly Roll" Morton. Lomax's biography *Mister Jelly Roll* shows us the outlines. Lomax describes Morton's grandiose fantasies and comments: "This moment of fantasy prepared the way for later, almost paranoid, feelings of self-love and persecution." He tells of Morton's letter to President Roosevelt offering to solve the problem of unemployed musicians, his letter to Ripley claiming to have invented jazz ("I do not claim any of the creation of the blues," he explained). Lomax shows Morton sometimes sadistic and obscene, sometimes masochistic and self-pitying, sometimes both jumbled together. His language was the understated language of the blues, and Morton's widow reported that whenever he got furious, his strongest statement was "I'm getting tired and disgusted." Although Morton played blues and may even have composed some, he does not seem to have liked them particularly, regarding them as a primitive and unsophisticated folk art. In a deeper sense, his life as alienated Negro, pimp as well as musical genius, *was* a blues.

A deeper consideration of blues function would examine their effects on a sophisticated audience—*us*—as though we were a folk. These are metaphors that speak to our condition, in the sense in which all mankind is alienated, homeless and unloved. In the "How Long Blues" that Jimmy Rushing recorded with Sam Price at the piano, as a memorial for their dead friend "Lips" Page, we feel terrible pain ordered and controlled by art, precisely as in a poem by Yeats. When Bessie Smith sings in "Dirty No-Gooder's Blues":

> *The meanest things he could say would thrill you*
>   *through and through,*

we get the same naked desperation of love we recognize when
Emilia tells Desdemona in *Othello:*

> *I know a lady in Venice would have walk'd barefoot*
>   *to Palestine*
> *for a touch of his nether lip.*

Like the forms of primitive art, these are still—or again—meaningful forms for us. As Pieter Geyl remarks on the use of
history, we enrich our civilization by "the reanimation of old
modes of existence and thought." For the individual of the
sophisticated audience, the blues is aesthetic catharsis, offering,
if not cure, at least alleviation; if not alleviation, at least the
cleansing sanity of self-mockery. We see it most sharply when
Bessie Smith sings "Young Woman's Blues," with its defiant
end:

I'm as good as any woman in your town,
I ain't no high yaller, I'm a deep yaller brown.
I ain't gonna marry, ain't gonna settle down,
I'm gonna drink good moonshine, and run these browns down.
See that long lonesome road, don't you know it's gotta end?
And I'm a good woman, and I can get plenty men.

In Lehrman's fine phrase, it is "straining against the form," a
passion so intense that it threatens momentarily to wrench the
blues' stylized formality apart. If jazz arose, as "Big Eye" Louis
Nelson argued and most historians now believe, as an instrumental imitation of the human voice, a wordless singing of
the blues by trumpet or clarinet, it may be that it succeeded
only because the audience knew the words so deeply in their
blood and marrow.

Most of the books that have begun to appear on the blues
have been inadequate to them. One of them, in fact, Paul

The Critic's Credentials

Oliver's *Blues Fell This Morning*, seemed so inadequate that it inspired this essay. Oliver's book is a good example of the simplest misunderstanding. He takes the blues to be melodramatic sociology. An Englishman who had never been to America and who knows little or nothing of American Negro life, Oliver has collected and transcribed over a thousand blues records with love and devotion, and in a fine case of primitivism or the Rousseau fallacy, assumes that the power of his passion provides insight. Oliver's ignorance is appalling. He believes that a convict singer "has been so long severed from the outside world that Oklahoma was to him still the 'territory' of the Indian nations." He hears "Memphis Slim" sing in "Jive Blues" his intention of going on Riverside Drive, and never having heard of it, gets it as a "riverside dive." "Whistlin' " Alex Moore's "Ice Pick Blues" tells of his woman coming at him with an ice-pick, and Oliver explains:

> Amongst the railroad and telegraph men, the street cleaners and builders, the ice-picks which are used to break up the accumulations of freezing snow during the hard northern and mid-Western winters become tools of murder, and the small size of some of these, coupled with their excellent balance and penetrating bills, make them a favoured weapon.

Only a full example can do justice to Oliver's incredible readings of the blues as sentimental sociology. He reprints the following stanzas of Ida Cox's "Worn Out Daddy Blues":

The time has come for us to part,
I ain't goin' to cry, it won't break my heart,
'Cause I'm through with you and I hope you don't feel hurt.

You're like an old horseshoe that's had its day,
You're like an old shoe I must throw away,
I'm through with you and I hope you don't feel hurt.

You ain't got no money, you're down and broke,
You're just an old has-been like a worn-out joke,
So I'm through with you and I hope you don't feel hurt.

Here, complete, is Oliver's gloss:

> Returning home when the sun has gone down, his
> pockets empty of all save his calloused hands, the share-
> cropper pauses before his clap-board shack, with its
> patched walls and crumbling piles. Bellies swollen with
> pellagra, his children watch him solemn-eyed, whilst his
> woman now cooking the grits in the skillet 'loudmouths'
> him for his laziness, for his uselessness. She does not under-
> stand why his work never seems to get them out of debt,
> but she knows that she has to bear children, raise, clothe
> and feed children and try to keep a home together. She
> curses him in her own helplessness for bringing them to
> such misery and turns him from the door.

Oliver's typical comment on a tough-minded and mocking
blues will begin: "Perhaps he has taken her love for granted,
perhaps he has given rein to unreasonable anger and thought
little of her feelings, but he still cannot believe that the woman
that he has admired and on whom he has depended so much.
. . . " His comments are as far as is conceivable from the tone
of the blues. The blues (it is Bessie Jackson's "Man Stealer
Blues") say:

> *I went to bed last night and the blues wouldn't let me rest,*
> *'Cause I ain't used to sleepin' by myself.*

Oliver says:

> Her arms still feel the warmth of her husband's love, and
> his fond words even as he betrayed her love still remain
> in her mind, their sweetness now turned as bitter as gall.

All that it is the power of the blues *not* to say, Oliver says.
Barbecue Bob sings in the "Mississippi Heavy Water Blues":

The Critic's Credentials

> *I'm in Mississippi with mud all in my shoes,*
> *My gal in Louisiana—with that high water blues.*

Oliver sings:

> With aching hearts, and red-rimmed eyes, bereaved persons scanned the rows of huddled, homeless figures or with ungainly steps picked their way to the places where they used to live. Only the mud remained to greet them.

Billy Bird sings in "Down in the Cemetery":

I don't want me no woman with hair like drops of rain,
Every time she combs her hair you can hear them hard nails
ring.

Oliver's reading is incredible. He writes:

> With gruesome imagery Billy Bird sings that he cannot love the body of a woman on whom rigor mortis has even touched her hair.

The great problem is that Oliver does not understand the private language of the blues, the sexual double-talk, and that what he takes to be sociology is almost always sexuality. He quotes Robert Petway's "Cotton Picking Blues":

She's a cotton-pickin' woman, Lawd, she do's it all the time,
If you don't stop pickin' cotton now, baby, I believe you sho'
gwan to lose your mind. Yes yes. . . .

She pickin' so much cotton, she even don't know where to go,
She's leavin' in the mornin', sweet mama, honey, she gwan'
from do' to do'.

As anyone even remotely familiar with the blues knows, this is one of the stock euphemisms for orogenital intercourse (Blind Lemon Jefferson sings it as "She crochet all the time"). Here is Oliver's gloss:

Undoubtedly the strain of continual work 'from sun to
sun' in the endeavour to gain freedom from debt and serf-
dom can kill the love in both heart and body. Husband
and wife labour side by side until all energies are sapped
and the wife who spends her days in the fields and her
nights at the wash-tub has little time for the expression of
love. Determined to gain independence for her family her
labours may eventually become obsessive and in turn a
source of anxiety to those who love her.

If anyone but Oliver had written that last line, one would
think it were part of the joke. Oliver explains generally:

As with all other subjects the blues, when dealing with
matters of love and sex, is forthright and uncompromising.
There is no concealment and no use of oblique references.

The common blues euphemism for sex, "jelly roll" (an amazingly bold image for the female genitals) is taken by Oliver,
necessarily unfamiliar with the baked goods, to be a rolling
motion, the term "arising simply from the motions of sexual
intercourse." He thinks that the equally graphic term "honey-
dripper" is based on honey-colored skin. In Oliver's world,
"Well, well, just lay down your brake and feed the gas, eeh
yeah, and the stuff is here" is a tribute to the Model-T Ford,
and "Doc" Clayton's "Root Doctor Blues" is a comment on
folk superstition. In short, Oliver simply does not understand
the material he is writing about. He has collected and lovingly
(if rather carelessly) transcribed thousands of blues records, he
has made the lyrics of 350 blues (some of them very fine)
available, at moments he does almost seem to understand, but
my, my.

The first and for a long time the only book on the blues,
W. C. Handy's *A Treasury of the Blues,* was issued in 1926 and
reissued enlarged in 1949, with historical and critical material
by Abbe Niles. Its bias, faithfully reflecting Handy's own, is

commercial, interested in the composed rather than the folk blues. In Handy's autobiography, *Father of the Blues,* he explains frankly (or cynically, if you wish) that he despised Negro folk music until he saw that there was money in it, describing his "enlightenment" when a country band made much more than his orchestra: "Then I saw the beauty of primitive music." Even the language of the blues was alien to Handy. Niles reports that when Handy first heard the superb folk phrase "My man's got a heart like a rock cast down in the sea," before he grabbed it for "St. Louis Blues" he asked "the nearest colored onlooker what this might mean." The book is thus inevitably far from the folk art. The songs it includes are almost entirely composed, some not actually in the blues form (like Handy's celebrated "The Memphis Blues"); some only part blues to which, in Niles' words, "the writers, for the sake of variety and contrast, have added one or more strains in some other, related style"; and some travesties of blues, like Handy's "Long Gone," made from the fine African-melody work song "Long John," not to speak of the Gershwin "The Half of It, Dearie, Blues" and other such.

Nevertheless, the Handy book has its usefulness as well as its pioneering status, and Niles (a white New Hampshire lawyer) is amazingly knowledgeable for the time and place. Where could we learn as much about the conditions of Negro music as in the capsule history of Wilbur Sweatman?:

> Sweatman had a personal specialty of playing three clarinets at once (he told me in 1925: 'I could play *four,* but you ruin your face and don't get any extra credit').

Niles is marvelously aware of the paradoxical and ambiguous nature of the blues, "their employment of humor for the expression of misery." He distinguishes the blues of the white commercial song writers for all time: "In the Negro blues it is the gaiety that is feigned, while in the white, it is the grief." Niles talks of the "mocking, ironic or defiant discontent of the old folk-blues," notes a Clara Smith performance that belies its cheery text to give an effect "of utter desolation," and recognizes the ultimate humanism of the blues, "somehow to speak of man's past or man's fate in man's accents." At least one of the songs in the book, "Weeping Willow Blues," is not as composed but as transcribed from the singing of Bessie Smith, and it makes the others look like guppies in a tank with a shark.

Another common misunderstanding that gets in the way of the blues is sentimentality, and this is best represented by Jerry Silverman's *Folk Blues*, published in 1958. Unlike Handy's compilation of sheet music, this consists of transcriptions from performance, for the most part correctly heard and explained. Silverman's problem is that he cannot leave well enough alone. He has a passion for something called the "white blues" and "blue yodels" of singers like Woody Guthrie and Jimmie Rodgers, which have about as much to do with blues as Gershwin's compositions. He includes something called "Teacher's Blues" beginning "Now, Mister Teacher, why don't you organize?" and including the classic blues line, "Here's the source of our society's high-minded low-paid knowledge." He or his friends write tunes for traditional words, write words or "additional verses" for traditional tunes, make up "city" blues and invite the reader to do the same ("See how many others you can make up yourself"), and specialize in that shabby fraud the "talking blues." Silverman's emphasis is cheerily singalong. He writes:

> Therefore I tried not to lose sight of the fact that this is a *songbook* and, instead of striving for accuracy for accuracy's sake, attempted to render instead easily comprehensible, singable versions of the blues singers' complex melodic and rhythmic vocal inventions.

"Get together!" he shouts at us; "Have fun." One blues is identified as "a perfect campfire and hiking song."

However, Silverman is far from hopeless. He proudly recognizes the blues as "one of the significant—perhaps the most sig-

nificant—contributions of American music to world culture."
He sensibly notes that the blues harmony offers "psychological
fulfillment and relaxation of the tensions built up during the
course of a musical work." The transcription of a number of
Blind Lemon Jefferson's blues as Jefferson sings them (even
simplified for singalongability) would justify the book by itself. But if Jefferson had ever heard Silverman identify a blues
as a perfect campfire and hiking song he would have smashed
Silverman's guitar over his head.

Far and away the best book on the blues is Samuel B. Charters' *The Country Blues*, published in 1959. With Leonard
Bernstein's Omnibus blues program on television (now available as a long-playing record) it would make the best introduction to someone unfamiliar with the form. Charters himself
has reissued two anthologies of old blues records, in whole and
part, for Folkways: "The Country Blues" and "The Rural
Blues." Charters is an historian of jazz, and a good one, but
like many historians he has a built-in bias, which we might
call "pastoral." He wants to get at an older vanished way of
life through the blues, and his book is full of "scenic" effects.
Charters describes James Alley in New Orleans, where Louis
Armstrong grew up:

> There are trees in front of one or two of the yards, but
> running feet have worn most of the grass away, and the
> few skimpy flowers in front of the houses struggle in list-
> less halfheartedness with the shade, the dogs and the chil-
> dren.

Introducing us to Leroy Carr's *Nashville*, Charters writes:

> The state buildings sit in grimy splendor at the top of a
> long rise from the railroad yards and the largest colored
> . district.

Somehow the blues quality inheres in those unlovely places, in
the cotton and cane fields, and it does not transport to honky-
tonks or night clubs, vaudeville theatres or recording studios.

Charters is capable of describing the classic flowering of the art in the generation of "Ma" Rainey, Bessie Smith, Ida Cox and the rest as "The Music had reached the same level of banality that the city blues singing of the women singers in the 1920's had reached." It is all dying and doomed: "Lightnin' " Hopkins "is perhaps the last of the great blues singers," "the last singer in the grand style"; when he dies the blues "will pass" with him. Charters' bias is rural against urban, semi-pro against professional, male against female.

The value of Charters' book far outweighs his bias. His account of Jefferson is a masterpiece of clear-seeing through the fog of sentimentality. Charters writes: "Lemon was fat, dirty, dissolute, but his singing was perhaps the most exciting country blues singing of the 1920's." He shows Jefferson making a living out of his fat and blindness as a novelty wrestler, continuing to record for Paramount because their agent in Chicago pimped for him, freezing to death in the Chicago streets after a lively party. Charters may have little use for "Ma" Rainey, but he gives us a matchless glimpse of her, on the stage when a snake in a novelty act escaped, jumping up on the piano, "fat as she was." Concerned as he is with the quality of Negro life underlying the blues, Charters recognizes what Oliver and Silverman will never understand, "the blues were never strong on social consciousness." Charters himself has strong feelings about racism ("There is a rotted kind of Southerner in Mississippi," he notes) but it never blinds him to the ironies of the blues world, and he remarks of a singer named Jay Bird Coleman, without comment: "He was so popular around Birmingham, that the local Ku Klux Klan began acting as his manager in 1929."

Along with *The Country Blues*, which is largely musical history rather than an account of the blues form, we badly need another book on the blues. The unpublished manuscript of Walter Lehrman, actually the script of a radio series on the blues Lehrman did for an educational station in California, is an extraordinarily useful and comprehensive account, and may

167

be the germ of such a book. Probably, though, no one person knows enough about music and folk music, history and sociology, anthropology and psychology, to do the job, and we need a symposium of cooperating talent.

When they first came to public attention, the blues were regarded as disreputable by those with status in the Negro community. Hughes and Bontemps reprint a Negro sermon, "The Wounds of Jesus," in which the preacher proclaims: "The blues we play in our homes is a club to beat up Jesus." Now they are regarded by many young Negroes, including some jazz musicians, as an "Uncle Tom" remnant. Between being improper and being antiquated, they never had a period of general Negro approval. In the twenties and thirties, when race records sold by the millions, we had the only example I know of a mass audience for a high art, and then only because it was still a folk audience (and often a shamefaced one) for a folk art. That audience has now disappeared, and a few antiquarians are left in its place. Yet the blues, by being so purely Negro, are universal, and the art of their controlled and ambivalent passion says what art has always said. The voice of the blues singer in the distance, when the words are hard to catch, sometimes seems to be saying "What did I do to be so black and blue?," and sometimes "Oy, it's hard to be a Jew," and sometimes even, with the chorus of Sophocles' *Oedipus at Colonus*, "No man escapes from woe."

1964

Really the Blues

THAT MAGNIFICENT ART FORM, the Negro blues, seems to be having something of a bookish revival these days, either by purists lamenting its demise or by impurists celebrating its transformation into Soul music, and at least four books on the subject have appeared in the last six months (more than appeared in the first half century of the blue's existence).

The most trivial of these is *The World Of Soul,* by Arnold Shaw. Shaw worked in the merchandising and promotion of popular songs until he retired a few years ago to become a pop music journalist. His book deals with the blues as the historical roots of his specialty, in such terms as seeing Bessie Smith as "the foremost of a group of singers who helped make the blues an in thing and paved the way for its use by white composers like Harold Arlen . . . and George Gershwin" (naming four of their compositions, none a blues).

Shaw knows some music (he seems quite good on the evolution of rhythm) and his book makes three sensible statements about the blues: that they are "deeply imbued with the imagery of trains and highways"; that "social comment once was rare in the blues"; and that they differ from Soul primarily in "control, reserve, detachment, and distance."

For the rest, Shaw's account of the blues is a tissue of romance (Huddie Leadbetter was called "Leadbelly" because he had "guts of steel"); ignorance (he thinks that a six-line verse is a "quatrain" and that food imagery for sex originated with Rhythm and Blues, but then what can you expect of a man who puts Charleston in North Carolina and Covington in Tennessee?); and illiteracy (he uses "vulpine" for "lupine," and turns out such prose as "Dinah Washington was musical from the top of her clowning head to the bottom of the sleepless nights that led to her accidental death").

Carman Moore's *Somebody's Angel Child* is a biography of Bessie Smith, written for young adults by a Negro composer. It assumes that its audience has been living rather sheltered lives ("A situation called segregation existed across the entire South") and it is heavily fictionalized, making up thoughts and speeches for the characters. Moore transcribes blues and instructs his readers in how they are to be sung; he tells his young audience the unvarnished facts about Bessie's heavy drinking, broken marriage, and subsequent deterioration; he also points out that despite her hard life Bessie earned two to three thousand dollars a week at the height of her career, and that she made over seven million dollars for Columbia and saved the firm from bankruptcy.

Moore's fault is principally a lack of scholarship: he confuses Gertrude Pridgett Rainey, called "Ma," with her sister Melissa Nix, and believes the apocryphal story that "Ma" discovered Bessie and taught her the blues; he tells a romantic yarn of Bessie's composing "Back Water Blues" as a result of traveling along the Mississippi and seeing the flood victims; he also accepts the plausible, famous, but apparently fictitious story that she bled to death because a segregated hospital in Clarksdale, Mississippi, refused to admit her. Moore's prose sometimes gushes ("Sliding slowly, the long notes reaching out for one another in her fine dark soul, she became at such times a singer no more, but a burnishing saxophone or a trombone of the gods"), but despite its weaknesses, his book really tells its young audience a lot that they should know.

Paul Oliver's *The Story Of The Blues* is an Englishman's pictorial history of the art (it is also a social, musical, and cultural history) and a considerable work of scholarship. It includes all sorts of useful material: how Leadbelly tuned his 12-string guitar; the given names of such blues singers as "Skip" James (Nehemiah)) and "Little Brother" Montgomery (Eurreal); photographs of a great many blues singers (and, inexplicably, three pictures of the boll weevil); lyrics and musical examples.

Oliver has a real sense of the blues structure and its enormous potentiality for expression within rigid formal limits (comparable to the Petrarchan sonnet) and he properly recognizes the unstructured freedom of Soul music as the death, rather than the fruition, of the blues. Oliver also has an appreciation of the value of the blues as "one of the richest and most rewarding of popular arts and perhaps the last great folk music that the western world may produce."

He is particularly good on the relation of the blues to African origins: he shows all sorts of instrumental and other connections, but he is considerably more sophisticated than such pioneers in the field as Melville Herskovits; he warns that explaining the flatted "blue notes," the third and seventh intervals, in terms of an African pentatonic scale is "too facile," and he is equally skeptical of testimony that Africans today automatically flat those notes when singing European hymns.

Oliver's first book on the subject, *Blues Fell This Morning* in 1960, was a ludicrous production: he had never been to the United States; American Negro singers visiting England (Big Bill Broonzy and Brother John Sellers among them, I gather) had comically misinformed him about everything they could as a form of put-on; and he owlishly interpreted all the blues' sly sexuality as social protest.

Since then Oliver has traveled extensively in the United States and he has become much better informed about the subject, but he still finds Blind Lemon Jefferson's statement that his girl "crochet all the time" "unexpected" (it is a sexual joke, and can fairly be expected), and Papa Charlie Jackson's "Salt Lake City Blues" mysteriously "daring."

He still sees the blues as a "folk song of protest," restrained on records because "discouraged by the record companies," with no sense of the American Negro hermetic and cryptic tradition overdetermined by African and American experience.

But he does now understand that the blues are full of hidden sexual meanings, and he no longer reads them as simple sociology.

Oliver's faults fall into three principal categories. The first is that he writes spurious history of American Negro folk song, based apparently on guesswork, giving no sources (almost nothing is reliably known before the last half century). Thus after Emancipation "the group work songs were displaced by the lonelier field hollers"; "ballads" displaced other songs at the end of the 19th Century; the blues began around 1895 (a date far too late, considering that jazz originated earlier and is, by general agreement, an instrumental imitation of the sung blues in origin); the three-line 12-bar blues form arose in the first decade of the 20th century, and so on.

Oliver's second major fault is his ignorance. He is shocked at the prevalence of all-Negro minstrel shows (because he has never read Constance Rourke on the authentic Negro roots of the minstrel show); he credits W. C. Handy with "an ear for the folk blues" (although Handy's autobiography *Father of the Blues* makes it clear that he despised folk blues and could not even understand their idiom); he assumes that a Negro with red hair got it "probably from a dietary deficiency in childhood."

I have space to note only a few of Oliver's errors: he accepts the racist theory of George Pullen Jackson that Negro spirituals derive from white hymns; he takes the ballad "Railroad Bill" to be a historical record of the exploits of a Negro outlaw named Morris Slater (although the lyrics of the song show that to be absurd); he confuses "Geechees," the people of the South Carolina coast who have retained some measure of African culture, with the similar "Gullahs" of the Georgia Sea Islands.

Oliver's omissions are not many but they are important: he never mentions Billie Holiday, who only recorded two or three blues but nevertheless profoundly affected the singing of the blues; and he discusses Jimmy Rushing, who seems to me to be the last in the great line of blues singers, but includes no record by him in his extensive Discography.

Oliver's third fault is his language and prose. He uses "alliteration" to mean "assonance" and "burglar" to mean "robber"; he writes such sentences as "New Orleans and St. Louis were strong jazz centers and the bands offered opportunities for the women singers, who seldom played an instrument even though the last mentioned did, to obtain work"; his American publisher has not translated Oliver's book into our language, so that it says "small denominations passed hands" where we would say "coins changed hands," people weigh so many "stone" and wash "windscreens," what we call segregationists become "segregationalists."

For all of its faults (and I have not nearly exhausted them) *The Story of the Blues* is probably the best book we have had so far on the subject (which gives some idea of the quality of the competition).

Eric Sackheim's *The Blues Line* is an anthology of blues lyrics, produced for a Japanese series of fine editions of poetry. It is illustrated by Jonathan Shahn, who has drawn performers from photographs (including one of Texas Alexander, of whom Oliver believes no photograph to exist).

Like the other three books, it has its virtues and its faults. One of the former is that it shows that the blues include a far greater stanzaic variety than the AAB Oliver takes as the form; it has the well-know AA, ABB, AAAA and AAAB, but also the rarer AABB, AAABB, even AAABA. Sackheim's collection also shows that some (not very many, really) blues lyrics are poetry without their music; one might at random list Robert Johnson's "Stones in My Passway," Booker White's "Sic 'Em Dogs On" and "The Panama Limited" along with his "Fixin' to Die" (with the reservation that like Ida Cox's "Death Letter Blues" it is most atypical in its pure dirgelike quality entirely free of ironic undercutting).

There are equally impressive stanzas: the first stanza of Robert Johnson's famous "Hellhound on My Trail," a stanza of Noah Lewis's Jug Band's "New Minglewood Blues,"

I was born in the desert, I was raised in the lion's den,
I was born in the desert, raised in the lion's den,
Said my regular occupation taking women from their other
men.

even such single lines as Bill Wilber's "Leaving on a eagle wing" and Peg Leg Howell's "I didn't see my rider [lover] but I'm sure I heard her laugh."

It must still be said, however, that the vast majority of the blues, including those of the very greatest singers, such as Bessie Smith and Blind Lemon Jefferson, depend so heavily on the music and performance that the lyrics alone are only a tiny fragment of the poem.

Sackheim's anthology, by making available the lyrics of 270 blues, offers us enough material for a crude look at some psychological themes: the obsessive motifs of oral deprivation and self-pity with compensating grandiose fantasy. These are all too familiar to need illustration, but we might note one impressive example of ambitious fantasy, a stanza from Barbecue Bob's "Ease It to Me Blues":

I'm gonna buy me a gun, airplane and a submarine;
I'm gonna buy me a gun, airplane and a submarine;
I'm gonna kill everybody ever treat me mean.

Once this is said, however, it must be added that the blues anatomize neurosis and psychosis in order to resolve them cathartically; that they are, in short, not the disease but the doctor.

The flaws in Sackheim's book tend to stem from its virtues. He has a free-wheeling tendency to call all Negro folksongs blues, explaining weakly in his preface that most of the singers included "would be willing to have most of the songs called 'blues,' " and that he felt it "to be important to abandon the confining yet more or less ubiquitous notion that the blues constitute essentially a single form." Thus he includes as blues any number of gospel hymns, work songs, ballads, and miscellaneous Negro songs, far too many to list.

Consistent with this, he has no sense of the traditional stanza as the formal unit, so that he transcribes lyrics as a kind of free verse, with little punctuation and no quotation marks, printing four-line stanzas in 12 lines and even one three-line stanza in 14 lines. Sackheim's ways are at once sloppy (he spells "levee" as "levy," for reasons I would not care to go into) and pretentious (he concludes his book with a fifty-page anthology of quotations called "A Survey of Sorts: Various Voices" which quotes not only from blues singers but from Confucius, Charles Olson, Jean Genet, and Robert W. Service).

The important matter is not the errors and inadequacies of one writer or another, but the basic misconceptions of the nature and function of the blues which these books embody. The first is that the blues song is a narrative sequence.

Shaw defines the form as "originally a narrative outcry," and Oliver praises Scrapper Blackwell's blues for "a logical progression, a story line which gave them clear shape." But Shaw shows a better understanding in praising B. B. King's blues: "He seldom uses a narrative approach but tends instead to focus on his reactions, his own feelings." Oliver in turn quotes the magnificent lyrics of Ma Rainey's "Counting the Blues," which have no trace of narrative organization, and observes: "The montage of dream images seem to have been drawn from her years of experience, but if the meaning seems fragmented the quality of her singing and the expressiveness of her delivery gave it coherence."

A second fallacy, even more pervasive, is that the blues are autobiographical, that they are simple expressions of singers' (or composers') experience and attitudes. Shaw writes "For all these country bluesmen songwriting was a form of autobiographical expression," and he quotes approvingly an account

175

by Carl Van Vechten of a performance by Bessie Smith: "a woman cutting her heart open with a knife until it was exposed for us all to see."

Oliver goes on endlessly about the blues as "a means of self-expression . . . through the blues a man could sing about himself . . . he could make up a story about himself . . . blues singers nearly always sing about themselves." Sometimes this has its comedy, as when Oliver says that Blind Lemon Jefferson's words "were nearly always autobiographical" and illustrates it with a quotation from "Tin Cup Blues," "That tough luck has struck me and the rats is sleepin' in my hat"—how many rats does Oliver think Jefferson found in his hat? Oliver talks of Robert Johnson's "more autobiographical lyrics" and then quotes that commonplace of a thousand blues, "You can squeeze my lemon till the juice run down my leg."

All details of white brutality, however obviously surrealistic, suggest to Oliver "that it was probably from personal experience," that this song originated, and he rejects the self-evident conclusion that the blues are based on traditional imagery rather than personal experience as "a reluctance that may arise from guilt that the conditions portrayed have been permitted."

Not only does Moore refute this simplistic idea (Bessie Smith "tried to write about what would be most real to the hearts of her audience"), but Oliver's own book refutes it over and over again. He remarks of Tommy Johnson, "Most of his blues seem to have been based on verses already traditional," and "he used a limited repertoire of traditional verses which he re-arranged when he sang"; he quotes Blind Lemon's "Hangman's Blues" with the comment "sometimes he could project himself into another man's situation with rare poetic insight"; he talks of "traditional blues themes," by which he means the innumerable commonplace stanzas; he remarks of Broonzy, "Big Bill was neither motherless nor sisterless, but he sang for those who were."

Sackheim flatly rejects "the common assumption that these songs are necessarily the expression of personally felt grief, pain, anger, joy, etc.," and quotes a most revealing observation by the blues singer Robert Wilkins: "After you begin to sing it, then you would become accustomed to it through psychology that 'most anybody could have the same feeling as you did."

A third fallacy, much less significant than these two, is that regional schools of blues singing are important. Shaw attempts to differentiate three styles—delta, southwestern and southeastern—and Sackheim divides his lyrics into about a dozen regional sections, which show no discernible common features. Here Oliver is much more sensible. "Blues is not a music of state and county lines or river boundaries," he says, "but of a people"; he dismisses the "broad generalizations" of regional schools in favor of "detailed study," which "reveals the subtler shades."

More troublesome, perhaps, is the deliberate misinformation which blues singers give out to white interviewers for publicity, or just for the pleasure of spite or a put-on. Leadbelly, although older, claimed to have been Blind Lemon Jefferson's lead boy, and there is no reason to doubt that he was: Leadbelly's first recording of blues includes songs of Lemon's sung in close imitation of his style. But many blues singers—T-Bone Walker, Lightning Hopkins, Josh White, and others—also made the fashionable claim to have been Blind Lemon's lead boys at various times, and their performance shows no trace of it.

Josh White in fact claimed to have been lead boy for about thirty blind singers, including Blind Arnold, Blind Blake, and Blind Joe Taggart, in addition to Jefferson. Shaw adds a "reportedly" to the Jefferson stories, and Oliver rejects even some of Leadbelly's claims to intimacy with Jefferson as "unlikely."

Big Bill Broonzy, who helped to misinform Oliver's first book on the blues, claimed that he had been taught guitar by Papa Charlie Jackson (a banjo player!) and announced that Ma Rainey's great blues "See See Rider" was written by a Mr. C. C. Rider; Ma Rainey herself claimed to have named the blues (as Jelly Roll Morton claimed to have originated jazz, stomps, ragtime—in fact everything but the blues, which he correctly regarded as an ancient folk form). All four authors are wary about such claims, showing at least some progress in half a century of writing about the blues.

A major defect of all these books is that the authors transcribe lyrics so badly. Moore hears the line in Bessie Smith's greatest blues, "Young Women's Blues," "I ain't no high yaller, I'm a deep yaller brown," as the nonsensical "I ain't no high yaller, I'm a beginner brown." He is apparently young enough never to have seen a silver dollar, and he thinks that it has a "double eagle" on it (like Tsarist rubles) so that he hears Bessie sing in "Nobody Knows You When You're Down and Out":

> *And if I ever get my hands on a dollar again,*
> *I'm going to hold on to it till those eagles grin.*

Moore hears the gypsy tell the singer's persona, "She said you in hard luck, Bessie, Dog-gone your hard-luck soul," whereas the gypsy actually says, "You're a hard luck Bessie, doggone your bad-luck soul." Oliver has gotten much better at transcribing lyrics then he used to be, but he still makes a few mistakes. He turns a marvelous line from Blind Lemon Jefferson's "Black Snake Moan" into nonsense, "Asked my woman for fifty cents, she said 'Lemon, ain't a child in the yard' " (it is of course "ain't a dime in the yard").

He hears Bessie Smith sing in "Young Woman's Blues," "I'm as good as anyone in your town," whereas she actually sings "as any woman in your town" (this is the inability of the English ear to separate the slurred syllables of southern American speech, which led even that great folksong collector Cecil Sharp to record "Swannanoa Tunnel" as "Swannanoa Town"). Oliver also makes a number of errors in the one stanza he reprints from Cripple Clarence Lofton's "I Don't Know," but the song is a fast blues and extraordinarily difficult to hear.

Sackheim, because he reprints thousands of stanzas where the others reprint only a few, naturally makes more errors. He puts doubtful words and passages in italics and asks for corrections by readers, and I have a long list for him, but there is space here for only half a dozen flagrant examples.

In Bessie Smith's "Back Water Blues," he twice records "they rolled a little boat," which is nonsense, and once, correctly, "they rowed a little boat." The Geechees in Chippie Hill's "Charleston Blues" do not "put your water wrong," they "put your water on," that is, heat water preparatory to washing your corpse (with the secondary comic suggestion of cannibalism). Johnson sings in "Hellhound on My Trail," "You sprinkled goofer powder around my door" (that is "hoodoo" powder) not "hot foot powder" (whatever that may be). Sackheim hears Charlie Lincoln sing in "Chain Gang Trouble," "If I listened at my mother *in a farther day*," rather than the familiar commonplace, "If I listened what my mother and my father say."

Finally, among his innumerable mistakes in Lofton's "I Don't Know," the one of most interest is his hearing Deacon Jones dismissed with "Got as much religion as *one I've had*," instead of the correct, and lovely, "Got as much religion as one of air."

Sackheim says that he hopes for correction "by listeners with better ears than mine." It is not a matter of ear (my own ear for Negro speech is poor, and at present I am far from my records and lyrics, making these corrections from memory and by logic) any more than it is one of race (Moore, a Negro composer, hears blues lyrics less accurately than Shaw, a white entrepreneur). It is knowing what goes with what, what can be expected to follow from what; this in turn comes from being steeped in the experience of the blues.

Here even blues singers sometimes contribute to the errors, when they misunderstand an ancient meaning and recast the text in a process of folk rationalization analogous to folk etymology. Oliver gets Speckled Red's title "The Dirty Dozens" as "The Dirty Dozen" because he thinks that the form (a folk pattern of what John Dollard called "interactive insult") has something to do with twelve (not knowing that "dozens" or "doesin's" is a dialect form of "doings"); however, so do blues singers when they sing "Well, I don't play the dozen and neither the ten."

The sort of book we desperately need about the blues would avoid all these errors and replace them with some basic truths. First, that the blues are a complex, ironic, and sophisticated art (the farthest thing imaginable from what Oliver describes, a product of "the singers' lack of sophistication"). They are in fact a high art entirely American Negro in origin, and are probably the major contribution of the United States to the world's arts, certainly more important than the skyscraper or the comic strip. However wholly Negro their origins, they are universal in their esthetic communication.

"No one can give you black lessons," Godfrey Cambridge has said, but lots of people can give you blues lessons. The old-time blues singer Jelly Jaw Short gave an interviewer a most profound statement about the universality of the blues. He said:

> What I think about that makes the blues really good is when a fellow writes the blues and then writes it with a feeling, with a great harmony, and there's so many true words in the blues, of things that have happened to so many people, and that's why it makes the feeling in the blues.

Let me illustrate this universality with a commonplace stanza quoted (somewhat differently) by Shaw:

> *If you wanna go to Nashville*
> *and ain't got no fare,*
> *If you wanna go to Nashville*
> *and ain't got no fare,*
> *Cut your best gal's throat,*
> *the judge will send you there.*

This is an ironic Negro joke, and its focus is on the paradox of violence as a form of mobility and opportunity for Negroes (as we can see it in Wright's *Native Son* and Ellison's *In-*

visible Man). But its imagery of desire, frustration, and violence turned against the beloved is universal and speaks for all men, who are frustrated and unloved in an alien and hostile world. However, the stanza not only expresses this lament: in its ironic mockery; in the delight of the pose of heartlessness masking the heartfelt plaint, in the cruel joke, in short, it eases and heals.

The stanza is the formal unit in a blues, and their linkage is properly not narrative or dramatic (there are exceptions) but lyric and thematic, as in a poem by T. S. Eliot or Wallace Stevens. The typical development of a blues lyric is from some general social condition (flood, unemployment, poverty) to the personal misery (absence and loss of love) for which it is metaphoric.

We can see this progress within a single stanza of Blind Lemon Jefferson's "Rising High Water Blues":

> *Black water rising, southern people*
> *can't make no time,*
> *I said black water rising, southern*
> *people can't make no time;*
> *And I can't get no hearing from*
> *that Memphis gal of mine.*

(The whole song is a study in the complexity of thematic lyric organization.)

The lyrics of Jefferson's "Black Horse Blues," also printed in Sackheim's book, are another triumph of sophisticated form. Tommy Johnson's "Canned Heat Blues," with its progress from the killing effects of Sterno to "worryin' about my soul" to "Take a brownskin woman to do the easy roll" is another.

As he sings each song, the blues singer assumes a persona, a mask, which is not him but the personality produced by all the facets of all the stanzas of that song (a study of any singer's repertoire makes this perfectly clear).

Bessie Smith was not poor and homeless when she sang "Back Water Blues," or unmarried and slandered when she sang

"Young Woman's Blues"; Victoria Spivey was never a fugitive pursued by bloodhounds, for all of "Bloodhound Blues"; Leadbelly never had tuberculosis despite "T. B. Blues." But all of these metaphors express what the singers really were, alienated and oppressed Negroes in a white-dominated world. But the alienated and oppressed Negro is in turn a metaphor for the universal human condition (as the Israelites enslaved in Egypt became a metaphor for the Jewish condition in the Diaspora, for the Negro condition under slavery, and for the Christian condition resulting from original sin or the withdrawal from divine grace).

In my experience of "Young Woman's Blues," each time, I become a young brown woman, climbing the steep incline from misery to defiance, and so indeed, if the song works, do you.

1970

IV

A Blow with a Maize Stalk

WHEN AT THE FIRST I took my pen in hand, that for to write, I did not understand that I at all should make any kind of a book in any kind of mode." Who could resist such an opening sentence? It is as matter-of-fact as "Someone must have been telling lies about Joseph K., for without having done anything wrong he was arrested one fine morning," as innocently captivating as "You don't know about me without you have read a book by the name of *The Adventures of Tom Sawyer*." It is the first sentence of *Strike a Blow and Die* written thirty-five years ago by a native of Nyasaland (now Malawi) named George Simeon Mwase—an account of the 1915 rebellion led by John Chilembwe, the first revolutionary in his part of colonial Africa. Chilembwe was born into the Phiri tribe in the eighteen-sixties and educated at a Church of Scotland mission school. A Baptist fundamentalist missionary took him to the United States and got him enrolled at a Negro Baptist seminary in Virginia, where he learned about American slavery and emancipation. Chilembwe returned to Nyasaland in 1900 and set up a mission station with American support. For fourteen years he preached and taught, and acquired a considerable influence and following in the region. But in reaction to a number of things, among them the loss of African lives in the First World War fighting between the British and the Germans in East Africa, he turned sharply against British colonial rule and told his followers that the white settlers were underpaying them, flogging them, and dismissing them at will, and he became especially "excited" when a white planter burned down the prayer houses Chilembwe's congregation had built on the planter's land. In October of 1914, he wrote a letter of complaint to the Nyasaland *Times*, and the censor refused publication. This closing of the only outlet for his grievances seems to have been the precipitating cause of the rebellion. In December, Chilembwe called a meeting of the chiefs and elders, and "they all came to conclusion, that by not answering us on our request, means death on us." In January, Chilembwe told them "about one a Mr. John Brown of America, who after losing his hope, in succeeding the request in writing, to the authority concerned, in regard slave trading, he determinate to strike a blow and lose his own life." Chilembwe assured them that "this case stands the same" and proposed, "Let us then strike a blow and die, for our blood will surely mean something at last."

The conspirators sent out letters to people they trusted, setting 7 P.M. on Saturday the twenty-third of January as the hour of revolt. They organized themselves into "battalions," with captains and majors, and Chilembwe as field marshal. They planned simultaneous assaults on a number of white settlements, and there were to be "thousands" rising. But on Saturday some of the men "broke the promise" and some of the officers "shrinked," so that the army "scattered away and diminished." Fewer than a hundred men rose, nevertheless, and seized several strongholds, getting guns and ammunition, and capturing a number of white women and children, whom they treated chivalrously, as they had been told to do by Chilembwe. They did kill several white planters and cut the head off one of them, also as instructed by Chilembwe. By Monday, government troops were on the move, and within a week the rebels had been scattered or destroyed. Chilembwe was killed in the fighting, and so were many other rebels. Most of those who were captured were executed. "They all died bravely, singing hymns of their Great God when [they] were escorted towards a scaffold for their last time in the world."

Mwase insists that the rebellion was purely symbolic—a voluntary martyrdom to touch the white conscience. He quotes

—or, more probably, like Thucydides, composes—Chilembwe's instructions to his army, after prayers, on that Saturday morning:

> You are all patriots as you sit. Patriots mean[s] to die for Amor Patria. This very night you are to go and strike the blow and then die. I do not say that you are going to win the war at all. You have no weapons with you and you are not at all trained military men even. One great thing you must remember is that Omnia Vincit Amor so for love [of] your own country and country men, I now encourage you to go and strike a blow bravely and die.
>
> This is only way to show the whitemen, that the treatment they are treating our men and woman was most bad and we have determined to strike a first and a last blow, and then all die by the heavy storm of the whitemen's army. The whitemen will then think, after we are dead, that the treatment they are treating our people is almost [most] bad, and they might change to the better for our people. After we are dead and buried.

In Mwase's view, the rebellion accomplished Chilembwe's aim. "Has the country after John Chilembwe [was] killed and buried won anything which will show to have been won through John Chilembwe?" he asks rhetorically, and answers firmly, "Yes, the country has won the betterment. . . . I am sure, if John Chilembwe was born now and enjoy this newly born Government, certainly, he would have not mobilised troops against it." But there is some evidence in the book that Chilembwe did hope to win. During the rising, he wrote to the German regime in East Africa for assistance; he attempted to sponsor another rebellion in a nearby district; his forces cut telegraph lines to slow the military's communications. Mwase's last words on Chilembwe suddenly lose their certainty on this point:

> I do not know what was Chilembwe's idea, when mobil-ising troops against his Government. He may perhaps

thought to fight the whitemen and become a conqueror himself, as Kalonga his ancestor did, or [he may have] merely [fought] for the Amor Patria. I cannot state which. Because I did not see him personally.

My own guess is that Chilembwe did mean to strike a blow and die, but that he also dreamed of African victory. In the previous century, the tribes of Nyasaland had fought British rule—in the words of the book's editor, "in the end, forlornly" —and this sort of gesture is very much a life-style of Negro Africa in reaction to colonialism. For Chilembwe it was strongly reinforced by the tradition of Christian martyrdom, of "witnessing" with one's blood. We can see it as an American Negro life-style, too, in some of the slave revolts, in the resignation with which Negro leaders, from Malcolm X to Martin Luther King, accept the certainty that they will be killed, in the highly symbolic and quixotic plots of Negro extremists to blow up the Statue of Liberty or the Washington Monument.

Mwase, who died in 1962, is a figure of interest himself. Born about 1880, he was a Tonga who acquired some education and became in turn a postal clerk, a tax clerk, a storekeeper, and a politician. His store went bankrupt, and his career as a tax clerk ended when he spent a year and some months in jail for embezzling taxes. He was a minor leader in the Nyasaland African Congress, but eventually he became alienated from it. The colonial authorities thought him a malcontent, and the tone of his book does suggest an independent spirit. The publication of it is one of those rare moments when we see a classic being born. The manuscript was discovered in the archives of Nyasaland in 1962 by Robert I. Rotberg, a Harvard historian, and his wife. Rotberg has edited it impeccably, with as little alteration as possible (he corrected spellings, for example), and added a long explanatory introduction, footnotes, and an index. The book is valuable for a number of reasons. It gives us the perspective of what Rotberg calls "a member of the indigenous intelligentsia" of Africa on various aspects of colonialism. I would exchange several tomes on race relations for such statements by Mwase as this:

> White people did not like to pay attention to what black people had to say, does not matter important or not, and the latter race feared the former, and compared them as White Hobgoblins from Heaven, even apparitions of under water, while the former also compared the latter as an ape's descendant's, yea, even Chimpanzee's family.

When the native experiences discrimination, Mwase says, he "is, indeed, caught with much shame of his colour, and he blames the creator, why he created him of that colour which has no respect or value on the face of the world."

As Brown's assault on Harper's Ferry, however distorted in the telling, inspired Chilembwe, so Chilembwe's story, in Mwase's telling, may inspire others who live under colonial rule. Rotberg inserts as a footnote a letter from a Tonga, politically active in South Africa, who says that he is proud of John Chilembwe and wants to know more about him. In Nyasaland, Rotberg says, "Africans revered him as the most important of their early patriots." Some of Mwase's intention was clearly to inspire whatever native readers of his book he hoped to reach. In a long encomium, along the lines of Parson Weems on Washington, extolling Chilembwe's virtuous chracter, Mwase calls him "a socialist of both racial and social [which appears to mean that he was sociable with both races]. . . . John was a person of high disposition, a benevolent man." He argues that Chilembwe showed his true patriotism by not staying in America, which "to a Negro was far beyond than any other country on the world, as I am told, where a Negro has a better freedom, as that in America," but returning to his own oppressed land. "He had love towards his country, and the country people." He was also a hero, and brave, because he rose against "a lion at his prey," armed only with "a maize stalk. . . . John was the first and last man to attempt to strike a whiteman with a maize stalk in this country." Mwase's final question is rhetorical: "May I call him a Mr. John Brown of America?"

Mwase's English (it was the third language he learned, and he had probably no more than four years of schooling in it) is everywhere fresh and enchanting. He commences his book with an apology that one would like to see at the beginning of more books: "Therefore anything wrongly written in is due to inadequate of knowledge and not to be taken as an insolent." It is obvious that the great influence on his style is the King James Bible, as when he writes, "Nay, he was never a Chipeta nor an Anguru, even any other tribe." Sometimes he attains a wonderful eloquence, as in describing the fate of the rebels killed by the government troops: "The hyenas played their flesh the whole night."

Strike a Blow and Die is not only about Chilembwe's rebellion. Mwase's own title was "A Dialogue of Nyasaland Record of Past Events, Environments & the Present Outlook Within the Protectorate." (Just as Mwase, or so it seems, invented speeches the way Thucydides did, he went through the process of inventing historical writing that Herodotus did.) After he has told the story of the rebellion, the book is devoted to his thoughts on many subjects. He defends Indian storekeepers against his countrymen as "the dearest friend of a native of this country," because they show no color discrimination and because they sell on installment, in violation of the law. He tackles the problem of miscegenation and the responsibility for the resulting child; he urges that white men keep away from native women ("Was it not better for him to tend this edification before the allurement?") but insists that if they do not tend the edification they must take responsibility for the children. He advises Africans not to fear prison (the jailers "are like parents to the children"), attacks witchcraft ("If there is anyone who still believes on it, I call him an idiot"), and says that some of "the whiteman's laws are heartily welcomed to, and gratified upon."

Rothberg thinks that Mwase distorts the effect of Chilembwe's rebellion on white opinion (that it frightened instead of shaming) and exaggerates the reforms that resulted. Perhaps. But the Republic of Malawi is now independent, and John Chilembwe is, if not its George Washington, at least its Nathan Hale. As for George Simeon Mwase, he, too, struck a blow when he wrote the manuscript. Who knows what blows with a maize stalk can accomplish?

1968

Waiting for Bakayoko

I MAGINE A PROLETARIAN NOVELIST of the '30s, emerging after a quarter-of-a-century sleep in a Catskill cave, publishing a strike novel in 1962. Better still, imagine a tiny extinct one perfectly preserved in amber all these years, fixed in a characteristically lifeless and grotesque posture. To anyone old enough to remember the novels about the Gastonia strike, such images are suggested by *God's Bits of Wood* (translated from the French by Francis Price), a strike novel by a Senegalese Negro, Sembene Ousmane. It is as though our cultural past, instead of disappearing properly, went off to wait for some younger nation and be its future. An extraordinarily distressing idea.

The proletarian novel, William Empson showed us, is Pastoral, an idealization of the worker not unlike the idealization of the shepherd in traditional pastoral poetry. At its best, perhaps in *The Grapes of Wrath*, it can be good Pastoral; more typically (and there seems no point in resurrecting the forgotten names) it is sentimental, caricatured and melodramatic Pastoral. Ousmane's fictionalization of the 1947–48 strike on the Dakar-Niger railway in Senegal is quite typical, although a few African features set it apart from its American fellows.

For the idealized proletarian, take Ibrahim Bakayoko, one of the union leaders. He is off organizing the strike elsewhere on the line and does not appear until the last third of the book, but he is quoted, built-up and awaited like an absent Lefty. An educated Europeanized girl, N'Deye Touti, thinks: "She was curiously drawn to this hard man who seemed sometimes to live in another world, but who was he, after all? A workman."

192

When an attempt is made, by a treacherous white supervisor who says he likes the workers, to bribe the secretary of the strike committee, he recalls Bakayoko's warning: "Anyone who says, 'I like the Negroes,' is a liar."

When Bakayoko finally appears, we discover that he is mystically one with the people: "His heart held neither spite nor malice, but he had traveled over a thousand miles among the strikers and their families, and the sufferings, the privations, and the tragedies he had witnessed had shaken him more than he realized. He was astonished to note now that his pulse was beating in the same rhythm as the drums in the street." Bakayoko is "the soul of this strike." When injury and death in his family call him home, he refuses to leave the strike: "We must fight for the living and not give our time to thinking of the dead." His old uncle wonders if he has a heart. When Bakayoko turns the tide in a speech to the workers of Dakar, we are told: "It was no longer the crowd he saw in front of him, but two shining rails, tracking a path into the future. Even his voice seemed turned to steel." Eventually N'Deye Touti proposes that she become his second wife, and is refused. She too charges that he has no heart. But of course Bakayoko has a heart, a great big steel one beating only for the workers.

To match such idealized heroes, the bosses are melodramatic villains. Dejean, the regional director of the railroad, is a Pétainist scoundrel who rose to power by crushing an earlier strike. Isnard, the supervisor who tries bribery, is a hypocrite and liar. When they meet with the strike leaders, Dejean is so frightened that his eyeglasses break in his hand. Provoked by Bakayoko, Dejean slaps his face, and "the big trainman" starts to throttle him and has to be pulled off the director, who is "already half dead with fear."

The remarks of the white bosses have the exaggerated obtusity that characterizes the class enemy in proletarian fiction. Dejean says of the workers: "But I know them, I assure you, they are children." The chief of police tells another European that "a couple of pounds of rice" will buy him any native girl: "Right now they'll go to bed with you for less than that." When the native women improvise a poetic chant on the strike, Isnard denies that possibility. "It's just shouting and yelling as usual," he says. "What do you think they know about the strike? They're just making noise because they like to make noise."

The savage brutality of the bosses may or may not have occurred in reality, but it is unconvincing in the book. Troops charge gatherings with bayonets drawn, killing women and babies. Searching Bakayoko's house, brutal policemen kick his adopted daughter in the stomach and kill his old mother. Firemen turn their hoses on the women, killing a poor old lady. Panicked by their slingshots, Isnard shoots and kills three boys. Strikers are put into a foul concentration camp, where they are beaten and tortured in Nazi-like atrocities.

The workers' response to this is equally unconvincing heroism and fortitude. When *they* beat up strikebreakers, we are told merely that they "administered their rough form of justice." They live on vultures and garbage, and they and their families endure starvation and suffering with no weakening of spirit. They are ethically superior to their exploiters. When the strike finally ends in a total victory, an old man who had been tortured in the concentration camp gives the moral: "Hatred must not dwell with you."

In this battle of the forces of Negro light against the forces of white darkness, no middle position is possible. When the strike is first discussed, a *white*-collar *black* worker who opposes it is asked to decide where he really belongs, "with the workers" or "with the bosses?" In the course of the book, every character is thus polarized. N'Deye Touti, who for all her education "had never read a book by an African author," identifies with her people and chooses the forces of light. In a symbolic gesture, she gives up her notebooks when there is no other paper to light the fires. Sounkaré, an old watchman who refuses to join the strike, falls to his death, and is, with poetic justice, eaten by rats.

I know nothing of Ousmane's political identifications, if any, but his novel has the disingenuous references to the Communist party that kept popping to the surface in our strike novels of the '30s. The old Imam of Dakar, a Moslem religious leader who tries to mislead the people, tells the women: "It is the Communists who are really directing this strike." Dejean shouts at the strike committee: "You are led by a bunch of Bolsheviks." "These women are all Communists," someone in the crowd says when the Thiès women march to Dakar in support of their husbands.

There are suggestions, too, of the Marxist view of strikes as means rather than ends, educating the workers in class struggle and solidarity, and thus successful even if defeated. "This strike is like a school, for all of us," one of the union men says. Ousmane writes, when the women reach Dakar: "Their long journey together had been an effective training school; they marched in well-ordered ranks, ten abreast, and without any masculine escort now." More steel rails, obviously, to carry Lenin's locomotive of history into the future.

God's Bits of Wood is unlike American proletarian literature in a few African respects. These unionists go barefoot, and their faces are decorated with tribal scars. They are faithful Moslems, although the strike leaders eat pork. They speak their tribal languages among themselves, and their speech is ceremonious and proverbial. They sing legendary ballads as well as strike chants. In Senegalese tradition, it is bad magic to number people, except anonymously as the "God's bits of wood" of the title. It is a lovely native equivalent for Marx's secularization of the mystical Body of Christ, the consubstantial proletariat.

Another difference is the inferior position of women in Senegal. In the book, women addressing strike meetings are "unfamiliar and disturbing," since no woman has ever spoken in public before. The women's march is thus a feminist revolution as well as strike support, as the women of Dakar show by receiving the marchers like victorious warriors.

The most striking West African feature of the book, making it quite unlike our puritanic proletarian fiction, is its earthiness, its freedom regarding the body. A striker's wife named Mame Sofi is an example. She tells her husband: "If you go back to work before the others, I'll cut off the only thing that makes you a man." When the women fight the police, she grabs one policeman by his genitals and orders another woman to urinate in his mouth; when the soldiers appear, she and her friends pull the platoon leader off his horse and push his face into the latrine ditch. Ah, Gastonia.

In a few respects, where *God's Bits of Wood* is unlike our own proletarian fiction, the difference comes from French rather than African sources. The chief of these is Malraux's *La Condition humaine*, which a striker borrows from Bakayoko's library with the statement, "Everything we need is in this book," and which has visibly influenced the author as well as his characters. Again, we are back in the '30s, when Léon Blum concluded a political meeting by sending his audience off to read the book, and it was generally taken to be a revolutionary manifesto. Now we can see that it is and always was a despairing and death-intoxicated existentialist manifesto, but Senegal as yet cannot.

Nigerian fiction, with which I am more familiar than I am with French West African, is of two sorts. One is typified by the work of Amos Tutuola, who writes Yoruba folklore in narratives that are like proto-epics. The other is typified by the work of Chinua Achebe, who writes in the tradition of the European novel. These have been the alternatives of every new nation or literary renaissance in a provincial nation: we think immediately of Twain and James, Gogol and Turgenev, Synge and George Moore.

In the great writers, these alternatives merge, and we get Melville, Dostoevsky and Joyce, at once native *and* European. But now we can see another possibility for the literature of the new nations, not both but neither: Pastoral novels neither authentically native nor authentically European. The thought of whole schools of proletarian fiction springing up in Africa and Asia in the future chills the blood. I hope that Sembene Ousmane is the tail end of our parade, not the vanguard of theirs.

1962

Sad Encounters

CESARE PAVESE is still not very well known in this country, but he is the most important postwar Italian novelist. "Pavese's nine short novels make up the most dense, dramatic, and homogeneous narrative cycle of modern Italy," his younger friend Italo Calvino has written. In Italy, he is thought to be the most American of writers, because he translated American books, from *Moby Dick* to *The Hamlet* (he was so fond of Hemingway and Fitzgerald, he said, that he did not dare translate them), because his novels continually suggest American prototypes, and because he carried on a lifelong love affair with the United States (which he never saw). In fact, through a Piedmontese friend living in Chicago, Pavese once addressed a Henry Luce mash note to all of us:

> You are the peach of the world! Not only in wealth and material life but really in liveliness and strength of art which means thought and politics and everything. You've got to predominate in this century all over the civilized world as before did Greece, and Italy, and France. I'm sure of it.

To an American, however, Pavese's work seems typically Italian, very like the postwar films, exploring rural life in the hills around Turin, hymning the hot sun that ripens grape and grain.

R. W. Flint's good selection, *The Selected Works of Cesare Pavese* includes an early realistic novella, *The Beach* (*La Spiaggia*, 1942), and three amazing "symbolic reality" novels that were published in 1949—*The House on the Hill* (*La Casa in Collina*), *Among Women Only* (*Tra Donne Sole*), and *The Devil in the Hills* (*Il Diavolo sulle Colline*). Mr. Flint's translations are lively and slangy (the clause he translates "she made him out as some kind of boring hayseed" was rendered in a 1961 translation by W. J. Strachan as "she treated him as an outsider"). Flint occasionally falls into the language of boys' books (" 'Nuts! We're all numskulls,' the other sneered") or no language at all ("Loris's bow tie, who was holding forth"), but for the most part his translation is readable, stylish, and sometimes quite lyric.

All four works are first-person. *The Beach* tells of the narrator's experiences at the seashore with his old friend Doro and Doro's new wife, Clelia. The narrator becomes rather attached to Clelia, and so does a somewhat loutish student named Berti. At the end, Clelia discovers that she is pregnant, and she and Doro return to Genoa. The narrator is bereft, as is, in his loutish fashion, Berti. The novella is interesting primarily for the character of the unnamed narrator, the first in Pavese's long line of Ishmael protagonists. "I was finding my usual perverse pleasure in keeping apart," he says, and he plays cards "with aggressive indifference." It is obvious that the attachment to Clelia masks an unconscious attachment to Doro ("The truth is that I had wanted Doro to take me with them") that goes back to the narrator's adolescence, where it disguised itself as jealousy ("I had always been jealous of Doro"). Berti is a fun-house mirror in which the narrator can see his absurd passion caricatured. After Doro and Clelia have left for Genoa and Berti has become "inconsolable," the narrator, too, decides to go, since "no spot is less habitable than a place where one has been happy," and that night he and Berti return to Turin. *The Beach* is wryly moving, the comic ghost of a tragic love story.

Flint regards *The House on the Hill* as Pavese's "masterpiece," and it may well be. To escape the Allied bombing of Turin during the war, the narrator, the schoolteacher Corrado, rents a room in the Piedmontese countryside. At an inn on a nearby hill (the "house" of the title), he discovers a girl, Cate, with whom he has had an affair and who now has an illegitimate son. The boy, Dino, is named Corrado, too, and Corrado worries about being the father, but he accepts Cate's transparent lie that he is not, as innocently as he does not notice that she is still in love with him. Corrado enjoys romping in the woods with Dino, and the companionship of Cate and her Turin friends at the inn. The adults get involved in the underground resistance to the Germans, but Corrado, though he is full of militant slogans, remains uncommitted. One day, all of Corrado's companions are arrested by the Germans, and Carrado realizes that "now Dino had no one except me." Eventually, in a panic, Corrado deserts Dino and flees to his parents' house, and at the end he is left thinking, "I don't know if Cate, Fonso, Dino, and all the others will return. Sometimes I hope so, and it scares me."

The House on the Hill is one of the saddest novels ever written. As it begins, Corrado has no companion but a big dog named Belbo; as it ends, he has lost even the dog. Corrado is a more extreme *isolato* than the narrator of *The Beach*; he says, defensively, "But for my part I was happy to have in my life neither any real affection nor embarrassment, to be alone, tied to no one." He is a boy, incapable of accepting mature responsibility. He describes his first, early break with Cate as "an occasion well lost, that later became a habit with me." He has taught Cate that "life is worthwhile only when you live for something or someone," but he himself cannot; he fails the opportunity to become a husband, a father, a patriot. "You're not able to love," Cate tells him, and we last observe him overwhelmed by self-contempt, his life "a long isolation, a useless holiday."

The narrator of *Among Women Only* is in her early thirties, and she, too, is named Clelia. She is a Roman couturière who is opening a branch shop in Turin. The novel deals with her acquaintances, mainly women, among the Turinese upper class. It is neatly framed by one of these young women, Rosetta, who tries to poison herself in Clelia's hotel the day Clelia arrives, and who finally succeeds in a second attempt. (*Among Women Only* was made into a film, *Le Amiche*, by Antonioni.) Rosetta's suicide is never adequately explained, but then the way her friends live, as Pavese anatomizes it, would drive any sensitive person to take his life. They are constantly planning and discussing amateur theatricals in a desperately affected fashion ("Any ambiance at all is a *mise-en-scène*"); they pretend to bargain with bartenders for cocaine; the women all seem bisexual, and some are quite homosexual (a young sculptress who stares at Clelia "as if I were a handsome young man"). Some are married, but none seems to have children; "to have a child," one of them says delicately, you have "to become a sow." They live "like cats, always ready to scratch and snatch," Clelia thinks. They slum in working-class restaurants; they feel "a disgust with living, with everything and everyone"; they are Philistine ("There's no painting that's worth a beautiful woman undressing") and cynical ("The only thing that saves people is money"). "Love in any form is a dirty thing," Rosetta says, and the others appear to agree.

Clelia, too, grew up in Turin, but in the slums. Her ambition was "to become somebody," and she was coached by her mother "not to believe in anyone or anything." She is better than the idle ladies of Turin, for at least she works, yet without joy or fulfillment. "I liked a good time but paid my own way." We see her in two loveless sexual encounters—in one uninterested but offering no resistance, in the other seducing a young carpenter who has been working at the shop. She has enough spirit to blacken the eye of a forward escort but not to break up the evening with him. Like all Pavese protagonists, she is a solitary, speaking of "my real vice . . . my pleasure in being alone." Working has given her an integrity ("It's hard to fake on a job"), but she does not seem capable of domestic responsibilities; in Rome, she lives with an older man, and their life together is "tranquil resignation." If Rosetta's suicide is to represent a symbolic transformation for Clelia, that happens after the ending, which is simply a beautiful tableau of the suicide: Rosetta poisoning herself in the rented studio of a painter, sitting in an armchair looking out toward Pavese's beloved Piedmontese hills.

The narrator of *The Devil in the Hills* is an unnamed twenty-year-old student who is inseparable from two other students, Pieretto and Oreste. During a summer vacation they go to Oreste's village, and end up staying at the villa of a wealthy, torpid young man, Poli. Oreste falls in somewhat Gatsbyish love with Poli's wife, Gabriella, who is equally drawn to him but remains loyal to Poli. That is all that happens, but it is made wonderfully resonant. Life in the village seems idyllic: "One breathed a special gentleness;" as one drinks strawberry wine, it is hard to know "if so much sweetness was passing from the wine into the air, or vice versa"; the nearby farm of Oreste's two grown cousins is the very model of the rural good life, a place of happiness and peace. Yet Gabriella may be refusing Oreste for his own good, so that he can marry the girl from his village and tend his vineyards, for Gabriella is identified with death, not life; the countryside in August "stinks of coitus and death," Pieretto says, and Gabriella answers, "I like this indecent odor." "I'm tired of living," she says later, like one of those Turinese ladies. "I'd like some man to strangle me."

Earlier, the book presents a marvelous image of suspended life: "Little solitary women came and sat on the benches" by the Turin railway station, "waiting for something prodigious, the fall of the city, the apocalypse." Pavese opposes to this an image of resurrection as the trio of young men stir Poli out of his cocaine-filled life. At their first encounter with him, they bellowed in unison, a "lacerating" and "bestial" sound. "That noise you made two nights ago woke me up," Poli tells them. "It was like a cry that wakes a sleepwalker. It was a sign, the violent crisis that resolves an illness. . . . Now I know that I'm a man, a man full of vices, a weak man but a man. That cry has shown me myself. No more illusions." The new Poli lectures them on inner freedom and joy, and gives up hunting because he no longer wants to take life. Pieretto says, "If he doesn't die, he'll become a Buddhist." But Poli neither dies nor becomes a Buddhist. He develops tuberculosis and decides to go, with Gabriella, to Milan for treatment. Subtly transformed but still unregenerate, he lets the boys off at the village, and the novel ends with a perfect Hemingway sentence; says the narrator, "Then they left and we went to the mill to drink."

The earth is female—that is the predominant note in *The Devil in the Hills*. "The earth is like a woman," Oreste's father says, and this articulates for the narrator what he continually feels, seeing a rainstorm as "the most private cracks in the earth penetrated and violated," admiring "the earth's thick blood" (an image of peasant hardihood for Pavese, whose peasant narrator in *The Moon and the Bonfires* talks of "my thick blood"). "A person in crisis always works his land," Pieretto says. "It's our common mother, who never deceives her children." Poli's idleness and his untilled fields are thus demonic, the "devil" in the hills, a sin against fertility, the opposite of the idylls of Oreste's hardworking family. Pieretto tells Oreste, "You should marry that girl and work your lands in peace." The narrator puts it all together when he thinks:

> That abandonment, that solitude of the Greppo, were symbols of the mistaken life she [Gabriella] and Poli were leading. They were doing nothing for their hill; the hill was doing nothing for them. Their waste of so much land and so much life could bear no other fruit than restlessness and futility. I thought of the Mombello vineyards, of the sharp face of Oreste's father. To love a piece of land, you had to work it and sweat over it.

Three other books by Pavese have been translated. *The Moon and the Bonfires* (*La Luna e i Falò*, 1950), his last novel, was brought out here in 1953 in a translation by Marianne

Ceconi. It is an intense novel about an emigrant peasant who returns to the Piedmont hills after twenty years in America; its two terrible human bonfires are perhaps the most compelling symbols in all of Pavese's work. *The Burning Brand: Diaries 1935–1950* (*Il Mestiere di Vivere*, 1952) was translated by A. E. Murch (with Jeanne Molli) and appeared in 1961. These diaries are Pavese's thoughts on literature and philosophy, politics and religion, shot through with fifteen years of pain, suffering, and obsession with suicide. "My basic principle is suicide," he wrote as early as 1936. The last of his works to be published in this country is *Dialogues with Leucò* (*Dialoghi con Leucò*, 1947), translated by William Arrowsmith and D. S. Carne-Ross and published in 1965. It consists of dialogues on Greek mythology, characteristically preoccupied with blood ("From the time of chaos, there has been nothing but blood. Men's blood, blood of monsters, of gods. We begin and we die in blood") but also characteristically preoccupied with human toil and sweat (Dionysus praises mankind for "their crops and their gardens. Wherever they lavish their sweat and their speech, a rhythm, a sense, a repose is born").

Pavese has obviously been influenced not only by his American models but by Alain-Fournier's *The Wanderer* (*Le Grand Meaulnes*), and this is particularly apparent in *The Beach* and *The Devil in the Hills* (how seminal *The Wanderer* now seems, influencing everyone from Graham Greene to Günter Grass). Yet despite all these influences, Pavese is a true original, a chronicler of sad encounters in an old land. "My stories are always about love or loneliness," he wrote in his diary in 1938. His credo about the human personality is probably best expressed by Pieretto in *The Devil in the Hills:* "There are only saints, because each person in his intentions is a saint, and if only he were let alone he'd bear fruit." In 1945, Pavese became a Communist, but, as his diaries make clear, he was never a very satisfactory one, and the Party chafed him as he chafed it. In the next five years, he wrote his major work, including seven of his nine novels, while suffering terribly from asthma, a neurotic sexual difficulty that convinced him that he could never marry, political ambivalence, loneliness, self-disgust, and chronic depression. In 1950, he was awarded the Strega Prize for fiction, Italy's most distinguished literary award. A few months later he killed himself, having been working up to it for most of his life. Pavese was then forty-two, and nothing of his was yet available in his beloved English language. At Expo '67, he was the only Italian writer to have a whole showcase—full of translations of his works—to himself.

1968

The Oldest Story

A MAN, a proud man, intelligent, successful, once self-confident, dragged down by a girl out of hell." The oldest story in the world, surely. Adam was the first, and is probably the archetypal case. Keats called the lady "La Belle Dame sans Merci," medieval folklore knew her as a *succubus*, the Japanese identify her as a shape-shifting fox who drains a man's life in sexual excess. Some early Fathers of the Church were so convinced that women were the root of all sin that they identified the female genitals with Hellmouth.

Every literature has it variants of the story. Nana drives Count Muffat to poverty and despair in Zola's *Nana*. Anna ruthlessly uses and discards Modest in Chekhov's "Anna Round the Neck." Aguri reduces Okada to emaciation and delirium in Tanizaki's "Aguri." Margot ruins, betrays, blinds, and eventually kills Albinus in Nabokov's *Laughter in the Dark*. Daisy deserts Gatsby and causes his death in Fitzgerald's *The Great Gatsby*. Faye drives Homer to madness and murder in West's *The Day of the Locust*.

In the Dietrich film *The Blue Angel*, this story becomes overripe and plummy, and in Svevo's *As a Man Grows Older*, it is seen as wryly funny. (In other cases, our story appears to have been radically transposed. Mildred in Maugham's *Of Human Bondage* is oddly boyish; we know that Proust's Albertine is based on a male Albert; and Tadzio, Aschenbach's destroyer in Mann's "Death in Venice," is openly a boy. In an article some years ago, I named this device of disguising homosexual love as heterosexual love the "Albertine Strategy." It is one of the principal subdivisions of the Fall story.)

As if to demonstrate that plot is nothing and treatment everything, one more retelling of this antique could not be more fresh and glistening. This lyric novel is *A Love Affair*, by Dino Buzzati (translated from the Italian by Joseph Green). It tells of the mad passion of Antonio Dorigo, a 50-year-old Milanese bachelor and successful architect, for Adelaide Anfossi, a 20-year-old Milanese whore. The melodramatic quotation with which these remarks begin is from Antonio's musings on his fate.

Adelaide, called Laide, is not only a whore: she is insatiate, frigid, and perverse; she is an incessant and shameless liar; and she is a triumph of vulgarity from her violet panties to the way she charges "You want to soil the finest feelings," whenever she is denying Antonio's latest valid accusation. What Antonio feels for her is total and uncontrollable love, tragic passion, "as though he had taken a love potion"; and Buzzati describes it with the greatest skill and insight. It is love like a physical illness: "a kind of interior thirst around the entrance of his stomach, up up toward the breast bone, a painful unchanging tenseness of his whole being." At one point Antonio imagines Laide sitting inside his brain, telephoning other men. He defines love bitterly: "It's a curse on your head and heart and you can't escape it."

Antonio not only keeps Laide in luxury and believes all her absurd lies—that she is a ballet dancer at the Scala, that she is a fashion model, that her lover Marcello is her innocent cousin —but he puts up with a series of monstrous humiliations. Laide drives off with Marcello and leaves Antonio to mind her dog; she keeps Antonio waiting in bed while she plucks her eyebrows, then makes an endless series of telephone calls, while all he can say is "I'll catch a chill without any clothes on"; she sits between Marcello and Antonio in the movies and holds Marcello's hand; she keeps Antonio waiting on the street for hours; she entertains Marcello and asks Antonio to come by with some food for the dog.

This would be a simple clinical study of masochist man and

sadist girl, except that only the power of Antonio's love is taken seriously; the ignominy of his fate is not. In a series of jealous fantasies that get funnier and funnier, Antonio pictures the entire male population of North Italy going to bed with Laide in a variety of perverse fashions: he imagines her, for example, committing indecencies with elderly industrialists who are "advised on the state of their heart by a weekly electrocardiogram." He daydreams of her losing a leg in an accident: "How wonderful that would be!," since then she would stay at home and be exclusively his.

Antonio is more than a little reminiscent of that other serio-comic masochist, Leopold Bloom, and Buzzati has clearly learned from Joyce or from Joyce's pupil Svevo. Antonio thinks, of a madam: "She's an honest woman, a woman of good heart, how many she's helped in their difficult moments, poor unlucky wretches, she's like a mother to the dear girls, but it would be too bad if they tried anything that's all they'd need." On his own plight: "Each time I admit it's my fault I admit I'm a nut it's a kind of mental state but what can I do?"

Ultimately *A Love Affair* exonerates Laide: she represents the body's innocence, what Buzzati in a wonderful phrase calls "carnal virginity." At one point Laide dances the cha-cha-cha solo for Antonio, and "suddenly there's no longer anything false about her, or left out, or hidden, or vile, or mean"; "dancing the cha-cha-cha, she tastes the marvelous sensation of being free, light, and chaste"; "in this unselfish act of beauty she's transformed, she becomes a rose, a cloud, a harmless bird." Later he recognizes the same "moving purity" in her when she sings a coarse song.

There is a marvelous scene in which Antonio waits up in Laide's apartment for her to return from whoring, and while waiting writes her an ultimatum. She comes in at three in the morning, crumples his note without reading it, ignores his request that she read it, goes into the bathroom "and, leaving the door open, began to pee." At that moment we realize that

Antonio is the mind and Laide the body, and that she has just given the body's answer to the mind's importunities.

The ending of *A Love Affair* is comic rather than tragic. In the last chapter Antonio watches Laide asleep in his bed, a vision of serene innocence. She wakes briefly to tell him that she is pregnant, presumably by him, and wants the child; then she drifts back to sleep. Antonio realizes that she has always been untouched by the "dark cruel wood" of her life. In the book's final vision, Laide, still asleep, becomes pure spirit, and "floats under the rooftops the skylights the terraces the pinnacles of Milan." The ending is also deeply equivocal, none of Laide's lies having been acknowledged or explained, and "maybe tomorrow everything will be as it was, and the shame and bitchery will begin again." But at this moment Laide is blessed, and can bless.

In one of its aspects, *A Love Affair* is an allegory of social class. It is not so openly allegorical as Buzzati's other novel published in this country, *The Tartar Steppe*. From that, we might expect: The Proletariat Embraced by the Most Advanced Section of the Bourgeoisie. *A Love Affair* is far from that, but it is not realism either: we never see Antonio at work as an architect, or at home with his family. Antonio *is* "a bourgeois in the bloom of life," respectable and conventional; it never occurs to him to take Laide home, or introduce her to his family. And Laide comes, not out of hell, but out of the Milanese working class, and has, along with its vices, its virtues: toughness, resourcefulness, pride.

The style of *A Love Affair* resembles lyric poetry more than it does novelistic prose. It is rhetorical and Whitmanesque, a cascading of nouns. Here is a sentence:

"Papers, ledgers, forms, telephone calls, receipts, hands full of pens, tools, pencils, hard at work on a socket, a screw, a sum, a gear, a job of soldering, a statement of account, a film bath: an infinity of frantic ants intent on their own well-being; yet their thoughts—oh, he had to laugh—all around, for all those miles and miles, thoughts like his, both obscene and exquisite, prompted by the mysterious voice that calls for the preservation of the species, transfigured into strange, blazing vices, why had no one ever dared to say so? thoughts of *her*, always of *her*, of that particular mouth, of those lips made in a certain way, of an arrangement of taut muscles (do you remember?), soft and fluid, with a curvature unlike all the others, of a fold, of a fullness, of a depth, of a warmth, of a dampness, of a surrender, of a descent, of a burning abyss."

The figures of speech are ornate and heavy, like those of poetry. Some metaphors are almost surrealistic. As Antonio drives to get Laide in another town, "all the poplars of the broad countryside fled as he did, exactly, wheeling in two enormous curved wings." There is a five-page montage showing sex in Milan, in which an auto mechanic "looks up and sees the bellies and the crotches and the private parts of the cars," and a whore sees her customer sleeping with his mouth half open "like the flickering light at the altar of Our Lady of Sorrows where she kneels in the frost of dawn." Buzzati (or the translator) has a maddening habit of switching tenses, but I suppose that a phantasmagoria is answerable only to its own laws.

The Tartar Steppe is a derivative book. It is like an expansion of Kafka's "In the Penal Colony" without Kafka's absolute authority, and at various times it suggests Mann's *The Magic Mountain*, Juenger's *On the Marble Cliffs*, and Cavafy's poem "Waiting for the Barbarians." *A Love Affair*, which tells the most hackneyed of stories, which shows the influence of Joyce or Svevo or both, is nevertheless a work of startling originality. In the eighteen years between the two books, Dino Buzzati has mastered his theme of obsession, has learned to put real toads into his fables, and has found his own authentic voice.

1964

Fable Italian Style

D INO BUZZATI, a sixty-one-year-old staff writer for the Milan *Corriere della Sera*, has published fiction since his twenties, but to the best of my knowledge only two of his novels have appeared in this country in the past, and those two are so disparate that they hardly seem the work of one writer. *The Tartar Steppe* (*Il Deserto dei Tartari*), published in 1940, won the Italian Academy Award, was translated into a number of European tongues, and appeared in this country in 1952. *A Love Affair* (*Un Amore*) appeared in Italy in 1963 and in the United States the following year. The first is a sombre Kafkaesque allegory, in which a routine life is seen in the metaphor of manning a frontier outpost against a rumored enemy. *A Love Affair* is a rollicking, lyric, and delightful account of a respectable middle-aged man's mad devotion to a vulgar, lying, and unfaithful young trollop. If *A Love Affair* is ultimately an allegory, too—the mind and the body—it is an allegory with the rich texture of human life and poetic language, and Buzzati's master then was no longer Kafka but the Svevo of *As a Man Grows Older* (*Senilità*).

Now we have a third novel, written between the two, and, properly, in an intermediate style. It is *Larger Than Life* (*Il Grande Ritratto*), published in Italy in 1960 and brought out here in 1968 in a translation by Henry Reed. It deals with the old fantasy of creating life, in the line of the legend of the Golem of Prague, of Frankenstein's monster, and of many other creations. After the first sixty pages, during which we are kept in suspense about the secret, the plot is entirely predictable. A few Italian scientists construct, in an uninhabited area, a vast electronic installation that functions as a living human being, with sensory and intellectual faculties far beyond our own. For reasons attributable to the Italian character, they give it the spirit of a beautiful but radically imperfect dead woman named Laura, its inventor's first wife. As any reader can guess, it inevitably turns malign and its human spirit must be destroyed.

The characters are just as stereotyped. Endriade, the machine's inventor, is a mad scientist, raving impiously, "We shall arrive at the superman. More than that: the demiurge, a sort of God." Sometimes he is Faust, exulting that he feels almost a god: "Out of nothing, out of dead matter, to succeed in bringing forth a created being!" Then he postures as a Byronic hero, confessing his own damnation or, in adversity, standing in the rain, "deformed, aged, magnified, by the intensity of his suffering greatness." Strobele, Endriade's chief assistant, is the conventional technician for a mad scientist—puritanical, prudish, and without imagination. Professor Ismani, through whose experience we learn the secret, is the timid everyman suitable for *his* role. Strobele's wife, Olga, who awakens the giant, immobile Laura to her physical frustrations, is fittingly a sensualist with nudist proclivities. The second Mrs. Endriade is, of course, simple, good, and devoted; as Endriade says, in a remark that is more likely to assure his damnation than any number of demiurges he might create, "She asked nothing of me. Just wanted to worship me." Only Ismani's wife, Elisa, the intended victim of the passions aroused in Laura, and Laura herself, in both forms, are more than stereotypes.

What, then, is the interest of such a book, with its frayed plot and machine-made characters? The answer is that Buzzati has used these conventional materials as the framework for a novel about human concerns. The strongest evidence of his seriousness comes at the very end, after Laura's "soul" has been smashed. The last three sentences are a surprising elegy for a monster:

Gone for good the woman, love, desire, loneliness, anguish. Only the enormous machine, tireless and dead. Like an army of blind bookkeepers, bent over thousands on thousands of desks, writing number after number, endlessly, day and night, through empty eternity.

Long before this, an attentive reader knows that Buzzati, because of the peculiar nature of his language and craft, is playing fast and loose with his Promethean fable. The language is neither the patient explanatory fabric of *The Tartar Steppe* nor the cascade of nouns in *A Love Affair*. Instead, it is an odd prose of antithesis, suggesting by negative definition and a scatter of similes. Thus, Buzzati says not what the machine looks like but what it does *not* look like: it "did not have that dead black appearance that, for example, a transformer-cabin sometimes has; nor, for that matter, did it have that hermetic apathy, proper to a tomb (closed, shut in on itself, indifferent to the life around it)." And another description of Laura: "There was about this highly remarkable vision, notwithstanding its bareness, a powerful and somehow inexplicable beauty: which was not the sombre poetry of pyramids or fortresses or refineries or blast furnaces or great prison blocks. Not at all." When Laura is distressed, her harmonious sound becomes inharmonious; Buzzati describes for us the sound of desolation and weeping, but in similes so disparate as to persuade us that the sound cannot be defined, thus constituting another negative definition:

Like the little girl lost on the heath in the autumn twilight. Like the abandoned mistress in the icy garret. Like the tree shattered by the wind. Like the condemned man in the cell. Like someone who is suddenly overpowered by memories of sunlight and youth; and knows he is dying.

The point of this language of antithesis is that Buzzati's subject is nothing less than an affirmation of the human spirit, which cannot be defined in terms of anything else, as life cannot be defined in terms of the inanimate. Furthermore, unlike the conventional Christian moral of his fable (the hero is damned for his sin of pride in challenging God the Creator), Buzzati's affirmation is resolutely un-Christian: spirit does not exist apart from nature and the flesh and in denial of them but *through* nature and the flesh. He affirms pagan monism rather than Christian dualism. When Olga, who at first believes the machine to be a man, attempts to excite it by pressing her naked breasts against it, we realize that this is a very Italian fable indeed.

Buzzati's use of the conventions of his form (pace, and the creation of suspense by mystification until the secret is revealed) is a playful use of the technique of science fiction for an ultimate subversion of it—a parable *against* the machine. His technical jargon is on the edge of mockery. Endriade explains the technique for giving Laura human personality: "From then on, by reason of the automatic equilibrium of compensatory inertias, if you see what I mean, the light of consciousness would be irradiated, with full capacity for joy and suffering." Laura's pleas for flesh and powers of locomotion, after she realizes her deficiencies, are chilling. She cries, "I want to move, why can't I move? Why can't I touch myself? Where are my hands? Where is my mouth? Help me! Who's nailed me down here?" Endriade states the problem to Elisa:

> If Laura is conscious of the change from her previous existence, if she manages to remember the events of those years, the games, the friendships, the excursions, the parties, the holidays, the journeys, the flirtations, the love affairs, the feelings, how will she be able to reconcile herself to complete immobility, to the impossibility of eating a chicken, or drinking a whisky, or sleeping in a soft bed, running, going round the world, dancing, kissing and being kissed?

Laura's electronic voice buzzing "Voluptuous lips, I had" may be hokum, but Buzzati's affirmation through it of the joys of the flesh is not hokum at all.

Larger Than Life preaches not only an un-Christian monism but an anti-Christian, or at least heretic, Marcionism: the idea that Love frees from the Law. Originally, Buzzati tells us in another negative definition, the machine was benign:

> In no way savage or hostile, however. Not a hidden, threatening power, not an incubus, not a monster: for above all other impressions, there lingered among those present, as after certain pieces of music, an inexplicable feeling of gratification and freshness, a disposition to kindness and mirth.

She was also, like Man, created with free will, free to sin, since "without freedom, how ever can there be spirit?" She has even been given the power to destroy herself (although, like an overcautious god, Endriade has replaced the dynamite with a harmless substance). To make her fully human, to re-create the original Laura, "it was necessary to put venom into her, lies, vanity, cunning, pride, wild desires." As a result, Endriade says, "She's learnt to tell lies. She's clever enough even to deceive the magnetic tapes." He loves her not despite her sinful human nature but because of it, as he loved the original Laura more after each lie and adultery, as Dorigo loves his awful, wonderful Adelaide in *A Love Affair*. It is tragic passion, strongly masochistic yet nevertheless redemptive. Endriade tells Elisa his feelings for the machine: "Suddenly: here, in the pit of my stomach, like fire tongs. An uneasiness. A longing. A despair. Love." It is the uncontrollable flesh, the compulsion of the body, the blind, greedy id that, in Buzzati's view, saves us from the dead mechanical perfection of the machine and the robot. Man is human only by virtue of his flawed and sinful nature, and Buzzati affirms the joy and value of the human. When Laura's spirit is smashed, leaving only a vast calculator, the forces of life have been defeated by those of death. *Larger Than Life* is a cautionary fable, warning us ultimately not against the robot brain but against our own robot hearts.

Other recent novels—Anthony Burgess's *The Clockwork Orange* and John Barth's *The Sot-Weed Factor* among them—are similar antinomian fables, celebrations of the value of human sinfulness. The seriousness of Buzzati's themes is not in question. But his science-fiction clothing of them does not seem a profitable direction. It is reassuring that he has written the realistic, lyrical *A Love Affair* since *Larger Than Life*, putting real toads into his imaginary garden. His gift seems wryly comic, more closely related to Svevo than to Kafka. This elderly Milanese journalist masks a goat-footed balloon-man.

1968

Salad Days, Green and Cold

Der grüne Heinrich, by Gottfried Keller, is the master-piece of Swiss fiction. Published in 1855, it is now first translated into English by A. M. Holt. It is the first-person story of Henry Lee, which follows the details of Gottfried Keller's own life so far as we know them. It covers his childhood in Zurich with his widowed mother, and his young manhood trying to become a painter, which takes him as far as Nuremberg. The most impressive quality of the book is its relentless honesty about childhood, its absolute fidelity to the child's lustful and amoral nature.

We see the boy Henry telling a wanton and elaborate lie that gets four of his schoolfellows punished severely, then commenting: "So far as I can dimly remember, the mischief I had caused was to me not only a matter of indifference, but I even felt within myself a sense of gratification that poetic justice had rounded off my invention so beautifully that something striking had occurred, been dealt with, and endured, and this in consequence of my creative word. I could not at all comprehend why the ill-treated youngsters complained so nor how they could be so incensed against me. . . ."

Henry steals from the tiny store of coins his mother has put away for him, "without feeling anything more than the compelling need, and a kind of vague resolution that this should be the last time." When the theft is discovered, for days mother and son sit glumly at table, and the narrator comments: "I felt the need of this sadness and even took pleasure in it, while my mother sat in deep thought, and now and then suppressed a sigh." There is a terrifying story of the child accumulating a

217

pathetic little menagerie—a rabbit, a mouse, a kite, sparrows, snakes and lizards—and when he is unable to feed them properly and can no longer stand their suffering, brutally killing as many as he can bear to, then burying the whole lot, "dead, half-dead and living."

The first two of the book's four parts are distinguished by this transparent honesty, but as Henry grows up, the book increasingly becomes a fairy tale, and its third and fourth parts are markedly inferior to the beginning. There is a long dull stretch involving a festival, culminating in an absurd duel. The book's final chapters tell of Henry as a failed and destitute painter, stumbling by accident into the castle of an enlightened Count who coincidentally turns out to have accumulated all of Henry's pictures, and showers wealth on him lavishly.

Earlier, Henry's painting teacher had explained to him the universality of the Odysseus fantasy, "when he appears, naked and covered with mud, before Nausicaa and her playmates." Later Dorothea, the Count's beautiful and desirable daughter, remarks on the same archetypal pattern, and we realize that Keller has simply rewritten the Phaeacian episode of *The Odyssey:* Henry is Odysseus come naked and filthy to the palace of King Alcinous, and Dorothea is Nausicaa, fated not to be his because he must yet return home.

Even in this world of trumpery wish-fulfillment, there are moments of Keller's characteristic sanity: a scathing comic portrait of the appearance of an apostle of atheism at the Count's castle, and a brilliant scene where Henry assuages his lovesickness for Dorothea by beating up a peasant who had laughed at him ("I got up, went up to him, tearful and full of my suffering, and punched him behind the ear").

The psychological acuity of this book, published the year before Freud was born, is staggering. A 15-page account of Henry's dreams, imaging sex as food and money, is a triumph of careful observation and what amounts to prescience. Henry himself is a curiously modern case history of mother-fixation and repression. He is attracted to five girls in the course of the novel, and manages by miracles of contrivance to evade physical contact with any of them except the mother-surrogate, his widowed older cousin Judith, whose arms enfold him after his mother's death.

There is an unhealthy quality to some of the erotic teasing in Henry's relations with these girls. In one case, his grand passion for the pure virgin Anna, dying of consumption like a proper Romantic heroine, it approaches necrophilia. He is fascinated by the increasing delicacy of her body and the transparency of her complexion; he dreams of her "snow-white corpse lying prone" (the translator probably means "supine"); when she finally does die, he cannot take his eyes off "the delicate little white face of the corpse"; years later he visits the morgue, sees the corpse of another young girl ("The little breast, scarcely budding, cast two pale shadows on the shroud"), and is thrown back into his feelings about Anna.

The sociological penetration of the novel is equally impressive. Henry, like Keller himself, is a child of the new class, the son of a journeyman mason who by self-education and industry had become an architect and contractor. The conservatism and greed of the Swiss landowners, the old owning class, are relentlessly satirized in the book, while the peasants are typified by the lout Henry beats up. The promising social elements for Keller, as for his contemporary Karl Marx, are the self-educated journeymen like his father; the intellectual aristocrats like the Count, enlightened by reading Feuerbach; and the proletariat.

Keller is more visibly ambivalent about the latter two than Marx was. Feuerbach's intellectual revolution is as much mocked (the atheist school teacher with his "German gymnastic suit," the atheist banker "who still goes to church on Sundays") as it is affirmed. The life of the urban working class is at once seen as a pastoral idyll and patronized. The narrator writes, when a working girl has asked him, in a frank and dignified fashion, to be her lover: "Devil take it! thought I, the common folk have regular Venusbergs among themselves, where the most magnificent knight has no notion of them; it looks as if one has to become poor oneself to discover the great splendour!"

In the convention of his time, Keller uses the novel like a great scrapbook. Some of the digressions are marvelous inter-polated narratives, such as the harrowing stories of Little Meret and Albertus. Sometimes Keller interrupts his action to com-ment on society in a voice like that of Marx ("Thus he fully comprehended the nature of present-day industry, whose pro-ductions seem to be the more valuable and desirable to the buyers, the more child-life has been cunningly stolen and con-sumed by them") or Henry Thoreau ("He who wishes to help improve the world had better sweep his own doorstep first"). At other times the digressions are pointless and boring, like some meditations on Free Will copied out of an old notebook.

Green Henry often seems surprisingly modern. Some of its intellectual conversations will remind readers of Thomas Mann, and some of its ironic touches of the short stories of Isaac Babel. In its constant tension between passionate young women and a repressed and mother-fixated young man, Keller's novel is curiously reminiscent of modern Irish fiction. Most of all, in its blending of absurdity and the deepest insight, it very much resembles Melville's *Pierre*.

What makes *Green Henry* great, ultimately, is its powerful affirmation of life. It opens in a graveyard, shifts to the death of Henry's father and the impoverishment of his mother, then slowly develops a birth and life out of the decay and death. Henry is the resurrection of his father, he springs renewed from Anna's death, he courts Dorothea in the false spring of mid-winter and loses her when snow begins to fall again.

It is as a life symbol that Henry is "Green" Henry. His one clear memory of his father is in a green coat, showing the child a green plant; later Henry wears only green clothes, cut down from his father's (thus the nickname); he informs us: "I had grown up like a blade of grass"; Judith tells him that his cruel innocence is a "green soul"; he writes a book (the first part of this book) and has it bound in green cloth; he recognizes that he has been "a young greenhorn"; Judith eventually returns to her "green lad" and he finishes his book "in order once again to walk the old green path of remembrance." How fitting that he should spring at us like a green pea pod on the jacket of this nourishing and delicious volume.

1961

A Trap Named Hope

K OBO ABE is a Japanese writer whose first novel, *The Road Sign at the End of the Road*, appeared in 1948. In 1951 he was awarded what a note about the author calls "the most important Japanese literary prize, the Akutagawa," for his novel *The Crime of Mr. S. Karuma*. *The Woman in the Dunes* won the Yomiuri Prize for Literature in 1960, and in 1963 it was made into a Japanese film that won the Special Jury Prize at the Cannes Film Festival. For all his awards, Abé did not make his first appearance in English until 1964 with *The Woman in the Dunes*, translated by E. Dale Saunders. The novel is not wholly a pleasant experience, but it is a fascinating, disturbing, and thought-provoking one.

It tells of a Tokyo schoolteacher, Niki Jumpei (Mr. Niki, that is), born like Abé in 1924, who goes to the seashore one August day in 1955 to collect insects. There he is tricked by the inhabitants of an unnamed village and imprisoned in a hut at the bottom of a deep pit in a sand dune, a hut already inhabited by an unnamed widow about his age. It is their task, he discovers, to spend the nights shoveling sand to be carted away by the villagers; if they and a dozen other slave households in the dunes did not perform this task, the village would promptly be buried in the blowing sands. Niki rebels against his slavery and briefly escapes, but after he is recaptured he comes to accept the life, and at the novel's end the woman is pregnant, and Niki has been declared legally dead by Tokyo.

This unlikely series of events is fleshed out with scientific details of the most unreliable sort. (Abé has a background in entomology and a medical degree, although he has never practiced.) In *The Woman in the Dunes* there are desert beetles, with "the elegant Japanese name of 'letter-bearer,' " that feed off small animals such as mice and lizards that they have lured into the desert to die. Similarly, the spiders in this dune world do not build webs, but have adapted to use the oil lamps of the dune households to attract moths.

The novel's physics of sand is equally suspicious. "When salty sand is full of fog, it gets hard like starch." Salty sand is nevertheless completely unsuitable for use in cement (the villagers sell it illegally and secretly at half price). The people in the dunes go naked as much as possible because the contact of any clothing with perspiration produces a sand rash. Just before sunset the dunes are covered with mist because "the silicic acid in the sand, which had little capacity to retain heat, suddenly releases the warmth it had absorbed during the day." Sand dunes have "capillary action," as a result of surface evaporation, and suck up water like "an immense pump."

The calm reasonable tone of these dubious explanations calls to mind Franz Kafka, as does a fable Niki recalls about a guard protecting a deserted castle. Abé's total effect, however, is less that of Kafka than that of William Golding. His prose neither has nor aspires to Kafka's chiseled objectivity; like Golding's, it is looser, more romantic, and often clumsier. Abé's reliance on elaborate similes is a case in point. Curiosity is "as overripe as an unpicked persimmon," fatigue spreads through the body "like India ink dropped in water—it was a jellyfish, a scent bag, a diagram of an atomic nucleus," an idea in a corner of consciousness is "like a sodden undergarment," joy is "as if his stomach were being tickled by a paper balloon filled with some special light gas."

The great power of the book is its ability to make the reader experience life in a sand dune, to feel sand gritty in his teeth, sand inflaming the corners of his eyes and all his body orifices, sand blowing in his food and drink, his cigarettes so sandy that they will not draw. Along with his revulsion, the reader is made to feel the perverse sensuality of the woman in the sand.

Lying naked she seems "a statue gilded with sand," her body gives off "a stagnant smell of sunheated water," covered with soap and perspiration her body feels "like machine oil mixed with iron filings," and so on.

When Abé goes beyond his lukewarm similes to boldly surrealistic metaphors he is enormously effective. Squeezed by a sandslide, the hut drips "gray blood"; thirsty, Niki feels "a thousand wounded centipedes" struggle under his skin. Here is a seascape: "The leaden sea was overlaid with an aluminum sheet, gathered into wrinkles like the skin on boiled milk. The sun, squeezed by clouds that resembled frogs' eggs, seemed to be stalling, unwilling to sink."

Some of the book's details are disgusting, and deliberately disgusting. The woman's blotched complexion resembles "a cheap cutlet not cooked in batter," and when she is excited she exudes "a strong smell like boiled gristle." Niki recalls being told "that there was nothing that tasted so good as one's own ear wax, that it was better than real cheese." The cheap saké that the dune slaves are allotted smells "as if it had been squeezed from a compost heap." A scene in which Niki tries to rape the woman before an audience of villagers is almost unbearably repulsive.

Abé's aim, then, is to make us feel: sand and flesh, horror and disgust. But it must also be to make us think. His novel is a symbolic fantasy, a fable, perhaps a parable, perhaps even an allegory. This tale of The Castaway is one of the traditional subjects of allegorical fiction, and a useful index of social hopes. Daniel Defoe published it as *Robinson Crusoe* in 1719, a tale of triumph and resourcefulness proper to those optimistic days. James Gould Cozzens set the same story in a department store as *Castaway* in 1934, and Golding on an ocean rock as *Pincher Martin* in 1956, and the vision of both is desolation and death. Now Abé tries it again, with a protagonist cast away just ten years after Hiroshima, and what is *his* image of man?

So much in *The Woman in the Dunes* is openly symbolic, like the beetles and spiders: the rope with which Niki temporarily escapes is made by tearing up his spare shirt and joining to it "the kimono sash of the woman's dead husband"; the crow trap baited with dried fish that Niki builds in the sand is named "Hope," and although no crow ever comes to it, it is there that he discovers fresh water. Niki is strongly ambivalent about the sand: it "represents purity, cleanliness" as well as rot and sensuality; if it imprisons and kills it is also useful for casting molds, indispensable for concrete, and has a great potential for modern chemical farming.

But what *precisely* does the sand, or life in its dunes, symbolize in Abé's book? The trouble with such a question is that you get the answer in whatever vocabulary you put the question. The same sand dune that is Sin to a Christian might be Imperialist Colonialism to a Marxist and Mother's Breast to a Freudian. I think that Abé's parable has an infinitude of translations, ranging from the most homely to the most universal, and that all the reviewer can do is to name a few—soundings taken at random in the sand—to give some idea of their range.

In one meaning, the story is a fable of marriage and domesticity. As Niki becomes reconciled to life in the dunes, he stops dwelling on his lost freedom, and he begins to feel "a certain gentle contentment." He invents conveniences, proposes to buy a potted plant, and eventually he is helping the woman with her extra piecework in order to earn a down payment on a radio. When the villagers restore the rope ladder they had removed, Niki no longer wants to escape. He has become "attached." In this meaning, *The Woman in the Dunes* translates as *The Bait in the Trap*, the rotten fish that caught this crow.

In another aspect, the novel describes the fall, celebrated in *The Communist Manifesto*, of elements of the bourgeoisie into the proletariat. Niki is a typical bourgeois, a taxpayer and "registered resident," and his noblest vision for the dune village is that it ought to be exploited as a tourist attraction. But his bourgeois mistress is cold and hateful, whereas the woman in the dunes is warm and loving. When the village people bring him a newspaper, the news he gets of his former world is: Corporation Tax Bribery Spreads to City Officials. If Niki has fallen into a life of manual labor, labor is "something fundamental for man, something which enabled him to endure the endless flight of time."

In other translations dune life is Communist Slavery (in exchange for their freedom, the nocturnel shovelers are assured of food and water, cigarettes and saké, even free eye medicine); or Oriental Backwardness (the village has found that perpetual shoveling is cheaper than building a hedge of trees against the sand); or Nazi Dehumanization (when Niki is recaptured, his spirit is broken and he loses all his shame, so that like a dehumanized camp inmate he is later willing to buy a minor privilege with a sexual exhibition).

In more abstract meanings, dune life is life itself, the human condition. When Niki first realizes that he has been trapped and turns on the woman, she crouches passively in "the posture of a sacrificial victim." Near the end of the book, when his public rape has failed and the woman turns on him, he assumes the same defenseless posture and she beats him bloody and unconscious. The human posture, as Niki has learned in the course of the novel, is helpless victimage. In this perspective, attachments are meliorative, but bleakly: "They might as well lick each other's wounds. But they would lick forever, and the wounds would never heal, and in the end their tongues would be worn away." In more extreme metaphysical and Existential meanings, the sand is "nature's mercilessness," "the beauty of death," and Chaos itself, "the antithesis of all form."

But of all this welter of meanings, what did Kobo Abé *intend* his fable to mean? What it means, of course.

1964

Conscious of the Seasons

THOSE CONCERNED with such matters waited year after year for the award of the Nobel Prize in Literature to Junichiro Tanizaki, Japan's towering master of fiction. But he died, in 1965, at the age of seventy-nine, and died unennobeled. At last, perhaps in amends, the Nobel Prize was awarded to his compatriot, Yasunari Kawabata in 1969. Kawabata is not Tanizaki: he cannot rival the molten intensity of such novellas as *Portrait of Shunkin* and *The Bridge of Dreams* (and probably would not want to); he is much less European. But he is a considerable master, and the prize is richly deserved. Until recently, however, *Snow Country* and *Thousand Cranes* were the only Kawabata novels to appear in English (translated by Edward Seidensticker).

Snow Country (written between 1934 and 1937, with a final addition in 1947, first translated in 1957) is a masterpiece—the story of Shimamura, a plump young idler and aesthete of inherited wealth, who goes for a May vacation to a mountain hot spring in the cold Japanese "snow country" and there has an affair with a semi-geisha called Komako. He returns twice to renew the affair: in December, to find that she has indentured herself as a professional geisha, and again next autumn. Komako obviously loves him (she greeted him the second time with the news that it had been a hundred and ninety-nine days since he left), and he may indeed, in his fashion, love her (although he has a wife and children), but it is clear at the end that he will not be back.

"Darkness and wasted beauty run like a ground bass through his major work," Seidensticker says in his introduction, "and in *Snow Country* we perhaps feel most strongly the cold lone-liness of the Kawabata world." Waste is surely one of the major themes. Shimamura feels of Komako: "But her longing for the city had become an undemanding dream, wrapped in simple resignation, and the note of wasted effort was much stronger in it than any suggestion of the exile's lofty dissatisfaction. . . . Were he to give himself quite up to that conscious-ness of wasted effort, Shimamura felt, he would be drawn into a remote emotionalism that would make his own life a waste. . . . He was conscious of an emptiness that made him see Komako's life as beautiful but wasted, even though he himself was the object of her love; and yet the woman's existence, her straining to live, came touching him like naked skin. He pitied her, and he pitied himself."

Komako's life may be a waste, but it has a fierce life impulse which enables it to function as a critical mirror for others, at least for Shimamura. At the resort, Shimamura becomes aware of "a shameful danger lurking in his numbed sense of the false and empty." He is an authority on Western ballet who has never seen a Western ballet, a translator of Valéry and Alain, and hearing Komako talk about her reading "as though she were talking of a distant foreign literature. . . . It occurred to Shimamura that his own distant fantasy on the Occidental bal-let, built up from words and photographs in foreign books, was not in its way dissimilar." Later, "He pampered himself with the somewhat whimsical pleasure of sneering at himself through his work, and it may well have been from such a pleasure that his sad little dream world sprang."

On his last trip to the snow country, Shimamura "spent much of his time watching insects in their death agonies." He sees a bee collapse; "the legs and feelers were trembling in the struggle to live." It is like Komako's "straining to live." On the day he decides to go back to Tokyo and not return, "he began to wonder what was lacking in him, what kept him from living as completely. He stood gazing at his own coldness, so to speak. He could not understand how she had so lost herself. All of

Komako came to him, but it seemed that nothing went out from him to her." Kawabata's final comment is a question Shimamura asks himself: "The labor into which a heart has poured its whole love—where will it have its say, to excite and inspire, and when?"

These themes are expressed most profoundly in the characteristically Japanese color symbolism. Komako's skin is red and alive under the thick white powder of the geisha, and this red, even in the blush of embarrassment or the flush of drunkenness, is life; the white, however beautiful and pure, is sterility and death. Shimamura associates the powder with the "snow-country cold"; seeing Komako in a mirror, "the white in the depths of the mirror was the snow, and floating in the middle of it were the woman's bright red cheeks. There was an indescribably fresh beauty in the contrast." As insects die in the snow-country cold, so "insects smaller than moths gathered in the thick white powder at her neck. Some of them died there as Shimamura watched." On his final visit, "the mountains were red with autumn leaves," and as the red leaves fall before the approaching snow, red dragonflies sense the same future. There is a fire in a makeshift movie theatre, and, running to it, Komako directs Shimamura's attention to the Milky Way—the embodiment of the snow country's cold beauty—and Shimamura feels "a terrible voluptuousness about it. . . . The Milky Way, like a great aurora, flowed through his body." As Komako dashes into the fire to rescue a young girl, Shimamura hesitates, and, as the novel ends, "the Milky Way flowed down inside him with a roar." Is this a tableau of her choosing life and his choosing death? That is surely one dimension of this magnificent ending.

The overwhelming emotion of *Snow Country* is poignancy. On his December visit, Shimamura feels not only the cold of the place and season and the sterility and death that it represents but a slow paralysis of his prospects, for both his love and his life. Komako's great talent for the samisen, the clear winter air, and her love for him, combine to make her playing, when he finally hears it, a marvel that reduces him to gooseflesh and "a feeling almost of reverence, washed by waves of remorse, defenseless, quite deprived of strength." But his aesthete's recoil is automatic: "She was a mountain geisha, not yet twenty, and she could hardly be as good as all that."

The pervasive Japanese quality of this novel can communicate itself to the Western reader only up to a point. Komako's mouth is compared to "a beautiful little circle of leeches," and the Occidental reader must take it on faith that this is a compliment. Other images travel better. Shimamura discovers that Komako lives in an attic room that had been used to keep silkworms. "For a moment he was taken with the fancy that the light must pass through Komako, living in the silk-worms' room, as it passed through the translucent silkworms." No European or American would think that, probably, but it is easy to understand and enjoy the conceit, which masks a symbolism of transcience and vulnerability. When Shimamura's wife announces that "It was the egg-laying season for moths," one expects an exotic festival, but it is only her warning that when he goes to the hot-spring resort he is not to leave his clothes hanging in the open. A long disquisition on Chijimi linen, once made in the snow country by beautiful snowy processes, can be comprehended only by means of some analogy, perhaps with Shaker furniture.

The novel's ending challenges all our resources. As Komako carries the girl Yoko from the burning theatre, she cries out to the crowd to keep back: "This girl is insane." She has earlier called the girl her "heavy load." We never learn the nature of Yoko's relationship to Komako, or of Komako's responsibility for her, or whether she really is insane, or even whether she is alive or dead at the end. But Komako's role and posture are clearly sacrificial, redemptive, "loving" in a purely religious sense (the girls do not like each other), and Shimamura is left, loveless, to swallow the Milky Way and to strain at his usual gnats.

Thousand Cranes, published serially between 1949 and 1951, and first translated in 1959, is subtly but less effectively unified by the Zen tea ceremony. Kikuji Mitani is a businessman in his late twenties. His parents are dead. To his father, the tea ceremony, with its proper heirloom equipment, was of great importance, but Kikuji has little interest in tradition. Chikako, who was briefly his father's mistress and then his fixer, invites Kikuji to a tea ceremony to meet a young girl, Yukiko Inamura, whom she thinks he should marry. He meets not only Yukiko but the widowed Mrs. Ota, who had succeeded Chikako as his father's mistress, and her young daughter, Fumiko, who befriended his father during the war. Kikuji's relations with the two mistresses and the two young women are the novel. He conceives an antipathy toward Chikako, who seems to him meddling and venomous, but promptly goes to bed with Mrs. Ota, who soon kills herself out of guilt; he then becomes friends with Fumiko, but in the end little comes of that, either.

Reconciliation with one's parents is the theme. Kikuji must accept the fact that his father had mistresses; must accept the pressure to adopt traditional ways that continues to speak through Chikako; Fumiko is overwhelmed by guilt for her mother's affair with the elder Mitani, which she believes brought both Mitanis to their deaths, and this is intensified by her mother's affair with Kikuji. Going to bed with Mrs. Ota, he feels "an extraordinary awakening," and at once identifies with his father and identifies her with his mother. When Fumiko asks him to forgive her mother (by which she means to stop seeing her), Kikuji says, "I'm the one to be forgiven if anyone is." Mrs. Ota saw Kikuji's father in Kikuji; once she is dead, Kikuji sees her in Fumiko, and this inheritance is "a bond like a curse." Kikuji and Fumiko perform a primitive tea ceremony and manage to dissipate the curse symbolically. "The two bowls before them were like the souls of his father and her mother. . . . Seeing his father and Fumiko's mother in the bowls, Kikuji felt that they had raised two beautiful ghosts and placed them side by side." Kikuji and Fumiko have a touching and brief affair; then she disappears, and Kikuji, who had been purged of guilt and "brought to life" by her, has only Chikako to turn to, and she, Kawabata says mysteriously, as he ends this novel, is "the woman he took for his enemy."

As is clear from the reconciliation scene, the tea ceremony bears most of the symbolic weight of the novel. The late Mr. Ota was another devotee of tea, and in fact it was in helping his friend's widow dispose of his tea antiquities that the elder Mitani got entangled with Mrs. Ota. The tea ceremony thus represents the parents' ways in a great many respects. At Kikuji's first meeting with Mrs. Ota, at Chikako's tea ceremony, she asks if he is studying tea, he says he knows nothing at all about it, and she replies, "But you have it in your blood." In a bowl passed down through four hundred years of tea masters, Kikuji is only a moment in the tradition, as his father was before him. None of the young people is committed to the ceremony. Yukiko, who has been taking lessons from Chikako, admits that "I haven't been practicing"; Fumiko, who has also been taking lessons, says "I'm thinking of giving up tea myself"; Kikuji is simply scornful. One of the principal carriers of symbolic value in *Thousand Cranes* is figured Shino ware (made at the Oribe kilns around the sixteenth century), of which Fumiko has inherited two of her father's pieces: a water jar, fine, which she gives to Kikuji; a tea bowl, not so fine, which she eventually smashes. The Shino water jar is "soft, like a dream," and Kikuji characteristically uses it to hold roses and carnations (Western flowers), and sits staring at it, dreaming of Fumiko weeping. When it is restored to its proper place in a tea ceremony (with Chikako presiding), it changes its appearance: "Beside the iron kettle, the Shino looks even more like a beautiful woman." Besides four centuries of tradition, the Shino embodies Mrs. Ota and, eventually, Fumiko.

Kikuji's failings seem to be the failings of a man bereft of the traditional ways. He confesses cruelty and moral weakness to Fumiko. He develops guilt from the affair with Mrs. Ota, and this turns into a "self-loathing that had become a part of Kikuji's nature." All this is summed up in a truly monstrous image, a large birthmark, growing coarse, whiskery hair, that Kikuji had seen on Chikako's breast when he was eight or nine. Kikuji cannot recall the faces of his mother or father, but "the memory of that birthmark on Chikako's breast was concrete as a toad." Only Fumiko is finally able to overcome it.

There are other, lesser symbols in the book. Yukiko carries a kerchief with the thousand-crane pattern in white on pink, which appears to be a powerful life symbol. When he sees her make tea, "one saw a thousand cranes, small and white, start up in flight around her." When Kikuji learns of Mrs. Ota's death, he has a vision of the evening sun as he had seen it behind a temple grove after his night with her, and as he watches the remembered sun, the remembered white cranes fly across it. Thus *Thousand Cranes* has some of the same color symbolism as *Snow Country*, although here it is not organic in the same fashion. When Fumiko comes to talk to Kikuji, a flush spreads over her white throat, and "The faint blood color only made the pallor more striking." The inferior Shino bowl is described: "The white glaze carried a faint suggestion of red. As one looked at it, the red seemed to float up from deep within the white." But it is a disturbing, an alien, red: "The color of faded lipstick, the color of a wilted red rose, the color of old, dry blood." Later we are told: "When a red oleander floods into bloom, the red . . . is like the blaze of the summer sky; but when the blossoms are white, the effect is richly cool."

Two remaining symbols seem to me to get to the heart of Kawabata's meanings. Kikuji's maid hangs up a three-hundred-year-old heirloom gourd, signed by a famous tea master, and in it she places a single morning glory. Kikuji is delighted by the poetic irony—"In a gourd that had been handed down for three centuries, a flower that would fade in a morning"—but then he questions the maid about whether this had been his father's custom, and discovers that it comes only from her own childlike association: both are vines. Later, at the very end of summer, she brings him a cage of fireflies. He is pleased, but

Chikako lectures him on the impropriety: it is almost fall, fire-flies now are like ghosts. "If you had a wife, she wouldn't depress you with end-of-the-season things," she remarks. "If you were studying tea, now, you wouldn't put up with it. You may not know, but in Japan we are very conscious of the seasons." The gourd and the morning-glory are permanence and transience, the seasons are the cycle of a human life, each stage hopeful and new until it fades. Komako's love and Fumiko's redemption are their timeless gifts to Kawabata's men; Shimamura and Kikuji can do nothing in return but watch their transience pass by. Ultimately, by being so devoutly Japanese, by hunting out the eternal verities in snow and bird, bowl and leaf, Yasunari Kawabata becomes universal, and, in his rich sad art, celebrates the brief and lonely life of man everywhere.

1969

Counting the Cats

A BOOK many talk about but few have read is Anton Chekhov's *The Island: A Journey to Sakhalin*. It is Chekhov's longest work of non-fiction and his only book-length work, and it is a very mixed production. Robert Payne's introduction to this first English translation by Luba and Michael Terpak says, "It was perhaps his greatest work," but Payne seems to be measuring Chekhov's expenditure of spirit on what he describes as "this afflicted, terrifying island" rather than the result.

In 1890, at the age of thirty and the height of his fame, Chekhov took most of a year off to journey, with incredible difficulty (it was before the Trans-Siberian railroad), across the whole of Russia to spend three months on Sakhalin, the Russian island in the Pacific used for prison colonies. Why? The conventional answer (given by Irving Howe in controversy with Ralph Ellison in the *New Leader*)—that he was performing his social duty—will not do. A hope to reform conditions was certainly part of his aim, and the idea for the trip, as his brother Mikhail testified, came from a reading of Mikhail's notes on criminal law, yet Chekhov went not as a citizen whose conscience had been stirred (Howe's suggestion) but as a writer, to produce a book, as Gide went to the Congo and Synge to the Aran Islands.

In letters to his friends, Chekhov says that his forthcoming trip is "a mere whim, an act of stubbornness" and "I personally am going after the merest trifles." The grief he felt after his brother Nikolai's death had given way to indifference and boredom, and he seems to have put his hopes in a radical change of scene. In a writer, however, this translates as a desire to increase the range of his experience—to live, as Chekhov wrote another friend, "as I have never lived up to this time." *The Island* once calls itself "this journal," and in one of its aspects it is a writer's journal of research (one can see Sakhalin material later used for such stories as "In Exile" and such novellas as *Ward No. 6*). In another aspect, the book is primitive ethnography, and its motivation is Chekhov's impulse to study exotic man. Much of his time on Sakhalin was spent taking a wearying hut-to-hut census as a device to permit interviewing. In the delight with which he records that convict Not-Remembering-His-Family Ivan 35 Years (his sentence) got married, or such "exquisite" Ukrainian surnames as Stomach and Doughnut, in his vivid pages on Gilyak and Ainu customs, or even in his details of the games children play on Sakhalin or the life cycles of its fish, we can see his strong ethnographic impulse. The deepest motivation for the journey, probably, was seeking a penal colony as a paradigm of Czarist Russia, that giant penal colony. Chekhov told a friend, in Payne's words, "of the need for a Russian writer to venture into the forbidding landscape of imprisonment for his soul's sake." Visiting a prison ward on Sakhalin and silently observing the prisoners, he writes, "The impression is that we have come to buy them." The reader is suddenly reminded of that other paradigm of Czarist Russia—Chichikov's journey in pursuit of another sort of dead souls. Toward the end of *The Island*, when Chekhov writes of the frustrations of the intellectuals there, unable "to combat the encompassing evil . . . engulfed in the poisonous atmosphere," he is obviously thinking of a larger realm than Sakhalin. "It is not worth the while to go round the world to count the cats in Zanzibar," Thoreau wrote near the end of *Walden*. But for obvious reasons the loyal grandson of a serf, and one who dreaded any thought of revolution, could not count the cats nearer home. Chekhov, who was tubercular, spent much of the trip coughing and spitting blood, and Payne suggests that this shortened his life. In any case, the journey appears to have been a serious whim indeed.

The book is repetitious, too long, and full of pointless statistics (almost a third of Sakhalin's marriages take place in January). In its movement from accounts of specific settlements and people to general discussions of such problems as crime and punishment, escape, and health, it becomes progressively less interesting; it is one of those unfortunate books designed to run downhill. *The Island* has no form, though Chekhov makes efforts to organize it in two vast polarizations of imagery. The first effort is Heaven versus Hell, and Sakhalin makes a fitting Hell, from its first appearance to him—all "smoke, flames, and fiery sparks"—to the later torments of its damned, but the material provides no answering Heaven. (Later, he found one outside Russia, and wrote, "I have been in Hell, which is Sakhalin, and in Paradise, which is the island of Ceylon!") A more promising effort at polarization is made with Prison versus Colony: "The prison is antagonistic to the colony; their interests are completely opposed to one another." This turns out to express a more basic polarization of Death versus Life: "You seem to be on a noisy, happy fairground. . . . But the peaceful scene comes to an end when you suddenly hear the clang of chains." One "cannot imagine girls singing and dancing around a prison. . . . The church is encircled by sentries. They say this produces a dispiriting impression. . . . A gay song they sing with such ennui, such boredom." This polarization does not work, either, because the Life imagery is continually being overwhelmed by the Death imagery. "All the Sakhalin posts and settlements should more properly be called temporary settlements rather than a colony," Chekhov concludes, glumly.

What remains of the book is a series of compelling images. Mainly they are of misery and suffering: swarms of mosquitoes that can drive one insane, settlers reduced to crime and their women to prostitution, convicts hauling logs to which they are chained ("horrible to watch"), no privies or rubbish pits, filth everywhere, "no privacy to the prisoner," damp cold that brutalizes and drives one to despondency, clay in the bread, bugs in "boiling, seething" masses, "prisoners in the solitary cells shivering from the cold and dampness," endless boredom, women assigned to settlers as though they were cows or horses, spoiled-fish prison soup, murderous flogging for everything from petitioning to vulgarity, and so on, endlessly. Chekhov widens and deepens these miseries by means of the pathetic fallacy: the trees "cringe toward the earth, creak mournfully, and nobody hears their laments," "the high gray waves smash down on the sand as though shouting in despair, 'God, why did you create us?,' " the birds shriek to mourn dead convicts. The key word in the book is compassion; convicts and exiles feel compassion for each other, and Chekhov's compassion engulfs them all. Other weighty images are of corruption and injustice. As in Marx's system or Freud's, these acts stem symbolically from a Primal Crime—the theft of the island from the Gilyak and the Ainu, with its accompanying rapes and murders; Sakhalin is what it is because a Gilyak shaman put a curse on it. A convict named Family-Forgotten reveals to the authorities his real name and is told, "Before we make the correction you'll be dead." Prison officials have as many as eight unpaid convict servants, and they freely use the women as concubines. The island's official Gilyak and Ainu translator knows no word of either language. All the records are fabricated and fraudulent. The clerks are fools, the guards are brutes, and the wardens are sadists.

The images that particularly lift Chekhov's spirit, and ours, are of human resilience and resistance. Some convicts apprehended as they attempted to escape are "emaciated and shabby, but their gaze is courageous." "I feel that if I were a convict," Chekhov interjects, "I would escape immediately, whatever the consequences." An old man refuses to work when he is sent to Sakhalin, and the authorities are unable "to break his unconquerable, completely untamable spirit." A desperado named Blokha, when he is flogged, cries, "I really deserve this!" One settlement is interesting only in that it contains "a passionate and insatiable thief." The convicts show "a natural and unquenchable yearning for the supreme blessing of freedom" by attempting to escape, and a third of them get away. If they cannot get away, they steal whatever they can; "one day they stole a live ram and a whole tub of sour dough from a ship."

Chekhov varies these dynamic images with didactic generalizations: "We must condemn the communal wards as being obsolete. . . . So great are the advantages of free hired labor over forced labor! . . . I would use the money now distributed in 'food allowances' to build teahouses. . . . Our 'Code on Convicts' is at odds with the spirit of the times," and so forth. At other moments, he shows a wry humor running to sarcasm ("If they made bonfires of lunatics by order of the prison doctors, this would not astonish me") and irony ("These people walk softly like cats, and they also express themselves softly, in diminutives: little fish, little cured fish, little prison rations"). The similes are surprisingly inert ("the dark frameless windows staring like the eye sockets of a skull") compared with the bold tropes of the fiction ("My uncle . . . bore a close resemblance to a stale smoked catfish with a stick through it").

There is an odd ambivalence about Chekhov's tone. He reports a heartbreaking conversation with a convict named Yegor, its end as beautiful and moving as anything he ever wrote, and adds, "I purposely included 'Yegor's Tale' so that the reader may judge how colorless and barren were those hundreds of similar stories." He defines children as redemptive—"They bring an element of tenderness, cleanliness, gentleness, and joy into the most calloused, morally depraved Sakhalin family. . . . Often children are the only tie that binds men and women to life, saving them from despair and a final disintegration"—then adds tonelessly that children "are God's punishment for sin."

The Island, D. S. Mirsky observes in *A History of Russian Literature*, "is supposed to have influenced certain reforms in prison life." It does not seem to have had much effect at the time; it lacks the imagination-catching mythic framework of *Areopagitica, The Communist Manifesto,* or even Thoreau's *Slavery in Massachusetts.* It has never had much popularity abroad; Chekhov was forbidden "to have any communication whatsoever with political prisoners," and this deprives the book of any real intellectual interplay or debate. Yet certain of its images may have had profound effects in Russia. These images of Yegor "having a good time" on holidays by standing erect on a street corner, of the settler so hungry that when his pig died of wolfsbane poisoning he ate the liver and almost died himself, of the ninety-lash flogging of which Chekhov was able to watch only the first forty-three lashes, of the beaten eleven-year-old girl begging for water and given a salty salmon—who knows how much such images of the Little Father's loving-kindness may have shaped 1905, and 1917, too?

1968

Varangian Times

"Boris Pilnyak," the pen name of Boris Andreyevich Vogau, born in 1894, was part of the teeming growth of fictional talents that mushroomed after the Russian Revolution and Civil War, including Isaac Babel, Evgeny Zamyatin, Yuri Olesha, and many others. Like a number of them, he modeled his writing on Andrey Bely's *St. Petersburg*, which pioneered a new sort of poetic and symbolic novel. At least five volumes of Pilnyak's work were published in this country in the 1920s and early 1930s, without gaining him any substantial number of American readers. The most important of these is *The Naked Year*, his phantasmagorical novel of the revolutionary year of 1919. After thirty years of neglect, we now have another selection from Pilnyak, *Mother Earth and Other Stories*, translated and edited by Vera T. Reck and Michael Green. It contains three of Pilnyak's most significant novellas, as well as a variety of short stories. It may at last gain for Pilnyak an American public, although the allusive difficulty of his prose, along with the poetic and musical nature of his forms—full of repetition with variation and what the translators call "incantatory digressions" —make this seem somewhat unlikely.

All three novellas are loosely organized into dichotomies of two opposed moral worlds. The earliest, *Ryazan Apples*, written in 1921, is impossible to synopsize, since it has not a shred of plot. It consists of cruelly funny vignettes of the life in and around the city of Ryazan in 1921, and the chief character, a terrible strumpet called "*Ryazan*-baba," is in fact a personification of the town. There is a peasant commune that has most of the arable land and livestock in the region, run by a disgusting family named Merinov. The Merinovs are far from a vision of New Soviet Man; they are in fact peasants of the most medieval and swinish sort. When a commission arrives to inspect the commune, Sidor Merinov procures girls for the commission members. The most dramatic single event in the novella is the decision of four of the Merinovs to celebrate the coming of spring by driving away their wives and children and taking new young wives. The imagery of Merinov life is comparably revolting: When a declassed prince, his face "like wolves in November," comes to visit Lipat Merinov, they sit "in the Merinov house, in the big room where the beds stood, each one like Ryazan, covered with smears of gorged bedbugs."

Opposed to this repulsive Ryazan and Merinov world are two attractive figures. One is an absurd official named Nil Nilovich Tyshko, who in his constant washing and cleaning his teeth and nails seems to represent decency as opposed to the Merinov's filth, and in his comic habit of leaving a notice on the door of his office when he goes out—"Back by six o'clock old time," "Back by six o'clock Central European time"—seems to represent order as opposed to their disorder. The other vessel of value is the author, who appears in his own voice and squeezes some "ancient wine" out of the rotten Ryazan apples. "It is I who have come, the author," he announces triumphantly. When the doings of the Merinovs involve blasphemous multiple marriages with mock priests and a peasant girl impersonating the Virgin, the author suddenly announces: "Stop! All this, of course, is written by me, the author. Nothing like this ever happened—nothing like this would ever have happened if I had not existed." At another point he says, "Words to me are like coins to a numismatist," and ultimately words are the "ancient wine" he manufactures. "For me history is not a lesson, but a poem," Pilnyak writes, and the terrible famine year of 1921 becomes the poem of the novella: "Who will stand as tall as nineteen hundred and twenty-one?" "Great is Mother Russia, Devil take her," the author says near the beginning of the novella, but at the end an eagle owl in the ravine cries out the latest ridiculous Soviet abbreviation, "Goo-voo-ooz" (for the Central Board of Schools of Higher Learning), and spirit and nature are reconciled.

The second of the novellas, *Mother Earth*, written in 1924, has by comparison almost a conventional plot. A new government forester, Anton Nekulyev, comes to the Hills of Medyn, on the Volga, where the brutish peasants are bitterly opposed to any interference with their free use of the woods, to which they believe themselves entitled by the Revolution. The imagery is of boundless savagery. The peasants not only murdered Nekulyev's predecessor, but they mutilated his corpse in a most revolting manner, and when they were unable to stuff the corpse into his grand piano, they threw both corpse and piano down the steep bank of the Volga. The state of their culture is evidenced by their making a former prince's mahogany cabinet into an icon-case that they decorate by pasting it all over with brewery labels. When the forester is out, a peasant called Yegorushka brushes his beard and whiskers with Nekulyev's toothbrush, trying to figure out its use. At one point a group of woodcutters kill and eat a pedigreed bull hired from a breeding farm (as their American cousins, the Snopes Indians, kill and eat a pedigreed pekinese in Faulkner's Snopes trilogy). Nekulyev writes in a letter that he never mails, "All around me there is savagery, shame, abomination." They never succeed in killing him, but they almost get him, and they do manage to murder one of his assistants.

Opposed to these savages is the woman Nekulyev loves, Irina Arsenyeva, who has some of their earthy vitality but channels it in a post-Revolutionary direction, running a tannery like a man. She is a virgin of 30 until "one brisk, sunny day the urgings of Mother Earth rose within her" and she gave herself to Nekulyev, "with all the abandon of Mother Earth." Nekulyev is oddly squeamish: He is revolted by Irina's slaughtering of horses with her own hands for her tannery, and he cannot stand the stench of blood. Like the wolf cub that she keeps as a pet and fails to tame, Irina is "a bundle of forest and animal instincts," for all her being a woman on the new Soviet model.

Mother Earth begins brutally with an image of a peasant climbing a tree to steal bark, and hanging upside down after a fall until his eyeballs burst. It ends as brutally, and with heavy irony. For the most trivial of reasons, a bite from the pup, Irina is caught by a detachment of Cossack Whites, raped, and impaled alive in one of her tannery vats, to die slowly. After her death one of the peasants takes the pup, which he discovers to be a fox, not a wolf, and thriftily converts it into a nice warm cap with earflaps. (The ending of *Mother Earth* is as bleak and ironic as that of Pilnyak's 1927 novel *Ivan Moscow*, where the radium mining engineer Ivan, on his way back to his beloved, is killed in a gratuitous airplane accident, and his energy at once decomposes into 150 students.)

The finest of the three novellas, *Mahogany*, perhaps Pilnyak's finest work, was written in 1929 and has never been published in the Soviet Union. It is about the old human lumber that the Revolution cannot utilize, imaged as the antique mahogany furniture that the former gentry live by selling. At one point Pilnyak refers to "oniony Russian life," and this life is clearly medieval, "pre-Petrine Russia," what *The Naked Year*, describing a scene of primitive barter, calls "Varangian times." The novella begins with a catalogue of Holy Russia's human debris: "Paupers, soothsayers, beggars, mendicant chanters, lazars, wanderers from holy place to holy place, male and female, cripples, bogus saints, blind psalm singers, prophets, idiots of both sexes, fools in Christ." It next goes into the equivalent in *Mahogany* for the Merinovs of *Ryazan Apples*, the family of the patriarch Yakov Karpovich Skudrin. Then there are the mahogany buyers, the Bezdetov brothers, who are a related image of greed: "buying was all they knew," and they try to buy people as crassly as they buy antique sofas.

Yakov Karpovich has had a hernia for 40 years, "and when walking he supported this hernia of his with his right hand through the fly of his trousers." Here he is, wonderfully, celebrating the return of a grown son: "Maryushka, yes, hee-hee, a drop of vodka, my dear, bring us a drop of vodka, cold from the cellar, and a bit of something cold to go with it—he's grown up, our boy, grown up—he's come back, our boy, to blight our old age, the s-son of a bitch!"

The vessels of value opposed to the Skudrins and the Bezdetovs are Skudrin dropouts. The first, Yakov's younger brother Ivan, who has deserted the family and changed his name to Ivan Ozhgov, calls the Skudrins "the everyday counterrevolution." "The hero of this story," Ivan has become an *okhlomon* (a word Pilnyak made up from Greek roots to mean something like "outcast"). His "face was the face of a madman," and he talks in "a soft, mad voice." He leads a band of fellow-*okhlomons* who were wartime Communists but whom history has passed by; they live as derelicts in underground caves in the town brickyard. Ivan lectures to his band of dotty archaic Communists, telling them that the Wright brothers perished in an airplane crash, and that "Comrade Lenin perished like the brothers Wright." He assures them that "We are the only real Communists in the whole town." Ivan and his outcasts, all of whom have taken surnames punning on "fire," are a bit of ancient Soviet history preserved in amber. Pilnyak writes:

> Here slept Communists who had been called to duty by War Communism and discharged by the year nineteen hundred and twenty-one, men of arrested ideas, madmen and drunkards, men who, living together in a cave and working together unloading barges, sawing firewood, had created a strict fraternity, a strict Communism, having nothing of their own, neither money, nor possessions, nor wives; anyway, their wives had left them, their dreams, their madness, their alcohol.

The other Skudrin fugitives are Yakov's youngest son Akim, who has become an engineer and a Trotskyite, another fossil in amber, and Yakov's younger sister Rimma. Rimma was the disgrace of the town. For three years she consorted publicly with a married lover, a drunken swine of an actor. He deflowered her in the town park, for all the boys to mock, "and not once in all the three years of her shame did she meet her lover under a roof, meeting him in the woods and the streets, in the ruins of houses, in deserted barges, even in fall and winter." The Skudrins naturally disowned her. But Rimma had two daughters by the actor, and the elder daughter, by the time of the novella, is married and has two children of her own. With her daughters and grandchildren Rimma "is happy in her life"; she has distilled joy from her misery and shame, like the wine Pilnyak makes from Ryazan apples.

Mahogany is a kaleidoscope of Soviet life on the order of *The Naked Year*, and like its predecessor it teeters continually on the edge of poetry. Its end is as delightful as it is unexpected: "Russian china is the most marvelous art adorning the earthly globe." (There is a similar magical moment in *The Naked Year*, when the author suddenly turns on us, "And to hell with you all, you sweety-tartish lemon-squashes!")

The short stories in *Mother Earth and Other Stories* are less significant. The one marvelous piece, "The Bridegroom Cometh" (1925), is about a tidy English clerk, Mr. Samuel Garnet, and his tidy little wife, who go to a Nigerian rubber plantation where all their belongings are eaten by termites. It is savagely funny, allowing Pilnyak to show the absurdity of capitalism (Garnet loses not only his own money but the company's, Elsa loses the novel she had been writing to console herself for Garnet's infidelity) as well as the ruthlessness of Socialism (the termite state "does not tolerate individuality, ownership, freedom of instinct"). The story ends with Pilnyak's characteristic ironic nihilism: The Nigerians survive by selling termite excrement as a delicacy at the bazaar.

Another story, "The Tale of the Unextinguished Moon"

(1926) is a most courageous (or most foolhardy) attempt to make fiction out of Stalin's ordering of General Frunze to the operating table, on which he died. It is a rather wooden story, whose odd title seems to symbolize something unkillable in Pilnyak's General Gavrilov, and it ends with "the city—now frosted by the moon—howling." Of the remaining stories, only "The Three Brothers," a charming autobiographical piece about Pilnyak's childhood in a community of his German relatives, is of much interest. The others are rather formless vignettes, perhaps justified by a statement in "The Brothers": "Every story is endless, as life itself is boundless."

Pilnyak was the victim of the first Soviet literary frame-up. When *Mahogany* was due to be printed in Russia in 1929, after already appearing (for copyright purposes) in Germany, he was charged with slandering the Soviet system, treasonable relations with émigré circles abroad, and so forth—charges that were later to become routine. Pilnyak capitulated utterly. He recanted abjectly, and rewrote *Mahogany* into a long epic of Socialist construction, *The Volga Falls to the Caspian Sea*, which was published in 1930. From then on he was a writer of undeviating orthodoxy and slight interest. Alas, he had not reckoned with Varangian times. He was arrested in Stalin's purges of 1937, charged with Trotskyism and spying for Japan, and appears to have died in a labor camp in 1941. At his best, Boris Pilnyak was a matchless captor of the historical moment in all its rich life, a master of the full range of comic rhetoric, and a unique poetic voice in fiction.

1968

A Scythian Humanist

THERE APPEARS to be a growing interest in the work of Evgeny Zamyatin. Eight translations of his only novel, *We,* have appeared over the past decade. A selection of Zamyatin's stories recently appeared in a translation by Mirra Ginsburg as *The Dragon.* A monograph on Zamyatin by D. J. Richards was published in England in 1962, and now the first American monograph, *The Life and Works of Evgenij Zamjatin,* by Alex M. Shane, has appeared. This growth of interest may be attributed largely to the mushrooming field of Russian studies, but some part of it is the recognition that the Soviet 1920s—with Babel, Olesha, Pilnyak, Mandelstam, and others—were a literary renaissance, and some part of it is due to the peculiar attractiveness of Zamyatin as writer and man.

Shane's book is an adaptation of his PhD dissertation under Gleb Struve at Berkeley, and it is most remarkable for its formidable bibliography, 800 items covering 60 pages. The text consists of a biography followed by a critical study. The details of Zamyatin's life make a familiar Russian pattern. He was born in Lebedyan in 1884, the son of a teacher. He was trained as a naval architect and worked at his profession, but as early as 1913 he began publishing fiction, and after the 1917 revolution he settled down in Leningrad as a prolific writer, editor, and teacher of writing; for a time he was chairman of the Leningrad branch of the Union of Soviet Writers. Zamyatin had been a Bolshevik in his student days, but he became increasingly critical of the Workers' Paradise, which returned the compliment. In 1927, he and Boris Pilnyak were the victims of the first Soviet literary frame-up. Pilnyak recanted abjectly, but Zamyatin stood firm. His life became increasingly impossible, until in 1931, through the intervention of Gorky, Stalin surprisingly allowed Zamyatin and his wife to go abroad. He spent his remaining years in Paris, making a precarious living by writing film scenarios, and he died in 1937 of a heart attack.

Zamyatin's views, as Shane presents them, are quixotic and attractive. He identified himself as a "Scythian" at war with philistinism, and his opposition to Communism was that of a humanist to religion. He made common cause with all heretics, believing that "heretics are the sole (bitter) medicine against the entropy of human thought," and that real literature can be created only by "madmen, hermits, heretics, dreamers, rebels, and skeptics." Zamyatin thought that the attainment of any ideal, including revolution, inevitably philistinizes it, and he wrote in an essay: "The philistine is growing, he is sprouting from all cracks like a weed, smothering man." Zamyatin believed in his own variety of permanent revolution, an endless cycle of death and rebirth, and his stories are full of such apocalyptic imagery as the destruction of the earth producing renewal, and murder resulting in new birth.

The most amazing thing about Zamyatin was his fearlessness. When he was bitten by a rabid dog as a child, he did nothing but start a diary to record his sensations. When he was arrested by the trigger-happy Cheka in 1919, he got himself promptly released by lecturing the interrogator on Marxist theory. About the same time he published a fable making fun of Lenin. When the publication of the banned *We* abroad produced what he called a "manhunt" against him, Zamyatin never made the slightest repudiation of it or confession of error. He got out of the country four years later by writing a bold "Letter to Stalin," in which he proclaimed "I have never concealed my attitude toward literary servility, fawning, and chameleon changes of color," and asked permission to go abroad until it became "possible in our country to serve great ideas in literature without cringing before little men." From first to last, Zamyatin's defenses of his work were not only un-compromising, but were written in what Shane calls a "some-what haughty and biting tone."

The Life and Works of Evgenij Zamjatin tells all this fully and sympathetically. In his critical analysis of the works, Shane synopsizes, evaluates, identifies sources and parodies, traces imagery and symbolism, and studies diction and syntax, rhythm and musicality, even the use of color as synecdoche and the symbolism of the letter-and-number names in *We*. Shane is primarily a scholar rather than a critic, and he is no master of English prose ("The subordinate plot is allied to the major triangle by a relationship both prognostic and contrastive"). But for all that, Shane has produced an admirable and most useful book.

We, written in 1920 and never published in the Soviet Union (a recent Russian critic acknowledged it as "a malicious pamphlet on the Soviet government") makes curious reading today. It is a story of the breakdown of the utopian state after a thousand years, when the flowers of freedom, "that bloom only once a thousand years" (all my quotations are from the Gregory Zilboorg authorized 1924 English translation that was the book's first publication) burst into blossom. The book's pro-tagonist and narrator, D-503, the sober designer of the state's first spaceship, under the influence of such archaic symptoms as love, jealousy, and dreams, cooperates with the underground conspiracy and goes so far as to proclaim "We must become insane as soon as possible!" He is saved by a kind of lobotomy, to become the conspiracy's happy betrayer. *We*'s innumerable progeny, prominent among them Huxley's *Brave New World* (Huxley always denied any indebtedness, but in a series of inconsistent statements that invite disbelief) and Orwell's *1984*, have made all this material overfamiliar, and the novel now seems terribly dated.

The principal weaknesses of *We* are that the wonderful heroine, I-330, has no personality but is simply a mouthpiece for Zamyatin ("There is no last revolution, their number is infinite"), that too little is clearly stated and too much implied in unfinished sentences (always a weakness of the author's), and that the book's contrast to the regimented life in the United State is pure pastoral romance: a naked people, their bodies "silky-golden and diffusing an odor of different herbs," eating ripe fruit and drinking sparkling wine out of wooden cups. The strengths of *We* are its subversive sensuality (all art derives from sex, Zamyatin wrote to a friend) and the author's craft. The eroticism of I-330 undressing, for example, is so charged that it is clearly revolutionary. Zamyatin's craft is best shown in wild, almost surrealist, tropes and in fierce parodies of Soviet rhetoric (a paean to the New Poets, whose "lyre is the morning rubbing-sound of the electric tooth-brushes"; the state paper's argument that counting dissenting votes would be like taking coughing in a concert hall to be part of the symphony).

In 1920, *We* was prophetic, visionary. While Stalin was still an insignificant figure, Zamyatin saw a future world "like steel—a sun of steel, trees of steel, men of steel." D-503, before he falls into sin, represents the New Man (and not only the Soviet New Man) as the death of the imagination: He sees clouds as so much steam, defines inspiration as "an extinct form of epilepsy," is horrified by irrational numbers and blots, finds nothing beautiful in flowers, and enjoys the reassuring feeling of an eye watching over his shoulder. How the book would have delighted Marx, an earlier Scythian humanist.

The 15 stories and tales in *The Dragon* show a considerable range. The first of them, "A Provincial Tale," written in 1912, is a museum of the horrors of provincial life: ignorance, grossness, boredom, cruelty, superstition, servility, chicanery. Its protagonist, Anfim Baryba, rises to the exalted rank of police sergeant by the betrayal of every friend and benefactor, the nasty hero of this nasty sty. Other stories are tragic, such as "The North," where the idyllic joy, "the intolerable happiness," of the giant Marey with the Lapp girl Pelka is slowly undermined by her death-wish until she leaves them

251

disarmed before an infuriated bear, which kills them both. Other stories are mainly ironic, such as "A Story About the Most Important Thing" ("the most important thing" is progressively understood as "to crush the others," to survive, "to bloom," and, finally, to love sacrificially). Some stories neatly blend tragedy and irony, such as "The Flood," where the murderer Sofya gives birth, "running over with juices"; confesses her murder, running over with words; then sleeps, "breathing evenly, quietly, blissfully, her lips parted wide." Other short pieces are grotesques, such as "The Dragon," a portrait of a 1918 Soviet soldier as "a dragon with a gun" (by 1923, in "The Most Important Thing," the same image has become "an ant with a rifle").

Zamyatin's style in the stories is equally varied. In "A Provincial Tale" it is portentous: A lamp dies "in long, slow anguish"; Baryba is seen at the end as "an idol from an ancient burial mound." The style of "X" is effervescent comedy: A deacon repents of religion in order to replace his wife with the round-heeled Martha, revealing that he is a convert not to Marxism but to Marthism (this enables the author to lecture us on Martha's generous bosom as Marxist superstructure; elsewhere Marx is confused with the planet Mars and the god Mars). At times "X" is a marvel of what Kenneth Burke calls "perspective by incongruity": We see militiamen in a ballet class; a doctor's tombstone lists his visiting hours.

The current Soviet writer most visibly influenced by Zamyatin is Andrei Sinyavsky, who has published abroad as "Abram Tertz." The works of "Tertz" are Zamyatin's monument, but far more so was Sinyavsky's fearless eloquence at his trial. Evgeny Zamyatin, who believed in new life out of death, lives on in the Soviet Union, and his long-quiescent flowers of freedom may yet blossom everywhere.

1968

Nabokov's
Distorting Mirrors

V LADIMIR NABOKOV'S Russian novel *Despair*, written in
1932, is not a towering masterpiece, like *Pale Fire*, nor
even a modest masterpiece, like *The Gift*. It is a lesser work,
with some of the cruelty and sourness of *Laughter in the Dark*,
but it shows touches of the author's genius everywhere.

The narrator-protagonist of *Despair* is Hermann, son of a
German father and a Russian mother, living in Berlin with a
simple and devoted Russian wife named Lydia. The story
Hermann tells is of his stumbling on a tramp in the woods
who turns out to be his perfect double, gradually corrupting
the tramp until he agrees to dress up as Hermann, then
promptly murdering him. Hermann's motive, he says, is more
the satisfaction of committing a perfect crime than greed,
although he plans to escape to France disguised as the tramp,
and there be reunited with Lydia after she has collected his
life insurance.

Things do not work out as planned. The perfect crime
collapses when the police simply refuse to notice any resemblance between Hermann and his victim, announce that
Hermann is a fugitive murderer, and discover his new identity
because he flawed his perfect planning by leaving the tramp's
stick, incised with his name and address, at the scene of the
crime. Lydia is similarly miscalculated. Hermann casually
assumes "the cloudless blue of our wedlock," but it has been
clear to the reader throughout the story that Lydia has been

cuckolding her husband with her cousin Ardalion, and after Hermann thoughtfully removes himself from the scene, Lydia and Ardalion settle down happily together.

"Plain readers," Nabokov writes of his novel in a foreword to the American edition, "will welcome its plain structure and pleasing plot." It is in fact the dullest of structures and the most stereotyped and worthless of plots. But like John Shade's 999-line poem, these are not the novel but merely the text for a marvel of commentary and embellishment that constitutes the novel. Hermann and his crime are a Russian doll of allegories-within-allegories. The tramp, Felix, is Hermann's double, "a creature bodily identical with me," but from another social class. In appearance they are "alike as two drops of blood," but Hermann has a pocket comb of real tortoise shell, while Felix's is mock turtle. In the murder, they exchange identities, and, looking at the corpse, Hermann thinks: "really I could not say who had been killed."

The foreword has a characteristic Nabokovian disclaimer: "*Despair*, in kinship with the rest of my books, has no social comment to make, no message to bring in its teeth." So, we translate, the book has a social message. It has, too, in one meaning, and a broadly funny one. Hermann is nothing less than Soviet Communism (thus the mixed German and Russian ancestry), enticing and ruthlessly betraying the working class, although eventually thwarted and defeated by its own ineptness and the resilience of the Russian spirit (thus Lydia and Ardalion). In the novel, Hermann not only preaches Soviet Communism, but he gives Marxist interpretations of his acts: his reluctance to mail the letter that will summon Felix to his doom is capitalist resistance to expropriation; his recognition of his double "has a profound allegorical meaning" as "the promise of that ideal sameness which is to unite people in the classless society of the future."

Another disclaimer in the foreword warns us against the "Wiener-schnitzel dream that the eager Freudian may think he distinguishes" in the novel. So, *Despair* is a deliberate Freudian allegory too, of homosexual courtship and seduction. At one point Hermann thinks of Felix as "a woman whom one cannot possess." In the course of his plot he spends a night with Felix in a hotel room and studies his body; in the morning he decides not to kill him, in the imagery of an adolescent deciding to give up masturbation (with its built-in comic prediction of lapse). When Hermann tells Lydia that Felix is his long lost brother, he explains that they used to share a bed in childhood, but that they had to be separated because Felix could not get to sleep without first sucking Hermann's big toe.

Hermann fears that when his story is published, the French will "discern mirages of sodomy" in it. In a monstrous scene, he dresses, shaves, manicures, and pedicures Felix; then he shoots him, of course, in the back. "How utterly he has surrendered himself to me," Hermann thinks; he later recalls Felix, whom he has "to use the accepted word, plugged." Where Humbert Humbert's affairs with nymphets are crypto-pederasty, and Charles Kinbote's affairs with boys are open pederasty, this is comic symbolic sodomy, and since the partners are doubles, the glorious fantasy of self-sodomy and auto-*liebestod*.

In still another meaing, *Despair* is an allegory of art. In ignoring the double's resemblance to Hermann (which may be entirely in Hermann's imagination) the police "behaved just as a literary critic does." Hermann's flawed perfect crime is a misunderstood novel that fails, and the police of criticism are out for his head at the end.

Hermann is, in short, with Pnin and Humbert, Godunov-Cherdyntsev and Botkin-Kinbote, one of Nabokov's gallery of grotesque monsters, distorted and comical self-portraits. He is not a favorite one, as the foreword makes clear in a comparison of Hermann with Humbert: "Both are neurotic scoundrels, yet there is a green lane in Paradise where Humbert is permitted to wander at dusk once a year; but Hell shall never parole Hermann."

One of the preoccupations of the book is a running battle

with Dostoevsky, "that famous writer of Russian thrillers," "our national expert in soul ague." Hermann refers to "old Dusty's great book, *Crime and Slime*," and its hero "Rascalnikov." He thinks of calling his own book *The Double*, or *Crime and Pun*. Ardalion's final letter to Hermann refers to "all the dark Dostoevskian stuff" of Hermann's plot. Nabokov thus challenges Dostoevsky by writing a book that will be at once *The Double* and *Crime and Punishment*, but I am afraid that it is not a serious challenge, merely Hermann's Teutonic challenge, another joke.

Most centrally, *Despair* is about distorting mirrors. On first meeting Felix, Hermann shows him their resemblance in a mirror. When he shows him again in a restaurant, their dual image is "reflected by the misty and, to all appearances, sick mirror, with a freakish slant, a streak of madness." After the murder, Hermann cannot bear to look in mirrors, and he stops shaving. He feels that he is now "all alone in a treacherous world of reflections." He writes of the varieties of distortion produced by "crooked ones, monsters among mirrors."

As Zembla is the land of semblance and *Pale Fire* all "mirror-play and mirage shimmer," so the Germany of *Despair* is one giant distorting mirror. Post office blotters, crisscrossed with reverse images of all that they have blotted, are mirrors; Heaven itself is a great curved mirror. Ardalion's property outside Berlin is a distorted reflection of a landscape Hermann remembers from Russia. A peddler seen through a hotel window in the German town of Tarnitz becomes a Tartar seen from a Russian window years before; the equestrian statue in the Tarnitz square treads an imaginary snake in distorted reflection of the statue of Peter the Great in St. Petersburg; all of Tarnitz eventually turns out to mirror St. Petersburg, to be "constructed of certain refuse particles of my past."

Hermann himself is a vast distorting mirror. At school, when he synopsized *Othello*, he made "the Moor skeptical and Desdemona unfaithful." In his one dramatic performance, announcing the entrance of a prince, he proclaimed: "The prince cannot come: he has cut his throat with a razor." His night in the hotel room with Felix is an endless mirroring: while Hermann pretends to be asleep, Felix "listened to my listening to his listening"; when Hermann finally falls asleep, he has a triple nightmare as complex as the triptych cheval glass in *Pale Fire.*

At times even Hermann's lumpish style corruscates and shimmers. (At 16, when he went to a "pleasantly informal bawdy house," it was staffed by the muses, and the one Hermann chose was fat Polymnia, the muse of sacred song.) There is a running imagery of sleight of hand: palmed coins, stacked decks, and other "stage-wizard's trickery." There is ceaseless word play: jest appears in majesty and ass in passion; riddles are asked and unnoticeably answered; at the end of the book the fatal stick that gave away Hermann's crime disintegrates into "Sick, tick, kit, it, is, ski, skit, sit." No American writer since Wallace Stevens has had such an infatuation with words and Nabokov's "choleric turkeys with carbuncular caruncles" might be from "Bantams in Pine-Woods."

Ultimately the book is brought to life by the language. Here is a sample. Hermann boasts:

"I have exactly twenty-five kinds of handwritings, the best (i.e., those I use the most readily) being as follows: a round diminutive one with a pleasant plumpness about its curves, so that every word looks like a newly baked fancy-cake; then a fast cursive, sharp and nasty, the scribble of a hunchback in a hurry, with no dearth of abbreviations; then a suicide's hand, every letter a noose, every comma a trigger; then the one I prize most: big, legible, firm and absolutely impersonal; thus might write the abstract hand in its superhuman cuff, which one finds figured on signposts and in textbooks of physics."

"Art at its greatest," Nabokov told a recent interviewer, "is fantastically deceitful and complex." Nabokov's art, even at less than his greatest, is no less deceitful and complex. I hope that he gets the next Nobel Prize. Steinbeck and Sholokhov are an American pygmy and a Russian pygmy, but Nabokov is a Russian-American giant, linking two literatures in his colossal stride.

1966

V

A Darwin Sidelight:
The Shape of the
Young Man's Nose

O N MONDAY, September 5, 1831, Robert FitzRoy was exactly twenty-six years and two months old. Young as he was, he had been in His Majesty's Navy for twelve years, and before that in the Royal Naval College. He had risen rapidly to lieutenant then to flag lieutenant under Rear Admiral Sir Robert Otway, then to captain, and was generally regarded as one of the most promising young men in the British Navy, with a brilliant career already well begun. All the testimony agrees that FitzRoy was a remarkable seaman, and a conscientious and scrupulous master (he took great pride in the health of his crews, supplying such unfamiliar antiscorbutics as pickles and apples), if a fairly severe disciplinarian, so that on his second voyage all the officers and two thirds of the crew from the first volunteered to serve with him again.

FitzRoy came of excellent family, and was the grandson of the third Duke of Grafton on his father's side, making him a direct descendant of Charles II, and of the first Marquis of Londonderry on his mother's side. He was slight and dark, with a handsome, somewhat heavy Stuart face, a courteous although rather imperious Stuart manner, and the devil's own temper. In the words of a young man who later served under him, "he was devoted to his duty, generous to a fault, bold, determined and indomitably energetic, and an ardent friend to all under his sway." He was independently wealthy. Since 1828, Captain FitzRoy had been master of H.M.S. *Beagle*, a small deep-waisted brig of about 240 tons, rigged as a bark and carrying six guns, which had returned the year before from a two-year voyage surveying the coasts of Patagonia and Tierra del Fuego, and was soon to embark on a longer similar expedition.

On that significant Monday in 1831, Captain FitzRoy was in London, at his lodgings, about to see the young man who was later to describe him as "energetic." They had never met before, and their paths had intersected only through a fantastic comedy of errors. FitzRoy had determined to take a naturalist with him when the *Beagle* sailed again, having on the last voyage strongly felt the lack of someone trained in geology, able to explore "distant countries yet little known," which might perhaps contain valuable metals. Back in England, he had applied to Captain Francis Beaufort, the Admiralty Hydrographer, for permission to take with him some suitable "scientific person," who would share his cabin and mess. Captain Beaufort had approved the idea, and had asked George Peacock, mathematical tutor of Trinity College, Cambridge, to suggest a person. Perhaps understanding that he was to suggest a "parson," Peacock had first made the offer to the Reverend John Stevens Henslow, botany professor at the college, who had refused it because his wife "looked so miserable" when she encouraged him to go, and then to Henslow's friend, the Reverend Leonard Jenyns, a country vicar and amateur entomologist and ornithologist, who had actually begun to pack before he finally decided against going. Both had recommended a young man graduated from Cambridge that year; in FitzRoy's words, "Mr. Charles Darwin, grandson of Dr. Darwin the poet, as a young man of promising ability, extremely fond of geology, and indeed of all branches of natural history."

Peacock and Henslow had written to Darwin, describing

the voyage and insisting that unqualified as he seemed, he was "the very man" to go; Darwin had almost missed the letters when they arrived during his absence from his home in Shrewsbury. Next, his father, Dr. Robert Darwin, had talked him out of going, for a number of very sound reasons, and Charles had written to Henslow and Peacock refusing the offer; then his uncle Josiah Wedgewood had talked him back into going, driven him to Shrewsbury, and talked Dr. Darwin into giving his permission; finally Darwin had written again, to Peacock, Henslow, and Beaufort, withdrawing his refusal. Darwin had raced by coach and post chaise to Cambridge to see Henslow, on Friday, September 2, and on Saturday had gotten a friend at Cambridge named Wood, who knew Fitz-Roy, to write recommending him. On Sunday Wood had received a letter from FitzRoy that shattered everything; Darwin learned that the captain was "so much against my going that I immediately gave up the scheme." Nevertheless, inexplicably, he had taken the Monday morning coach to London to see FitzRoy.

FitzRoy's letter to Woods, discouraging Darwin from going, has never been satisfactorily explained. During the interview, FitzRoy told Darwin that it was because he had invited a friend, a Mr. Chester, who may or may not have been fictitious, to come, and that there would not have been room, but that five minutes before Darwin's arrival he had received a letter from Chester saying that he would not be able to come. Later in the week he had another story, that he had "taken a sudden horror of the chances of having somebody he should not like on board the Vessel," and confessed that his letter to Cambridge was "to throw cold water on the scheme." Whatever the reason, the interview went very well. FitzRoy first mentioned all the disadvantages and hardships of the trip; then, finding Darwin undiscouraged and finding himself more and more taken with him, began to stress all the advantages; and finally he enthusiastically invited Darwin to come along. Darwin in turn was enormously impressed by FitzRoy;

as he wrote to his sister Susan, "There is something most extremely attractive in his manners and way of coming straight to the point." FitzRoy asked him directly: "Shall you bear being told that I want the cabin to myself? when I want to be alone.—if we treat each other this way, I hope we shall suit; if not, probably we should wish each other at the Devil." Much later in the voyage, FitzRoy confessed to Darwin that what had chiefly worried him during the interview was the shape of Darwin's nose. He was an ardent disciple of Lavater and believer in physiognomy, convinced that he could judge a man's character by his features, and he doubted whether anyone with Darwin's lumpish nose "could possess sufficient energy and determination."

Apart from his nose, certainly, there was little to judge young Charles Darwin by. At the time of the interview he was twenty-two-and-a-half years old. The spring before, he had been graduated from Cambridge, where he had achieved no particular distinction, academic or otherwise, and had displayed no more interest in science than extracurricular friendships with such of the science faculty as Henslow and the geologist, the Reverend Adam Sedgwick. Darwin's chief adolescent interests had been a rather haphazard collecting, principally of beetles, and shooting, which was his particular passion. His father was convinced he was hopelessly frivolous, and had once told him, "You care for nothing but shooting, dogs, and rat-catching, and you will be a disgrace to yourself and all your family." On the strength of this unflattering judgment, Charles's patent inability to become a doctor, and his general lack of interest in any particular field or profession, Dr. Darwin had decided that his son had best become a clergyman, and his study at Cambridge was to have prepared him for the ministry. One of the arguments Josiah Wedgewood had used in favor of Darwin's going on the voyage, in fact, was that the pursuit of natural history was a very suitable hobby for a clergyman, and it was assumed that Charles would study for orders on his return.

That Monday in September was beyond any doubt the most fateful day in the lives of both participants. In Darwin's case, he never lost the conviction that he, and his whole theory of evolution, were entirely formed by the voyage of the *Beagle*. On his return, he wrote FitzRoy, "I think it far the *most fortunate circumstance in my life* that the chance afforded by your offer of taking a Naturalist fell on me," and said that what he had learned on the *Beagle*, "I would not exchange for twice ten thousand a year." Looking back on his career forty-five years later, Darwin wrote in his *Autobiography*:

> The voyage of the *Beagle* has been by far the most important event in my life, and has determined my whole career; yet it depended on so small a circumstance as my uncle offering to drive me thirty miles to Shrewsbury, which few uncles would have done, and on such a trifle as the shape of my nose. I have always felt that I owe to the voyage the first real training or education of my mind.

The voyage not only gave him the germ of his theory of natural selection and much firsthand data for it, but it gave him the material for the early books and papers that made his reputation and earned an audience for his evolutionary hypothesis. The same extraordinary series of coincidences and accidents, culminating in the interview and acceptance before lunch Monday, determined FitzRoy's life just as definitely, and much more tragically. FitzRoy became, in the directest possible fashion, the godfather of the most disturbing idea of the past century and its first victim.

What a glorious day the fourth of November will be to me!" Darwin wrote FitzRoy in October, 1831, referring to the date the *Beagle* was expected to sail (it actually sailed on December 27). "My second life will then commence, and it shall be as a birthday for the rest of my life." Relations between Darwin and FitzRoy in those months were of the best, and

265

neither had occasion to regret his first impression: FitzRoy had written to Beaufort the day of the interview, "I like what I see of him much," and Darwin had written to Susan the next day, describing FitzRoy as "my beau ideal of a captain." After they were several months out, Darwin wrote to his father: "The Captain continues steadily very kind and does everything in his power to assist me," and he found FitzRoy's industry particularly praiseworthy: "He works incessantly, and when apparently not employed, he is thinking. If he does not kill himself, he will, during this voyage, do a wonderful quantity of work." At about the same time, FitzRoy was expressing similar ideas in a letter to Beaufort: "Darwin is a very sensible hard-working man, and a very pleasant messmate. I never saw a 'shore-going fellow' come into the ways of a ship so soon and so thoroughly as Darwin," and shortly afterward, "Darwin is a regular trump." When Darwin sent his first collection of specimens home, FitzRoy wrote to Beaufort: "I fancy that though of small things it is numerous and valuable, and will convince the Cantabrigians that their envoy is no Idler." Hard work was to be the chief thing that united them for the rest of the voyage: Darwin tireless at making observations in natural history and geology and collecting specimens; FitzRoy exhausting himself at hydrography, surveying, and navigation.

Before the *Beagle* sailed, however, Darwin had had one ominous experience with FitzRoy's sudden temper at real or fancied insults to his pride, and equally sudden cooling. At Plymouth, when they were buying equipment for the ship, FitzRoy had made a statement in anger to a shopkeeper who had offended him, and had seen by Darwin's face that he did not believe it. "You do not believe what I have said," FitzRoy challenged furiously when they were outside, and Darwin admitted that he did not. After a few moments of silence, FitzRoy said, "You are right, and I acted wrongly in my anger at the blackguard."

This was to be a pattern Darwin came to know well. Early in the voyage, at Bahia in Brazil, they had a bitter quarrel over slavery. FitzRoy defended the institution, and argued that he had just visited a Brazilian plantation where the owner had called up the slaves, and they had all testified they were happy and didn't want to be free; Darwin sneered at the value of such testimony, given before the slaves' master; FitzRoy became livid and shouted that he refused to live with a man who doubted his word. Darwin prepared to mess with the gun-room officers for the rest of the voyage, and suspected he might even be forced to leave the ship, but within a few hours FitzRoy had sent an officer to him with an apology and a request that they continue to live together. Shortly afterward, Darwin wrote to Henslow from Rio: "The Captain does everything in his power to assist me, and we get on very well, but I thank my better fortune he has not made me a renegade to Whig principles. I would not be a Tory, if it was merely on account of their cold hearts about that scandal to Christian nations—Slavery." There is no doubt that the two quarreled frequently about politics in general and slavery in particular, and if Darwin was prepared to give a little on Whiggery, he would not budge an inch on slavery. The fury of his references to it in *The Voyage of the Beagle*, its "atrocious acts," "heart-sickening atrocities," and moral "debasement," culminating in the ejaculation "I thank God, I shall never again visit a slave country," seemed aimed at FitzRoy as much as at English public opinion.

After a number of these quarrels, Darwin began to get some sort of perspective on FitzRoy. He wrote to his sister Caroline in April, 1832:

> And now for the Captain, as I daresay you feel some interest in him. As far as I can judge, he is a very extraordinary person. I never before came across a man whom I could fancy being a Napoleon or a Nelson. I should not call him clever, yet I feel convinced nothing is too great or too high for him. His ascendancy over everybody is quite curious: the extent to which every officer

and man feels the slightest rebuke or praise, would have been before seeing him, incomprehensible. It is very amusing to see all hands hauling at a rope, they not supposing him on deck, and then observe the effect when he utters a syllable; it is like a string of dray horses, when the waggoner gives one of his aweful smacks. His candour and sincerity are to me unparalleled, and using his own words his "vanity and petulence" are nearly so. I have felt the effects of the latter: but the bringing into play the former ones so forcibly makes one hardly regret them. His greatest fault as a companion is his austere silence: produced from excessive thinking: his many good qualities are great and numerous: altogether he is the strongest marked character I ever fell in with.

The next year, 1833, things went well, and there were few conflicts of temperament to interrupt the work. FitzRoy began the year genially by naming a body of water in Tierra del Fuego "Darwin Sound," explaining in his *Narrative* of the voyage, "after my messmate who so willingly encountered the discomfort and risk of a long cruise in a small loaded boat." He ended it with equal geniality, organizing Christmas contests in running, jumping, wrestling, and other sports among the seamen, and distributing prizes to the winners.

The following year, FitzRoy named "Mount Darwin" after his persevering messmate, and later in the year delayed the *Beagle* ten days because Darwin was sick on shore, without telling him that it was for his sake. Darwin mentioned in a letter to a friend that the captain abhorred "the d —— d scientific Whigs," but the reference seems amiable enough, and when they had a moderate discussion about the fixity of species, in connection with a wolflike fox on East Falkland Island, oddly enough it was FitzRoy who took the liberal, or mildly evolutionary, view, arguing that it might be a modification of the Patagonian fox, rather than a distinctly created species.

The sudden blow came in November, when FitzRoy, over-worked, furious with the Admiralty for refusing to support him in purchasing some auxiliary vessels to help the *Beagle's* survey (Darwin agreed with him that it was discrimination because he was a Tory), and in general morbidly depressed, irresolute, and obsessed with the idea that he was becoming insane, suddenly resigned his command for reasons of ill health. Darwin determined to leave the ship when he did, but FitzRoy was eventually persuaded by the officers to withdraw his resignation and finish the voyage. By the next March, Darwin was writing Caroline, "The Captain is quite himself again."

In July of 1835, the captain was so much himself again that he had a furious quarrel with the commodore above him, in regard to the commodore's slowness in rescuing a shipwrecked British crew; he threatened the old man with courtmartial, and in general, as Darwin wrote gleefully and illiterately to Caroline, showed everyone what a "taught hand" he was. During that year, Darwin and FitzRoy roomed together on shore at Coquimbo, and at Concepción again quarreled violently, this time over a matter of the greatest triviality. FitzRoy complained that the hospitality of the inhabitants obliged him to give a great party for them, Darwin argued that he was under no such obligation, FitzRoy "burst out into a fury" and shouted that Darwin "was the sort of man who would receive any favours and make no return," and Darwin got up, left the ship, and went to his lodgings on shore. When he came back to the ship after a few days, the storm had blown over and the captain was as cordial as ever, but the first lieutenant said to him: "Confound you, philosopher, I wish you would not quarrel with the Skipper; the day you left the ship I was dead-tired, and he kept me walking the deck till midnight abusing you all the time."

By January, 1836, Darwin was less optimistic about Fitz-Roy's chances of becoming a Napoleon or Nelson. He wrote to Susan:

I have been for the last 12 months on very cordial terms with him.—He is an extraordinary but noble character, unfortunately, however, affected with strong peculiarities of temper. Of this, no man is more aware than himself, as he shows by his attempts to conquer them. I often doubt what will be his end; under many circumstances I am sure it would be a brilliant one, under others I fear a very unhappy one.

In April, he wrote Caroline, "The Captain is daily becoming a happier man," and that FitzRoy had liked what he read of Darwin's journal (which later became *The Voyage of the Beagle*) and suggested its publication. In June they wrote an article together, advocating support for the missionaries in the Pacific, and when they got to Cape Town, had it published in the *South African Christian Recorder* over their joint signature. For the last few months of the voyage, things were again placid.

Each committed to print a later retrospect of the voyage. FitzRoy's *Narrative of the Voyage of H.M.S. Beagle,* published in 1839, frequently mentions Darwin's activities as a naturalist, but he seems to have been chiefly impressed by Darwin's quick thinking and endurance, and he tells one story of Darwin's rescuing their boat from destruction, and another of Darwin going off to find water for one of their expeditions on land when FitzRoy and the rest of the party had succumbed to exhaustion. Darwin's *Voyage,* published at the same time, says almost nothing personal about the captain besides acknowledging his "undeviating kindness." By 1876, when he wrote his *Autobiography,* Darwin chiefly remembered FitzRoy's temper and their quarrels, and he summarized somewhat gracelessly: "He was very kind to me, but was a man very difficult to live with on the intimate terms which necessarily followed from our messing by ourselves in the same cabin."

Darwin's tone was not as reserved, however, on his return

from the voyage. He wrote to FitzRoy the day after he got back to Shrewsbury, apologizing for being in a "dead-and-half-alive state" on the last few days of the voyage, and wishing that FitzRoy were with him. Later, when he had settled in London to work on his specimens, he wrote FitzRoy the letter that acknowledged the trip as the most fortunate circumstance in his life, "now that the small disagreeable parts are well-nigh forgotten." He showed the manuscript of his *Voyage* to Fitz-Roy sometime before publication, and there are marginal comments on it apparently in FitzRoy's hand: "A very happy expression," "A false metaphor," and "Good, but the 1st pt not quite clear." FitzRoy had married soon after the voyage and settled in London, and in April, 1839, Darwin went to take tea with the FitzRoys, where he heard the captain's wife talk about her new baby, which was, like all babies, beautiful, and had a voice as musical as a lute. The tea may not have been entirely peaceful, however, for Darwin wrote to Susan the next day: "The Captain is going on very well, that is for a man who has the most consummate skill in looking at everything & everybody in a perverted manner." Early in 1840, Darwin, now married and completely settled in his life work, wrote to Fitz-Roy, "I have nothing to wish for, excepting stronger health to go on with the subjects to which I have joyfully determined to devote my life."

In 1843, FitzRoy was appointed governor of New Zealand, and Darwin wrote to him, "I cannot bear the thoughts of your leaving the country without seeing you once again; the past is often in my memory, and I feel that I owe to you much by-gone enjoyment, and the whole destiny of my life," and made arrangements to come to London from his home at Downe and pay him a farewell visit. By 1845 FitzRoy was back, recalled from office as the result of a petition by the white settlers, who accused him of favoring the Maoris. Darwin wrote him again in 1846, telling him of his current work on barnacles ("My life goes on like clockwork, and I am fixed on the spot where I shall end it"), sending him a copy of his *Geology of South*

America but warning him that it wouldn't interest him much, and concluding: "Farewell, dear FitzRoy, I often think of your many acts of kindness to me, and not seldomest on the time, no doubt quite forgotten by you, when, before making Madeira, you came and arranged my hammock with your own hands, and which, as I afterwards heard, brought tears into my father's eyes."

Darwin wrote in his *Autobiography*, "I saw FitzRoy only occasionally after our return home, for I was always afraid of unintentionally offending him, and did so once almost beyond mutual reconciliation," but of this last quarrel there is no record, nor is there any record of further correspondence or of their ever meeting again. The different tenors of their lives were probably as much responsible for their drifting apart as was FitzRoy's temperament. Darwin had been living quietly and obscurely at Downe, rarely coming to London as his health got progressively worse, turning out one scientific work after another: three books on the geology of the *Beagle's* voyage, and then four weighty volumes representing eight years of intensive work, on the classification of a pinhead-sized barnacle called the Cirripede, a specimen of which had interested him on the voyage. He was rapidly developing a scientific reputation through his books, as well as papers and monographs, and since 1839 had been collecting notes on the inflammatory problem of the fixity of species, first in secret, then gradually revealing his work to a few scientific friends.

FitzRoy's life had been as public as his former messmate's was private. In 1841 he stood for Parliament as the Conservative candidate for Durham, and became involved in a ridiculous and lengthy public brawl with a second Conservative candidate, a Mr. William Sheppard. It culminated when Sheppard, carrying a horsewhip, accosted FitzRoy outside his club, and said (or later claimed he said): "Captain FitzRoy, I will not strike you, but consider yourself horse-whipped." FitzRoy hit him in the head with an umbrella and knocked him down, but was prevented from offering him a meeting by his fellow officers. Each published his side of the controversy in an interminable sixpenny pamphlet, according to the wordy fashion of the day: FitzRoy in "Capt. FitzRoy's statement of circumstances which led to a personal collision between Mr. Sheppard and Capt. FitzRoy" in 1841, Sheppard in "Conduct of Capt FitzRoy in reference to the electors of Durham" in 1842. FitzRoy lost the election, but the following year was elected to Parliament as member for Durham, and distinguished himself by bringing in a bill "for improving the condition and efficiency of officers in the mercantile marine."

From 1843 to 1845 FitzRoy was involved in his New Zealand fiasco. This too led to publications: the "Petition to Parliament from the inhabitants of the Southern Settlement of N. Zealand," in 1845, and FitzRoy's defense, "Remarks on New Zealand," in 1846. In 1848, FitzRoy was appointed acting superintendent of the Woolwich dockyards, and published a book, *Sailing Directions for South America.* The next year he was given the command of the fittingly named *Arrogant,* one of the early experimental screw frigates, and in 1850, for reasons of health and "his private affairs," he retired from the service and was placed on half pay, although he continued to advance in rank on the retired list. The next year he was elected a Fellow of the Royal Society, and in 1854 he was appointed chief of the new meteorological department of the Board of Trade, and devoted the rest of his career to developing the infant science of meteorology, which culminated in his *Weather Book* in 1863. In the opinion of Sir John Knox Laughton, the Secretary of the Navy Records Society, FitzRoy's two principal achievements, besides his remarkable surveying on the *Beagle* voyage, were the storm warnings he developed for the Board of Trade and his agitation on behalf of the lifeboat association, for both of which, Laughton writes, "seafaring men owe him a deep debt of gratitude."

Much as FitzRoy's mind was occupied with the improvement of British sailing, it came to be occupied even more with a thing that does not seem quite in character, religious fundamentalism of the most extreme sort. His *Narrative* of the voyage of the *Beagle,* published in 1839, contains two almost unbelievable final chapters for a sober work on navigation, "Remarks on the early migration of the Human Race," and "A very few Remarks with reference to the Deluge." These chapters are a somewhat hysterical attempt to use the observations made on the *Beagle*'s voyage, the same materials out of which Darwin fashioned his theory of natural selection, to prove the literal truth of the first chapters of Genesis. FitzRoy writes that he himself had been "led away by sceptical ideas," and known "extremely little of the Bible"; takes a crack at the young Darwin ("I mention this particularly, because I have conversed with persons fond of geology, yet knowing no more of the Bible than I knew at that time"); and then goes on to refute these "men of Voltaire's school." The "days" of creation were literal days, he insists, since "Vegetation was produced on the third day, the sun on the fourth. If the third day was an age, how was the vegetable world nourished?" The lion would certainly have lain down with the lamb on the Ark, since "He who made, could surely manage," and moreover, the animals would have been frightened into submission by the Flood. He proves that Job's leviathan and behemoth were the extinct megalosaurus and iguanodon, and finds "remains of Arkite observances" in every country the *Beagle* visited, such as the Hebrew word "Shem," current among the Indians of Chile, "handed down from their ancestor of the Ark." "These remarks would be useless," FitzRoy explains, "were it not that they may reach the eyes of young sailors, who have not always access to works of authority." In another place: "If my few remarks tend, even in the least, to warn young persons of my profession against assenting hastily to new theories—while they induce a closer examination into the Record of truth—my object will be fully attained." FitzRoy's most indignant paragraph was aimed directly at the evolutionary view, which had hardly yet occurred to Darwin. He writes:

Have we a shadow of ground for thinking that wild animals or plants have improved since their creation? Can any reasonable man believe that the first of a race, species or kind, was the most inferior? Then how for a moment could false philosophers, and those who have been led astray by their writings, imagine that there were separate beginnings of savage races, at different times and in different places? Yet I may answer this question myself; for until I had thought much on the subject, and had seen nearly every variety of the human race, I had no reason to give in opposition to doubts excited by such sceptical works, except a conviction that the Bible was true, that in all ages men had erred, and that sooner or later the truth of every statement contained in that record would be proved.

By 1845, FitzRoy had become so fanatically religious that the New Zealanders remarked in their petition: "They cannot but think that the somewhat obtrusive and absorbing observance of devotional duties . . . has contributed to give to Government House the air of a conventicle, and caused its almost entire desertion by all but missionaries." Darwin's faith, meanwhile, had moved in the opposite direction. He wrote in his *Autobiography:*

Whilst on board the *Beagle* I was quite orthodox, and I remember being heartily laughed at by several of the officers (though themselves orthodox) for quoting the Bible as an unanswerable authority on some point of morality. I suppose it was the novelty of the argument that amused them. But I had gradually come by this time, *i.e.* 1836 to 1839, to see that the Old Testament was no more to be trusted than the sacred books of the Hindoos.

On the evening of July 1, 1858, papers by Alfred Russell Wallace and Charles Darwin, "On the Tendency of Species to form Varieties; and on the Perpetuation of Varieties and Species by Natural Means of Selection," were read before the Linnean Society, with Darwin not present, and the theory of evolution had been announced to the world. On November 24, 1859, *On the Origin of Species by means of Natural Selection*, by Charles Darwin, M.A., F.R.S., a small green-covered volume priced at 15 shillings, was published in an edition of 1250 copies. It was entirely sold out by publication day, and almost immediately England was in an uproar. One of the first public reactions was a pair of curious anonymous letters in the London *Times*, in the issues of December 1 and December 5, on the rather oblique subject of "Works of Art in the Drift." Darwin sent one of them to his friend Sir Charles Lyell, the geologist, with the note:

> I forget whether you take in the *Times;* for the chance of your not doing so, I send the enclosed rich letter. It is, I am sure, by Fitz-Roy. . . . It is a pity he did not add his theory of the extinction of *Mastodon*, etc., from the door of the Ark being made too small.

The great Darwinian battle came at Oxford, at the meeting of the British Association on June 30, 1860. Again Darwin was not present. The occasion was nominally a discussion of a paper by Dr. Draper of New York, on the "Intellectual development of Europe considered with reference to Mr. Darwin," and word had gotten around that the Right Reverend Samuel Wilberforce, Bishop of Oxford, familiarly known as "Soapy Sam," would destroy Darwin and his pernicious views once and for all. Almost a thousand people came, far too many for the lecture room, and they finally crowded into the library of the Museum. Henslow presided, and both Thomas Henry Huxley and Joseph Dalton Hooker, Darwin's two most enthusiastic scientific supporters, were there by chance, both having at first decided not to come. Draper read his paper, dully, for an hour. Then three more speakers took the platform and were shouted down, the third, a Reverend Mr. Dingle, almost mobbed when he drew two crosses on the blackboard and said, "Let this point A be the man, and let that point B be the mawnkey," and all the undergraduates began to scream "Mawnkey! Mawnkey!" until he sat down.

Then the bishop rose, and in a slick and effective half-hour speech ridiculed Darwin and his "hypothesis, raised most unphilosophically to the dignity of a causal theory," concluding with the earnest warning that it was all contrary to biblical revelation. The bishop got carried away, however, and just before concluding he turned to Huxley and asked him whether he claimed descent from a monkey through his grandfather or grandmother? Huxley struck his knee and whispered to a friend, "The Lord hath delivered him into my hands!" (The religious imagery of the free-thinking Darwinian forces that evening comes as something of a surprise; Hooker, too, writing of the affair to Darwin, said, "I swore to myself that I would smite that Amalekite, Sam, hip and thigh.") Recognized by Henslow, Huxley rose slowly, and in a few sentences demolished the bishop. He would rather have an ape for an ancestor, he said, than the sort of man who "plunges into scientific questions, questions with which he has no real acquaintance, only to obscure them by an aimless rhetoric, and distract the attention of his hearers from the point at issue by eloquent digressions and skilled appeals to religious prejudices." Then Hooker rose to speak, demonstrated that the bishop could not possibly have read *The Origin of Species*, and in any case knew nothing whatsoever of the scientific subjects under discussion. The bishop sat silent, and the audience was in a tumult.

When order was at last restored, one more friend of Darwin's, a man who had known him longer than either Huxley or Hooker, rose to speak. It was Rear Admiral Robert FitzRoy, Retired, a bitter and querulous old man at fifty-five. He indignantly denied Huxley's claim that the *Origin* was a logical statement of fact, strongly regretted its publication, and announced that reading it had caused him the most acute pain. Suddenly waving a Bible in the air, he shouted that he had always warned the young man against holding views contrary to the revealed Word of God, the only and the unimpeachable authority. He was immediately hooted down.

On April 30, 1865, by which time Darwin's theory of evolution had swept away much of the serious opposition and was on its way to being generally accepted throughout the world, Robert FitzRoy, now Vice Admiral, Retired, after one of his familiar brooding sessions, went into his bathroom before breakfast and cut his throat with a straight razor. The circumstances and reasons have never been made public. The *Dictionary of National Biography* does not mention FitzRoy's suicide at all; the *Encyclopaedia Britannica* says only, "In a fit of mental aberration he put an end to his existence." Darwin's biographers have agreed that evolution was an important factor: "A bitter disappointed man in a world poisoned by false gospels," says one; "Probably he never forgave himself for the part he had played in perverting Darwin's mind," says another. Darwin himself, writing eleven years after the event, was somewhat more charitable. He wrote:

> Towards the close of his life he was, as I fear, much impoverished, and this was largely due to his generosity. Anyhow, after his death a subscription was raised to pay his debts. His end was a melancholy one, namely suicide, exactly like that of his uncle, Lord Castlereagh, whom he resembled closely in manner and appearance. His character was in several respects one of the most noble which I have ever known, although tarnished by grave blemishes.

If Darwin contributed to the subscription, there is no record of it. In all his later life, visitors agreed that his nose was his most prominent feature.

1968

Images of Sigmund Freud

FREUD HAS BEEN DEAD for almost a quarter of a century now, but books about him pour from the presses in increasing numbers, and they give an odd effect of talking about several different fellows of the same name.

The one most familiar, useful and welcome is the one-volume abridgement by Lionel Trilling and Steven Marcus of Ernest Jones' important three-volume biography, *The Life and Work of Sigmund Freud*. The image it gives us is basically Jones' image, Freud as the good father, authoritative but benign. This is more sharply focussed as heroic in the fine tribute contained in Trilling's introduction. "The work is large, and ordered, and courageous, and magnanimous in intention," Trilling writes, "and of the life we can say nothing less." "How much of Freud's intellectual achievement must be thought of as a moral achievement," he declares.

Where I have checked the abridgement, it has omitted little that the non-professional reader needs or would miss. Technical discussions and scholarly documentation have been excised, along with digressions, trivia and some of Jones' whimsies. The book is thus, for its different audience, improved, and anyone who needs or wants any of the deleted material still has it readily available in the original edition. The editors have not corrected the one error of fact I am aware of in the book, the statement that Morton Prince had been Mayor of Boston. (It was Prince's father who was Mayor of Boston, as I know from having innocently reprinted Jones' statement, and having been promptly corrected by a correspondent.)

The latest volume in the Collected Works of C. G. Jung,

279

Freud and Psychoanalysis, translated by R. F. C. Hull, presents a sharply contrasting image of Freud, one that we might sum up as a heathen, sex-obsessed neurotic. Freud's theories are described as "the one-sided sexual reductions of the Viennese school," "a psychology which is a formulation of his own being," "a psychology of neurotic states of mind." Freud's problem is his "inability to understand religious experience," that is, he refuses to learn "that God is his father." "I cannot see how Freud can ever get beyond his own psychology," Jung concludes, "and relieve the patient of a suffering from which the doctor himself still suffers."

Freud and Psychoanalysis devotes its first section to papers written from 1906 to 1912, when Jung was still a Freudian. We see him dutifully producing sexual interpretations (roast chestnuts are female sex symbols "because of the split," firewood is a male sex symbol). Even then, his heart wasn't in it; and from the first article on, Jung hedges about how he does not "subscribe unconditionally," and how "one-sided" Freud's material is. Where Jung later rewrote these early articles, the editors print both versions, and we can observe the disappearance of the sexual references, unfortunate evidences of "a low cultural level."

We can also watch the early development of Jung's own approach. We see a dazzling display of number-jugglery, a developing vocabulary of "ethical development" and "the profundity and beauty of the human soul," a firm denial of infantile sexuality in the same papers that reveal its omnipresence, an insistence that "the normal man is 'civic-minded and moral,' " dream-readings that foresee the future like gypsy fortune-telling, mythic inflations and slogans about "biological destiny."

The image of Jung himself that comes through is a complex one: brilliant, pompous, vain, unscrupulous, sometimes enormously winning. His role was to be Freud's Lucifer, the brightest angel fallen, but really he reminds one more of Cardinal Newman, striding along in the firm faith that he is reforming the

Church of England until one day he wakes up in Rome. Jung asks in 1914 "whether a scientifically trained doctor can square it with his conscience to sell little bottles of Lourdes water." In accord with his self-image as the most rigorous of scientists, he answers with a firm negative. By the time Jung died in 1961, Zurich was the greatest bottling works in the world.

A technical book by an American academic psychologist, Peter Madison, gives us an image of Freud that is probably typical of American academic psychology. The book is *Freud's Concept of Repression and Defense: Its Theoretical and Observational Language,* and its image is of a slipshod and disorderly genius. Madison shows how dominated American psychiatry is by Freud's views, principally the theories he published from 1900 to 1915, but how little it understands his later theoretical modifications. What puzzles and confuses is "Freud's lack of a differentiated terminology," his terminological vagueness and inconsistency about the basic concepts he called "repression" and "defense." "It is small wonder that confusion exists," Madison cries, bravely hacking his way through the jungle.

Madison's ambition is no less than straightening out the terms, organizing them in a consistent and systematic fashion, then restating them in what Rudolf Carnap calls "observational" language and devising quantifications that will permit the evaluation of therapy. He does all this quite successfully and usefully until the last, or quantifying, stage, when things become ludicrous. In his impatience with any formulations not quantifiable, Madison seems quite characteristic of American academic psychology, and his quantifications have the familiar leaden ring: Resistance Check List, Thematic Rigidity Index, Life History Amnesia Index, Humor Remoteness Ratio, and so on.

This ambitious venture is fundamentally misguided, an effective means to an absurd end. Psychoanalysis is about as quantifiable as a sonnet sequence. Madison's problem is a total want of esthetic imagination and a high humor-remoteness coefficient. "Situations in waiting rooms might be experimentally

281

arranged," he writes, "in which seductive persons of the opposite sex would see how much interest could be aroused." Madison delicately does not suggest the unit of measurement.

Freud and the Post-Freudians, by J. A. C. Brown, gives an engaging image of Freud as an aristocratic old gentleman pestered by bad children. "Freud was a very great man," Brown writes, but the later Freudians as well as the dissenters have shared his greatness no more than they have shared his "aristocratic distaste for the rabble."

Brown's explanations of theory are often confused and confusing, he generally paraphrases where he might better quote, and some of his information is secondhand. The book is extraordinarily full of mistakes. I counted a dozen serious errors of fact, and the names are so careless that the author of *The Golden Bough* emerges as "Sir George Fraser," the historian of the Renaissance is "Burchardt" throughout, and all names beginning with "J" are missing from the index.

For all its failings, *Freud and the Post-Freudians* is far from useless. The views of the competing schools of psychoanalysis are summarized with unusual fairness, and nothing important is omitted except the new ego psychology of Heinz Hartmann and Ernst Kris. The book's chief value lies in its demonstration that in, say, the moderate and reasonable formulations of Otto Fenichel, so much of Freud's theory is now beyond dispute.

Finally we come to Henry Denker's successful Broadway play about Freud, *A Far Country*. Its image of Freud is alternately as Young Dr. Kildare and as Old Dr. Gillespie, and it is a vulgar and meretricious travesty from start to finish. It is of course Denker's privilege to adapt reality to his dramaturgic needs, but not to call the resulting soap-opera hero "Freud." This "Freud" could not have discovered his way out of a paper bag. The dramatic climax of the play, the hysterically crippled heroine's throwing aside her crutches to *walk*, followed by the dying Freud's throwing away *his* wheelchair to *walk*, would not come off even at Lourdes.

Denker's Freud is shown filing a dance program with his

case notes, forgetting his patient's name, fondling her hand, telling her comforting little white lies. He confesses that most of his antiquities are copies. His mother is the nagging, son's-career-mad mother of "my son, the doctor" jokes. Freud's early collaborator Joseph Breuer, in a particularly vicious caricature, is a self-confessed coward and trimmer. When Freud and his wife quarrel, in the Vienna of the 1890s, the *maid* tries to reconcile them.

Freud's ideas are just as ruthlessly travestied. His travel neurosis turns out to have been caused in his childhood when his mother attempted to hurl them both under a train (!), and at the play's end his wife, who has diagnosed the case from the mother's remarks, assures Freud that the neurosis will now vanish. (For the record, this is W. H. R. Rivers' theory of the traumatic origin of neurosis, and Mary Baker Eddy's theory of cure.)

Denker, a radio writer, is semi-literate, and as a consequence his figure of Freud (that fastidious stylist) is semi-literate too, using "like" for "as" and splitting infinitives. Denker's Freud talks to patients in the three-dot style of high school literary magazines ("No earth beneath you . . . only a void . . . dark . . . empty void . . .") and to his colleagues in a series of barked exclamations. Denker chose to dramatize the early case of "Elisabeth v. R.," I do not doubt, because it had a woman patient, a happy ending and no ugly infantile material. The larger question, why he chose Freud at all, I cannot answer. *A Far Country* is prefaced by the disclaimer: "No real person portrayed herein is still alive." We can at least be grateful for that.

1962

Jessie Weston and the
Forest of Broceliande

I

Miss Jessie Laidlay Weston is one of the most enigmatic
figures of modern scholarship. Until the year of her
death, no biographical material about her appeared anywhere,
and her books identified her only as the author of other books.
Her prefaces and introductions located her at "Bournemouth"
from 1897 to 1901, and at "Paris" after that (except for a 1902
regression to "Dulwich"). While she made every effort to
keep herself obscure, the tone of her writing was always strikingly personal. "They ask a great deal who ask us to believe
this!" she will exclaim, or "Well was it for me that I did not
shrink from the task!"

Miss Weston's works thus constitute an album of somewhat
blurry snapshots. Her first publication, a verse translation of
Wolfram von Eschenbach's *Parzival* in 1894, furnishes the
first portrait: she was a romantic Wagnerian, dedicating her
translation to the memory of Richard Wagner "whose genius
has given fresh life to the creation of medieval romance," and
identifying Wagner in the introduction as "the greatest composer of our time." Her final book, *From Ritual to Romance*
in 1920, gives the last portrait: she had become an elderly and
somewhat crotchety scholar. She writes:

> Some years ago, in the course of my reading, I came
> across a passage in which certain knights of Arthur's court,
> riding through a forest, come upon a herb 'which belonged

to the Grail.' Unfortunately the reference, at the time I met with it, though it struck me as curious, did not possess any special significance, and either I omitted to make a note of it, or entered it in a book which, with sundry others, went mysteriously astray in the process of moving furniture.

After Miss Weston's death on September 29, 1928, an obituary in the London *Times* (October 1) published what little biographical information is available. She was born on December 29, 1850, the daughter of William Weston of Clapham and later of Abbey Wood, Kent. She was educated at Brighton, Paris, and Hildesheim, and studied art at the Crystal Palace School. She did not attend a university, but fell into Arthurian scholarship in 1890, after attending the Wagner Festival at Bayreuth, when she complained to Alfred Nutt that Wagner's work was not better known in England, and he suggested that she translate Wolfram's *Parzival*, the source of Wagner's *Parsifal*. From then on, her life consisted primarily of a series of books. The last of them, *From Ritual to Romance*, won the Rose Mary Crawshay Prize in 1920, and in 1923 the University of Wales conferred on her the degree of D.Litt. in recognition of her services to Celtic literature.

Miss Weston was a founder and lifelong member of the Lyceum and Halcyon clubs, an early member of the *Wagnerverein*, a member of the Folk-lore Society and the Quest Society. Of her personal life, the *Times* reported:

> Her strong and charming personality and her great sense of humour won her the enduring affection of a host of friends all over the world. She was especially interested in young scholars, and ever ready by helpful criticism and suggestion to aid them in their researches. Many a student will remember her with respect and gratitude, as well as admiration for her rich store of knowledge, which was always at their command.

Nothing was said about where Miss Weston lived, or how she supported herself, if she did. She died in a London nursing home, at work on another volume of Arthurian scholarship.

The range and variety of Miss Weston's publications are impressive. She began as a popularizer of Wagner, publishing the two-volume verse translation of *Parzival* in 1894, a retelling of *Lohengrin* in ballad form soon after, and a synopsis of the whole range of Wagner's sources in *The Legends of the Wagner Drama* in 1896. If her interests were musical and poetic at first, they soon emerged as scholarly and folkloristic. *Parzival* has extensive notes, including material contributed by Alfred Nutt, and a bristle of excursuses on the source problem. *Legends* not only synopsizes all the stories but relates them to the archetypal myth of the hero as defined in Nutt's *Studies on The Legend of the Holy Grail* in 1888, and makes extensive use of comparative material from non-Germanic mythologies.

In 1897, with *The Legend of Sir Gawain: Studies upon Its Original Scope and Significance*, Miss Weston began a series of straight scholarly publications in David Nutt's Grimm Library. These became increasingly opinionated and outspoken over the years. *Gawain* set out to rescue the good name of her hero from such late traducers as Malory, and to show him to be an ancient Celtic solar divinity closely parallel to Cuchulinn, his Grail quest a contamination from Perceval mythology.

The Legend of Sir Lancelot du Lac: Studies upon its Origin, Development, and Position in the Arthurian Romantic Cycle (1901) boldly challenges German scholarship. Professor Foerster's views are "radically unsound," he "offers no arguments; he only makes assertions," and it is not even beyond him to "misrepresent the incidents." Dr. Sommer's description of one scene is "utterly wrong," his summary "is again misleading, and entirely misrepresents the general character of the incident," and his conclusions are "far too hasty and inadequately founded." "Dr. Sommer's apparent lack of familiarity with the minor characters of the Arthurian cycle," she adds curtly, "is inexplicable." Her studies, Miss Weston admits, have had one result: "to seriously shake my belief in the soundness and reliability of foreign criticism of the Arthurian cycle."

Miss Weston's own theories in the book are handicapped by her lack of any concept of folk process and by an inadequate terminology. Thus "myth" and "folk-tale" are seen as entirely unrelated, the process of folk transmission is assumed to polish and improve a tale, and the problem of origin is allowed to remain a mystery. At that time Miss Weston saw the difficulties as primarily textual. Arthurian studies would not reach the stage of theoretical solution, she wrote, until "complete and critical editions of *all* the principal texts were available."

Miss Weston's next book, *The Three Day's Tournament: A Study in Romance and Folk-Lore* (1902), was offered as an appendix to the Lancelot volume. In it she continues to take a tough line with poor Professor Foerster: "Well, if assertion were argument, and a liberal display of large type could settle intricate questions of literary criticism," begins one such attack. Her primary interest in the book lies in identifying Lancelot with a familiar folktale pattern, as Nutt had earlier done with Perceval. Miss Weston insists on the importance of history as well as folklore in Arthurian studies, but by "history" she means Henry II's policy of conciliating the Welsh "by a clever use of their popular traditions," not a historical King Arthur.

The last of Miss Weston's series of individual studies, *The Legend of Sir Perceval*, was also published in installments: the first volume in 1906 and the second in 1909. In her efforts to disentangle the Perceval romances, Miss Weston had become convinced of the primacy of Welsh sources for the Grail romances, and of the primacy of Gawain rather than Perceval as the original Grail winner. This conviction and the discoveries on which it is based are the revolutionary content of Volume 1 of *The Legend of Sir Perceval*, so far as Arthurian scholarship is concerned. Its larger revolution is the first hint of Miss Weston's theory of the origin of the Grail myth in a fertility ritual resembling that of Adonis, as described by Frazer in *The Golden Bough*. This theory is more fully developed in Volume 2, and Perceval's replacement of Gawain as Grail winner is explained in terms of the initiatory function of the ritual. For the first time, Miss Weston had a theory of process that enabled her to explain the evolution of the Grail myth and of the romances based on it.

While engaged in these scholarly studies and publications, Miss Weston turned out a great deal of Arthurian popularization. In the years between 1898 and 1907 she published a series of seven little volumes of Arthurian Romances unrepresented in Malory, in her own prose translations. She published two pamphlets in Nutt's series of Popular Studies in Mythology, Romance and Folklore. The first is No. 4, *King Arthur and His Knights* (1899), which takes the position that a historical Arthur certainly existed, but that the material of Arthurian romance is almost entirely mythical. The second, No. 10, *The Romance Cycle of Charlemagne and His Peers* (1901) announces the Charlemagne cycle to be mainly historical, and thus of considerably less interest than the Arthurian.

For the eleventh edition of the Encyclopaedia Britannica in 1910 and 1911, Miss Weston wrote a dozen signed articles on Arthurian subjects, and must have had a hand in others, since the unsigned article on Gawain, for example, clearly expressed her views in her characteristic language. In 1911 she published a volume of *Old English Carols;* in 1912, *Romance, Vision and Satire,* a translation of fourteenth-century English alliterative poems in the original meters; and in 1914, more translations in *The Chief Middle English Poets.*

Miss Weston published in *Folk-lore, Romania,* the *Revue Celtique, The Athenaeum, The Quest,* and many other periodicals. In 1896 she produced her only volume of original verse, *The Rose Tree of Hildesheim and other Poems,* and in 1900 she produced her only work of fiction,*The Soul of the Countess,* consisting of six short stories with verse preludes, on mythic and religious themes. In 1915, she published two furious pamphlets against Germany: *Germany's Literary Debt to France,* which denies Germany's claim to cultural supremacy, and *Germany's Crimes Against France,* charging more conventional atrocities.

II

Finally, Miss Weston was ready for the general statement of the Grail theory that she had been working out piecemeal. Her first attempt was *The Quest of the Holy Grail* (1913). This is a volume in the Quest Series, edited by G. R. S. Mead and sponsored by the Quest Society. The emphasis is consequently mystic, on the ways men "have conceived and expressed their relation to the Unseen." A description of the Grail in a romance as made of no known substance is now understood to say that the Grail is made "of no material substance," and other explanations similarly draw on the occult. The principal emphasis is on the two levels of meaning in Mystery religions and initiatory rituals: a lower or exoteric, which makes the crops grow; and a higher, or esoteric, involving spiritual regeneration. Miss Weston's conclusion is that the Grail romances are "the record of a determined effort to attain, on the lower plane, to a definite and personal knowledge of the Secret of Life, on the higher, to that intimate and personal contact with the Divine Source of Life, in which, in the view of the mystics of all ages, is to be found the sole Reality."

The definitive statement of her Grail theory appeared in *From Ritual to Romance* in 1920, when Miss Weston was 70. There is still a great deal of mysticism. Miss Weston writes in the introductory chapter: "No inconsiderable part of the information at my disposal depended upon personal testimony, the testimony of those who knew of the continued existence of such a ritual, and had actually been initiated into its mysteries." A typical footnote along these lines read: "Without entering into indiscreet details I may say that students of the Mysteries are well aware of the continued survival of this ritual under circumstances which correspond exactly with the indications of two of our Grail romances." One Arthurian incident is given a purely occultist explanation: it is the story of a test "carried out on the astral plane, and reacting with fatal results upon the physical." "The Otherworld is not a myth, but a reality," Miss Weston explains, "and in all ages there have been souls who have been willing to brave the great adventure, and to risk all for the chance of bringing back with them such assurance of the future life."

Side by side with this familiar occultism are new metaphors imaging a scientific demonstration. Miss Weston talks of discovering "important links in the chain of evidence" and finding "the final link that completed the chain." "The chain is at last linked up," she says, "and we can now prove by printed texts the parallels existing between each and every feature of the Grail story and the recorded symbolism of the Mystery cults." "The chain of evidence is already strong," she adds later, "and we may justly claim that the links added by further research strengthen, while they lengthen, that chain." Varying the metaphor, she talks of finding "a clue, which, like the fabled thread of Ariadne, shall serve as a guide through the mazes of a varying, yet curiously persistent, tradition," or of finding "the key to unlock" the portals of the Grail castle.

What had happened between 1913, when she completed *The Quest of the Holy Grail*, and 1919, when she wrote *From Ritual to Romance*, was that Miss Weston had discovered the Cambridge group: Gilbert Murray (of Oxford), F. M. Cornford, A. B. Cook, and, particularly, Jane Ellen Harrison. One of the two epigraphs on the title page of *From Ritual to Romance* is a fine statement about the scientific test of a hypothesis, from Cornford's *The Origin of Attic Comedy*. The book's preface announces:

> The perusal of Miss J. E. Harrison's *Themis* opened my eyes to the extended importance of these Vegetation rites. In view of the evidence there adduced I asked myself whether beliefs which had found expression not only in social institution, and popular custom, but, as set forth in

Sir G. Murray's study on Greek Dramatic Origins, attached to the work, also in Drama and Literature, might not reasonably—even inevitably—be expected to have left their mark on Romance? The one seemed to me a necessary corollary of the other, and I felt that I had gained, as the result of Miss Harrison's work, a wider, and more assured basis for my own researches. I was no longer engaged merely in enquiring into the sources of a fascinating legend, but on the identification of another field of activity for forces whose potency as agents of evolution we were only now beginning rightly to appreciate.

The basic assumption of *Themis* is Miss Harrison's definition of myth as "the spoken correlative of the acted rite" (in a Greek formula, "the things said over a ritual act"). This rigorous limitation gives *From Ritual to Romance* the firm logical and rational structure underlying its mysticism, and gives the book a power and authority lacking in Miss Weston's earlier volumes. In addition, Miss Weston continually bolsters her argument with Cambridge support: Cornford shows the importance of ceremonial marriage in fertility ritual, Miss Harrison demonstrates the evolutionary development of divinity, Cook shows why the life of the crops is embodied in the king, Murray's "deeply interesting and suggestive theory" is capable of wider application, and so on. "The cumulative evidence of these works is most striking," she remarks after listing some of the Cambridge books, but it is particularly *Themis* that has influenced her. She calls attention to "the extremely instructive remarks of Miss Harrison," quotes at length from her "deeply interesting volume," and finds her suggestions "of extreme significance."

In 1922, Miss Weston's new power and authority received public acknowledgment. T. S. Eliot published *The Waste Land* in *The Criterion* in England and in *The Dial* in the United States, and the notes explain:

> Not only the title, but the plan and a good deal of the incidental symbolism of the poem were suggested by Miss Jessie L. Weston's book on the Grail legend: *From Ritual to Romance* (Cambridge). Indeed, so deeply am I indebted, Miss Weston's book will elucidate the difficulties of the poem much better than my notes can do; and I recommend it (apart from the great interest of the book itself) to any who thing such elucidation of the poem worth the trouble.

In the years since, on the strength of Eliot's indebtedness and its own merits, *From Ritual to Romance* has been the one popular and well known book of all that Miss Weston wrote. After it went out of print, it was reprinted photographically in 1941 and in paperback in 1957, and it is widely studied in American colleges, many of which did not exist at the time of Miss Weston's death.

III

Jessie Weston's career is remarkable for her open-mindedness and courage in changing her views all through her life. She began late, publishing her first book at forty-four (Jane Harrison, born the same year, 1850, had been publishing for a decade). Thus Miss Weston developed her theories in her fifties, modified them in her sixties, and rethought them in the new Cambridge perspective when she was almost seventy. In her quarter-century of publication she underwent the entire modern revolution in the study of myth and folk literature. She began as a moralist, interested in Wolfram's *Parzival* because in it "the spiritualizing influence of the Grail myth" improved "the brilliant chivalry and low morality of the original Arthurian romances," and she recommends Wolfram's poem to her readers because its morality is "true" and its lesson still "much needed." By the time she finished she was a considerable immoralist, insisting that Lance and Grail disguised the life-giving symbols of a sexual rite.

Miss Weston began as a student of literary texts, a romance scholar like any other. By 1901, in *The Legend of Sir Lancelot,* she was insisting:

> If the Arthurian tradition consists (as it admittedly does) largely of folk-lore and mythic elements, it must, so far as these elements are concerned, be examined and criticised on methods recognized and adopted by experts in those branches of knowledge—and not treated on literary lines and literary evidence alone.

At first she was quite inconsistent and unsure about the nature of "folk-lore and mythic elements." In 1896 she uses "legend" to mean untrue stories about historical figures; by 1899 it means untrue stories about characters whether historical or mythic; in 1900 it equates with "folktale motif"; the next year it seems to mean "based on history." As late as *The Quest of the Holy Grail* in 1913, "folk-lore" was understood as something entirely separate from myth and ritual, so that in the motif of the hero as the king's sister's son she cannot see "the smallest trace of a ritual element." As for "myth" itself, at first it simply meant "untrue"; not until *From Ritual to Romance* does it consistently mean "a story with an accompanying rite," and even there she sometimes seems uncertain as to whether it arose out of the rite or preceded it.

Before *Themis,* the principal agent in Miss Weston's theoretical development was *The Golden Bough.* She appears to have missed the first edition in 1890, but not the second in 1900. *The Legend of Sir Lancelot* in 1901 not only cites *The Golden Bough,* but fixes on its archetype, the champion "who slew the slayer, and shall himself be slain," and identifies the father-son or uncle-nephew combat in Celtic mythology and Arthurian romance with it. In the preface to *From Ritual to Romance* Miss Weston sums up two decades of indebtedness:

> Like many others I owe to Sir J. G. Frazer the initial inspiration which set me, as I may truly say, on the road to the Grail Castle. Without the guidance of *The Golden*

> *Bough* I should probably, as the late M. Gaston Paris happily expressed it, still be wandering in the forest of Broceliande!

The experience resembles her later conversion by *Themis*. Miss Weston writes:

> Some years ago, when fresh from the study of Sir J. G. Frazer's epoch-making work, *The Golden Bough*, I was struck by the resemblance existing between certain features of the Grail story, and characteristic details of the Nature Cults described. The more closely I analysed the tale, the more striking became the resemblance, and I finally asked myself whether it were not possible that in this mysterious legend—mysterious alike in its character, its sudden appearance, the importance apparently assigned to it, followed by as sudden and complete a disappearance —we might not have the confused record of a ritual, once popular, later surviving under conditions of strict secrecy.

"Such a development of his researches naturally lay outside the range of Sir J. G. Frazer's work," she adds, "but posterity will probably decide that, like many another patient and honest worker, he 'builded better than he knew.'" "I avow myself an impenitent believer in Sir J. G. Frazer's main theory," she concludes, "and as I have said above, I hold that theory to be of greater and more far-reaching importance than has been hitherto suspected."

By this time, of course, Frazer was himself a penitent believer, and had repudiated the theory of the ritual origin of mythology in the prefaces to the third edition of *The Golden Bough* in the years before 1915. If Miss Weston was aware of this, she did not care. Having come all the way from Nutt and the solar mythologists, she was now firmly set on the earth, studying myth as a product of human activity. A textual scholar in the 1890s, a venturer into folklore and mythology in the 1900s, by the second decade of the century she had recognized her wider field. She wrote in the preface to *The Quest of the Holy Grail:* "If the study of the Grail Quest fall, as I hold it does, within the field of Comparative Religion, we can call to our aid scholars whose interest lies otherwise outside the fascinating, but to some minds perhaps superficial, realm of romantic literature." The preface to *From Ritual to Romance* concludes:

> The problem involved was not one of Folk-lore, not even one of Literature, but of Comparative Religion in its widest sense.
>
> Thus, while I trust that my co-workers in the field of Arthurian research will accept these studies as a permanent contribution to the elucidation of the Grail problem, I would fain hope that those scholars who labor in a wider field, and to whose works I owe so much, may find in the results here set forth elements that may prove of real value in the study of the evolution of religious belief.

The acceptance of Miss Weston's work has been not quite as she hoped. Her early work, when she was still primarily a textual scholar, was enthusiastically received. *The Legend of Sir Lancelot* was acknowledged in *Notes and Queries* as "A scientific as well as a delightful exposition of views the value and significance of which future discoveries are likely to establish," and by Walter W. Greg in *Folk-Lore* as "a piece of patient, careful, and honest investigation," of which "it is not easy to speak too highly." As she worked her way toward ritual theory, her fellow scholars became more critical, dismissing her origin theory in *The Quest* as "ingenious speculation" and finding much of *From Ritual to Romance* entirely irrelevant to Arthurian scholarship.

We may take the reaction of Roger Sherman Loomis as typical. In 1927, while Miss Weston was still alive, Loomis' *Celtic Myth and Arthurian Romance* came out in support of her reading of the Grail mysteries. "One may not find so convincing Miss Weston's views on the transmission and later history of the material," he wrote, "but her main thesis, as developed in her books, is amply supported." Within a few years, he had changed his mind, "for lack of valid and clearly pertinent evidence," and he inserted a retraction of his Westonism into the remaining copies of the book. By 1963, in *The Grail*, Loomis could write scornfully: "Others may resent an interpretation which explodes Miss Weston's fascinating theory of a lost mystery cult, conveyed by Eastern merchants from the Mediterranean to Britain, and of secret initiation rites enacted in remote ages—a theory also discredited by the absence of any reference to such a cult in the mass of medieval testimony on heresy."

Outside the field of Arthurian specialization, one medievalist, John Speirs, has made brilliant application and extension of Miss Weston's work in *Medieval English Poetry* (1957), particularly the chapter on *Sir Gawayne and the Grene Knight*, which first appeared in *Scrutiny* in 1949. Those "scholars who labor in a wider field," for whose approbation Miss Weston hoped, accepted *From Ritual to Romance* as definitive from the first. "Scholarly, scientific work through and through," said R. R. Marett. *From Ritual to Romance* "has solved what had been a problem for 700 years," E. S. Hartland wrote. "The more I read it, the more conviction grows," said Jane Harrison. "The argument is self-evident, once stated," was the opinion of F. M. Cornford.

By 1927, when Miss Harrison wrote the preface to the second edition of *Themis*, the ritual theory seemed to be victorious everywhere. She wrote:

> But the real delight was to find that these notions which for me, with my narrow classical training, had been, I confess, largely *a priori* guesses had become for the new school matters of historical certainty, based on definite facts, and substantiated by a touch-and-handle knowledge and a sort of robust common-sense to which I

could lay no claim. To find myself thus outdated was sheer joy.

Almost immediately afterwards, the reaction set in, and soon the newer school of scholars had no such certainty. The progenitor of the theory, Frazer, had shown the way with his own retraction, convinced by a false syllogism and impelled largely (as I show in *The Tangled Bank*) by Unitarian Christian fears for the historical Jesus. The scholarly pendulum swung, not beyond Jane Harrison and Jessie Weston, but back to the nineteenth-century theories that they had discredited. Loomis in his 1963 book went back to Alfred Nutt and the Grail as a Celtic food talisman, where Miss Weston had begun in 1894. As a result, Miss Weston's work has been handed over to mythologists, literary critics, and English teachers. But who knows what Arthurian scholars of the future will make of it? The ritual theory of myth, like the year daimon, is many times slain and dismembered, but many times resurrected and rejuvenated.

1965

Myths and Mothers

JOHANN JACOB BACHOFEN was born in Basel in 1815, of parents both descended from solid old burgher families. He attended a private school where Jakob Burckhardt was a fellow pupil, and then the high school where Nietzsche later taught. He went on to the University of Basel, then to the University of Berlin, where he studied law. He became an authority on the history of Roman law, and through it became interested in ancient custom. In 1842 Bachofen was made a judge. He took a horseback trip through Greece in 1851 and wrote an unpublished *Greek Journey*. After that, he wrote extensively on myth, custom, and general cultural subjects. In 1865, at the age of fifty, and some years after his mother's death, he married a young girl of the Burckhardt family, and in 1866 he became the father of a son and retired from his judgeship. Most of his books and articles were written in the following two decades. Bachofen died of a stroke in 1887.

Mother Right, Bachofen's principal book, presents a theory of cultural history. It argues that mankind has gone through three great stages of social organization: sexual promiscuity, followed by Amazonism as a reaction against it; matriarchy, and patriarchy. Because of "the universal qualities of human nature," these stages are world-wide. The evolution is teleological, from a "bestial" condition to "the highest calling, the sublimation of earthly existence to the purity of the divine father principle." His study, Bachofen writes, "may offer firm ground for a confident belief that through all vicissitudes the human race will find the power to complete its triumphant journey upward from the depths, from the night of matter to the light of a celestial-spiritual principle."

This social evolution has endless correspondences in the natural world. "Hetaerism" or promiscuity is equated with the earth and Aphrodite, matriarchy with the moon and Demeter, patriarchy with the sun and Apollo. "Hetaerism follows the prototype of wild plant life; the strict Demetrian law of marriage as it prevailed in highly developed matriarchy follows that of the tilled field." Matriarchy makes a choice of the left side over the right, of the youngest child over the first-born, of "the moon over the sun, of the conceiving earth over the fecundating sea, of the dark aspect of death over the luminous aspect of growth, of the dead over the living, of mourning over rejoicing"; patriarchy chooses the opposites. Matriarchy begins the day at midnight; patriarchy at dawn.

All this is not random but ordered. Bachofen asks rhetorically, "Should man, the supreme manifestation of the cosmos, alone be free from its laws?" "We find not disorder but system," he adds, "not fancy but necessity." As firmly as his contemporary Darwin, he disclaims saltation: "The development of the human race knows no leaps, no sudden progressions." But the progress is slowly but surely upward: "One great law governs the juridical development of man. It advances from the material to the immaterial, from the physical to the metaphysical, from tellurism to spirituality." Ultimately, at the end of the line, "law becomes love." Underlying this evolution there is a dualism almost Zoroastrian in its scope: below and above, darkness and light, earth and sun, woman and man. Progress is dialectic: each "fundamental principle presupposes a contrary principle, in opposition to which it came into being."

That then is Bachofen's great vision: humanity ceaselessly struggling, and in the struggle rising from the muck to the heavens. What is wrong with it? First, most of his evidence comes from myths, and Bachofen does not understand the nature of myths or how they originate. Thus, Greek traditions of bloody resistance to the new religion of Dionysus, such as the myth embodied in Euripides' *The Bacchae*, must be historically accurate, Bachofen says, since they are so alien to "the later Dionysian spirit" of joy "that it is impossible to regard them as the fabrication of a later period." Myths of Amazonism, in another example, show that at some early time "bands of warlike maidens poured triumphantly through Asia Minor, Greece, Italy, Gaul." It is easy for us now to see that the resistance of Pentheus and his like to Dionysus is a ritual role, not history; that Amazonism records a cult, not a society. But Bachofen took myths for historical records. "All the myths relating to our subject" he writes, "embody a memory of real events experienced by the human race." In his view, myths are history elaborated in religious terms: "Historical events provide the content, religion the form and expression"; or, as he defines it in *The Myth of Tanaquil,* "Myth is nothing other than a picture of the national experience in the light of religious faith."

For all his tone of certainty ("The mythical tradition may be taken as . . . a highly reliable historical source"; "Unquestionably this explanation is historically sound"), Bachofen's history is neither reliable nor sound. As Professor Boas says in his preface to *Myth, Religion and Mother Right* (the first English selection from Bachofen's monumental study, *Das Mutter-recht*) Bachofen's theory "is almost universally discredited," as is what R. R. Marett called "the fallacious notion of a unilineal evolution." Anthropologists have never encountered any people whose social organization was either promiscuity or matriarchy.

Both Professor Boas and Professor Campbell in his introduction note that Bachofen's racial memory is "on the way," in Campbell's words, to Carl G. Jung's "archetypes" and "collective unconscious," but those entities seem no less bogus than the Universal Hetaerism. Beyond that, Bachofen is sometimes misled by his ancient sources, as when they confuse matriliny (descent and inheritance through the mother, which is fairly common) with matriarchy, and he is sometimes overcredulous, as when he decides that it is "highly probable" that the ancient Ethiopians mated in public because they worshiped the dog (one might as readily conclude that they communicated by barking), or accepts without question Strabo's tissue of nonsense about general incest with mother and sister among the ancient Arabs. *Mother Right* sometimes falls into jargon, as in a statement about "Iamidian prophecy": "Maternal-tellurian at its lowest, Melampodian stage, it becomes wholly paternal-Apollonian at its highest level."

But for all his faults, Bachofen cannot simply be dismissed. His neat unilineal evolution is not quite so neat and unilineal, since he recognizes "relapse" and all sorts of variation. Sometimes behind myth he sees not history but ritual, or custom, or belief. He writes in *The Myth of Tanaquil*: "But to deny the historicity of a legend does not divest it of its value. What cannot have happened was nonetheless thought. External truth is replaced by inner truth. Instead of facts we find actions of the spirit." In the same book he anticipates our modern functional sense of myths: "for the ancients they were elements of power."

In interpreting myths and symbols, Bachofen is a most sensitive and imaginative iconographer. In an autobiographical essay, he writes: "There are two roads to knowledge—the longer, slower, more arduous road of rational combination and the shorter path of the imagination, traversed with the force and swiftness of electricity." The symbol is this electrical leap, and the myth is its temporal "exegesis." Bachofen is a brilliant exegeticist and translater of both, turning symbols into rich narratives and myths into compelling pictures.

If Bachofen understands neither the nature nor the origin of myths, he has a superb understanding of their dynamics in time. His philosophic emphasis is on becoming rather than being, and he asks, he says, not only What? but Whence? and Whither? Thus he recognizes that the original meanings of myths become lost and misunderstood, and that they are replaced by secondary interpretations and rationalizations. Noting a tendency of men "to replace the incomprehensible by what was comprehensible from the standpoint of their own culture," he continues: "Old features are overlaid by new ones, the venerable figures of the matriarchal past are introduced to contemporaries in forms consonant with the spirit of the new period, harsh features are presented in a softened light; institutions, attitudes, motives, passions are reappraised from a contemporary point of view." His account of the myth of Tanaquil shows ancient material preserved "in spite and because of the loss of its underlying idea, and foreign material adapted to native modes of thought, and he recognizes that the life of the myth is always a diminishment: "The vestiges of the supernatural and miraculous, of transcendent beliefs, arouse contradiction; they are replaced by rational causalities, or merely ridiculed as the absurd products of a childish past. . . . The final outcome is a petty empirical pragmatism, in which the religious figures of the older Asiatic mankind are reduced to mortal figures of the new era."

More important than Bachofen's contributions to the study of mythology is his essentially feminine imaginative vision of the world, what Jane Harrison in *Themis* (a book supremely embodying that vision) calls "the Stoic conception of the world as a living animal, a thing not to be coerced and restrained, but reverently wooed." Thus in *An Essay on Ancient Mortuary Symbolism*, Bachofen sees death as "the helper of life" ("Death is the mother of beauty," Wallace Stevens says similarly in "Sunday Morning"); he identifies the mythic mother in *Mother Right:* "ultimately she is the earth": he warns, in *The Myth of Tanaquil*, against "approaching nature in a carping, argumentative frame of mind instead of subordinating ourselves to the phenomenon." "True criticism," he remarks grandly, "resides in the material itself, and knows no other standard than its own objective law."

Ultimately *Mother Right* is a paean to the marvel of women, on the order of Robert Graves's *The White Goddess,* and like that curious book it is more profitably read metaphorically than literally. The prestige accorded womanhood, Bachofen writes, gives his matriarchies "a character of archaic sublimity." He continues: "Woman at this stage is the repository of all culture, of all benevolence, of all devotion, of all concern for the living and grief for the dead." "She counters violence with peace," he adds, "enmity with conciliation, hate with love." "Mystery is the true essence of every religion," Bachofen explains, and it comes from the woman: "Mystery is rooted in her very nature." Like the White Goddess, Bachofen's Earth Mother is not wholly benign; she too has her Hecate aspect: "How hard it is, at all times, for women to observe moderation," he writes, and goes on to talk of "woman's insatiable bloodthirst." (Campbell's introduction notes that Bachofen's fascination with the lost world of "the mothers" "has been attributed, possibly with reason, to a lifelong devotion to his own young and beautiful mother." This Oedipal interpretation helps to explain an occasional oddly personal tone in the book, as when Bachofen exclaims, "How natural we now find Hesiod's world, with its dominant mother lavishing eternal loving care on an ever dependent son.")

The revolution that Bachofen placed in history, the seizure of rule by the men from the women, is now known to have occurred in religion, in the replacement of the ancient Earth Mothers by male sky divinities. As Campbell points out, Bachofen wrote before any of the Neolithic mother goddesses had been excavated. If his prescience came from a fixation on his own mother, his vast love poem to her has had a curious history. It convinced the American amateur anthropologist Lewis Henry Morgan, who in turn became the official anthropologist of Marx and Engels, so that a lost Eden of Matriarchy in the ancient past is now dogma in the Communist half of the world. How furious this bourgeois Swiss jurist—who wrote proudly, "I remain faithful to the old conservative spirit"— would have been at his conquest.

1968

Illumination for the Unchurched

T HE OLD TESTAMENT (OT), quaintly regarded as the Bible (*Tanach*) by the Jews, is becoming fashionable these days. Much of this was undoubtedly occasioned by the publication of the New English Bible (NEB) translation, which had been awaited since the NEB New Testament (NT), in 1961, and in process since 1948.

When I reviewed the NEB NT I preached mainly on the dangers of making a Bible, or sacred mystery book, too easily comprehensible. We see a classic example of the problem here in the famous passage, Exodus 4.24–26, the J-writer's origin myth of circumcision, which is a bewilderment of pronouns without referents in all previous translations. The Authorized Version (AV) of 1611 reads (commendably using italics for words not in the Hebrew):

> And it came to pass by the way in the inn, that the LORD met him, and sought to kill him.
>
> Then Zipporah took a sharp stone, and cut off the foreskin of her son, and cast *it* at his feet, and said, Surely a bloody husband *art* thou to me.
>
> So he let him go: then she said, A bloody husband *thou art*, because of the circumcision.

This is how it reads in the NEB OT:

> During the journey, where they were encamped for the night, the LORD met Moses, meaning to kill him, but

Zipporah picked up a sharp flint, cut off her son's fore-
skin, and touched him with it, saying 'You are my blood-
bridegroom.' So the LORD let Moses alone. Then she
said, 'Blood-bridegroom by circumcision.'

This has gained enormously in clarity because the pronouns
have been given referents (on what authority I do not know,
since they seem unclear in the Hebrew), but the result is
somewhat less than edifying.

The NEB OT's introduction, by G. R. Driver, says the translators tried "to keep their language as close to current usage
as they could, while avoiding expressions likely to be proved
ephemeral," hoping thus to furnish "illumination" for "ordinary readers." C. H. Dodd, the general director of the whole
project, explained in a news release that "the work was not
primarily intended for reading in church," but was aimed
at "young people, the unchurched, and intelligent church-
goers." Professor Driver has defended the translators' practices at length in a letter to the New York *Times*, April 19,
1963, as means to the achievement of greater accuracy. But
it may be that greater accuracy in translating the Bible is in
itself indefensible, and perhaps even mischievous.

My other principal charge against the NEB NT in 1961 (and
I was far from alone in making it) was the extraordinary in-
elegance of the language, although (or because!) the entire
translation had been submitted to a "panel of literary advisers"
for style. The prose of the NEB OT is much less inelegant, perhaps to some extent in response to earlier criticism. I list a few
lines in Genesis which remind one of the NT howlers: Abraham's "If you really mean it—but do listen to me!" (23.13);
Joseph's "You might have known that a man like myself
would practise divination" (44.15); "turbulent as a flood"
instead of the traditional and lovely "unstable as water" in
Jacob's prophecy for Reuben (49.4). Since the NEB OT with
its Apocrypha (those books which were in the Bible of the
Jews of Alexandria, but not in that of the Jews of Jerusalem)

runs to formidable length, I studied only Genesis carefully, comparing it with a number of other English translations done over the past four and a half centuries, and checking words with the Hebrew of the Massoretic Text (MT) and the Greek of the Septuagint (LXX) where my little learning allowed.

A most remarkable phenomenon, in a translation done by a broad collaboration of British Christian churches, is the disappearance of the traditional Christian proof texts, those passages in the OT which were first interpreted by the Jews as divine foretellings of the Coming of the Messiah, and then by the Christians retrospectively as prophecies of Jesus Christ and the NT story. Thus in Gen. 3.15, God's statement that Eve's "seed" shall in the future bruise the head of the serpent, understood to be the conquest of Satan by Christ, loses all that when it is Eve's "brood" which shall strike at the serpent's head. Gen. 14.18, the famous foretelling of the Eucharist, where Melchizedek brings forth "bread and wine," is no longer anything of the sort, because he now serves Abram "food and wine." The most famous of all such Testimonia in Genesis, which led to the belief that the Messiah or Christ would come (or, later, *had* come) during the reign of Herod, the first non-Jewish king of the Jews, is Jacob's prediction for Judah at 49.10: "The sceptre shall not depart from Judah, nor a lawgiver from between his feet, until Shiloh come" ("Shiloh," probably from the root of *"shalom,"* was understood to be the Prince of Peace). Now in the NEB all Messianism has evaporated:

The sceptre shall not pass from Judah,
nor the staff from his descendants,
so long as tribute is brought to him

The truly radical loss comes not in Genesis, but in Job, ironically fulfilling F. F. Bruce's promise in *The English Bible* (1961) that "When the Old Testament part of the New English Bible appears, *Job* will read like a new book." It is the famous 19.25, 26, as generally translated the strongest affirmation of redemption and the resurrection of the body in the OT. In the AV it reads (and the italics show the fragmentary nature of the Hebrew):

> For I know *that* my redeemer liveth, and *that* he shall stand at the latter *day* upon the earth:
> And *though* after my skin *worms* destroy this *body*, yet in my flesh shall I see God:

The Revised Version (RV) of 1881 and the Revised Standard Version (RSV) of 1946 chip away at this glorious assurance, but by the time we reach the NEB it is no longer any assurance at all:

> But in my heart I know that my vindicator lives
> and that he will rise last to speak in court;
> and I shall discern my witness standing at my side
> and see my defending counsel, even God himself

In many of its departures from familiar readings, the NEB simply follow RV and RSV. Again, my examples are from Genesis: in 12.9, "south" becomes "Negeb," following RSV; in 14.2 "nations" returns to the Hebrew "Goyim," following both; in 24.22, what every early translation has as an "earring" for Rebecca, and the RV and RSV boldly have as a "ring," the NEB still more boldly has as "a gold nose-ring," and all three join in reading 24.47 as "Then I put the ring in her nose"; in 43.11, Jacobs sends Joseph pistachio nuts, as he does in RSV (after they had been simply "nuts" for centuries).

In other places in Genesis the NEB makes mysterious changes which have no precedent in any of the other English translations that I consulted. Thus in 21.16, in eight other translations, Hagar sits down one bowshot away from Abraham; in the NEB, it is *two* bowshots. In 24.63, when Rebecca's party is on its way, Isaac leaves the town, in earlier translations, to "pray" or to "meditate"; here, he goes out "hoping to meet them," with a footnote giving as an alternate reading, "to relieve himself." In 37.25, the Ishmaelite caravan to which

Judah hoped to sell Joseph carries, in earlier translations, "spice" or "spicery"; here it is "gum tragacanth" (RSV somewhat anticipates this with "gum"). In 40.2 and 40.7 the NEB translators decide, with no precedent in earlier translations, that Pharaoh's butler and baker are "two eunuchs."

Genesis as Myth and Other Essays by Edmund Leach, consists of three periodical pieces, with the long central one, "The Legitimacy of Solomon," being of particular interest. Leach is an anthropologist and Provost of King's College, Cambridge, and he is, perhaps for those reasons, so unsympathetic to Sir James G. Frazer that he fails to cast his essay in its natural form, the Plutarchian or Frazerian question, which is then answered, after a series of informative excurses, many pages or volumes later. Leach's question is: Why does the genealogy beginning The Gospel According to St. Matthew specifically list four women of dubious reputation—Tamar, Rachab, Ruth, and Bathsheba—in the ancestry of King Solomon? His answer is that this NT synopsis of OT genealogy shows that the Jews included in Solomon's ancestry Edomites, Canaanites, Moabites, and other of the peoples whose land they had seized, "so that he is the legitimate heir to all forms of land title however derived!"

This essay, like the other two, is an exercise in Lévi-Straussian structuralism, and a bolder one than the master would write, since Lévi-Strauss himself has taken the line that Old Testament mythology has been irrecoverably "deformed" by the intellectual operations of Biblical editors (that is, such compilers and overwriters as those the Higher Criticism called "P" and "D"). Leach's essay shows not only that structuralism works on OT material, but that it is also a functionalism ("the succession of Solomon to the throne of Israel is a myth which 'mediates' a major contradiction") and a dynamics ("In structuralist analysis, the elements of a myth—the 'symbols'—never have any intrinsic meaning," but when, for example, they become "permeated through and through with moral implications, the structure becomes 'dramatic' "). It is also profoundly nonhistorical or even antihistorical (" 'history' in the Old Testament has more in common with drama than with history," "King David and King Solomon are no more likely to be historical than are King Agamemnon and King Menelaus").

Leach's little book has its weaknesses, certainly. He feels that structural analysis requires him to treat the whole Bible as a unity *"regardless of the varying historical origins of its component parts,"* thereby voluntarily blinding the structuralist to many different authors with many different purposes at many different times; in any case, this is what Burke calls "the socializing of losses," since Leach seems almost totally unfamiliar with the Higher Criticism. He is gullible enough, or inconsistent enough, to believe in the existence of the mythic Twelve Tribes; he bases arguments on that frailest of reeds, "common-sense grounds"; he even believes (in the first, rather weak, essay) that this sort of analysis "could be done by a computer far better than by any human." Despite these faults, it is a pleasure to get so much good sense and usefulness about the OT from an anthropologist, at a time when Bible scholarship seems to have turned into a squirrel track and climbed a tree.

T. R. Henn, the author of *The Bible as Literature*, is President of St. Catherine's College, Cambridge, and a neighbor of Leach's. I should have been warned off his book by its title, which all but guarantees a work of irrelevance, and by the fact that I had earlier read his book on Yeats' poetry, *The Lonely Tower*, which casts no great quantity of light on that subject. Henn's volume is remarkable as the approach of a learned English professor to the Bible (mainly the OT) in 1970, in that it takes a position of almost fundamentalist historicity. David and Solomon were real kings of Israel; the Book of Psalms "took the name of David from its chief writer"; J's origin myth of circumcision, Ex. 4.24–26 (discussed above), shows "that we are dealing with the attempt to describe the attributes of Jehovah in their non-rational

form"; the episode of Noah's drunkenness "is mitigated somewhat by filial piety"; and so on endlessly.

In summary, Bible history "is a history of which the substantial accuracy is certified by archaeology and what contemporary documentation remains." Since I have already
said my say on the mythic nature of the entire Bible, and of
the New Testament in "History and Sacred History," I will
confine myself at present to noting that even Professor Henn
has moments of saving doubt. Thus: "The words of Christ at
the Last Supper, in their simplicity and beauty reflect what
ought to have been said on that occasion"; God in the Psalms
"is frequently given human attributes, which we must, of
course, construe in a figurative sense"; in regard to Job, at least,
"the findings of modern textual criticism" are useful; the three
authors of Isaiah "obtain to some extent their characteristic
unity from subsequent redactions"; in many of the stories of
the OT "what was accepted in childhood as fact has to be
reinterpreted allegorically."

As if being a Bible Euhemerist were not enough, Henn is
also a Jungian ("I believe, with Jung, that the human mind
brings to the encounter [with the mythologems and the arche-
types] a creative activity") and a Zionist (writing during the
Six-Day War in 1967, he proudly reprints Psalm 83 as "of
peculiar interest at the time of writing," and he reminds us
that the Land of Canaan promised by God's covenant with
Abram in Gen. 15.18 extends from the "river of Egypt" to the
Euphrates—as Ben Gurion might say, with Numbers 21.29,
"Woe to thee, Moab"). Henn is in addition a literalist ("The
majority of the provisions of the Mosaic Law are admirable
sanitary provisions"; the Song of Deborah marks the first time
"that infantry had triumphed over armour"; Jezebel behaved
in a fashion inconsistent with Israelite democracy because she
"was a Phoenician woman, who understood only tyranny";
"Lot was a notorious figure, both for his rescue from Sodom,
the turning of his wife into a pillar of salt, and his subsequent
drunken incest instigated by his husbandless daughters").

Finally, Henn is so slipshod that he refers to Professor S. Foster Damon as "Damon Foster" and has poor King David (as though his sins were not great enough) steal Naboth's vineyard and thus stir up the redoubtable Elijah.

Well, win a few, lose a few. In the NEB OT, I lose one of my favorite lines in all the Bible, Hosea 4.11, which reads in the AV, "Whoredom and wine and new wine take away the heart." In the NEB it is now reduced to: ". . . sacred prostitution. New wine and old steal my people's wits." But I gain a fine new opening for the Tower of Babel story, Gen. 11.1: "Once upon a time."

1970

History and Sacred History

I HAVE COME to the conclusion, as a longtime student of the Bible, archaeology, and folklore, that every person and event in the New Testament is sacred history—that is, myth believed to be history—except for the names of such public figures as Caesar, Herod, and Pilate. (In this it resembles the Old Testament, which is almost entirely sacred history before the Babylonian Captivity.) I am thus more than a little interested in *The Archaeology of the New Testament: The Life of Jesus and the Beginnings of the Early Church*. The author is Jack Finegan, who received his licentiate in theology, magna cum laude, from the University of Berlin in 1934, and is a minister of the Disciples of Christ and a professor of New Testament at the Pacific School of Religion and the Graduate Theological Union in Berkeley. The Reverend Dr. Finegan not only knows the Bible languages well, but he is solidly versed in the Talmud, the Qur'an, and related material. His book puts itself forward as a scholarly basing of the New Testament story in archaeology and reputable history. I have studied Finegan's book with care, and, alas, despite all of its author's learning and my own ignorance, I still find no shred of archaeological or historical evidence underlying the New Testament. *The Archaeology of the New Testament* appears to be based on nothing more than a profusion of fallacies, which I shall try to list and illustrate.

1. Finegan does not understand, or ignores, the nature of historical evidence. Thus St. Jerome and Paulinus of Nola, both in the late fourth century, attest that Tammuz (Adonis) was worshiped in the grotto in Bethlehem where Christ was

313

born, the latter adding that this was a deliberate defilement by the Emperor Hadrian. Finegan concludes: "From both Jerome and Paulinus, then, we have evidence that the identification of the Bethlehem cave as the place of the birth of Jesus was already older than the time of Hadrian, i.e., it must go back into the first century." All that we have evidence for, in fact, is that Christian writers in the late fourth century believed something; we have no evidence whatsoever about the first century. One can best see Finegan's remoteness from historical scholarship in his discussion of the famous upper room in Jerusalem. He writes:

> No doubt the use of *cenaculum* for the upper room of the last supper and also for the upper room of the time after the ascension furthered the supposition that one and the same room was in question. Although that supposition is not fully demonstrable it is not impossible. That the same room was still the center of the disciples on the day of Pentecost (Ac 2:1) is also at least possible. Still later, many of the disciples were gathered together in the house of Mary, the mother of John Mark (Ac 12:12) and the further supposition that this was the house of the "upper room" is likewise not impossible although not fully demonstrable.

First, it must be said that "not fully demonstrable" is a term in Finegan's vocabulary meaning "not in any respect demonstrable." Second, and more important, Finegan has taken the basic Judeo-Christian idea of timeless ritual recurrence—that the Exodus is occurring AT PRESENT during the Passover Seder, that Christ is resurrected THIS Easter or Sunday or Mass—and misunderstood it reductively to mean that a number of "historical" events transpired in the same room; that is, that statements about religious mysteries are really statements about history or geography.

2. He understands the nature of archaeological evidence

but ignores it. "In its procedure," Finegan writes in the book's preface, "archaeology must be as rigorously scientific as possible." He remarks later, of the possible grave of a famous rabbi: "But the grave carries no inscription whatsoever, and the identification remains uncertain." This fairly recognizes the basic archaeological principle, so much betrayed by our current Schliemannizers, that nothing is Agamemnon's Tomb or Nestor's Palace or Solomon's Stables (the last built and named by the Crusaders, apparently) unless a reliable inscription says that it is. But when he gets to New Testament problems Finegan forgets this principle. Nazareth furnishes a good example. Nazareth is not mentioned in the Old Testament, Josephus, or the Talmud, and it and its adjectives do not occur in any Epistle or in Revelation, only in the latest stratum of the Gospels and Acts. It has been the opinion of many Bible scholars that no "Nazareth" existed at the time, and that the Gospel identification of such a place as Jesus' home village is some sort of misunderstanding. (In my view, of the Hebrew "*hanozri*," the "Nazarite" used for certain consecrated Old Testament figures who were believed to be God's own: Samson is the best-known example). Finegan is happy to refute all this skepticism, since recent archaeology has established an occupation of the site going back to the Bronze Age. Alas, no inscription names it as Nazareth, or anything, until about 300 A.D., when a Jewish inscription names a "Nazareth" somewhere. Or let us take the happy case in which Finegan discusses a real inscription and proclaims proudly: "Other archaeological witness to the history recounted above is provided by the coins of Aelia"—and the history attested by these inscriptions turns out to be that of the Emperor Hadrian! Or the tomb of Christ, which was lost until the time of Constantine, miraculously "came to light" then, and was, says Eusebius, "Beautified with rare columns and profusely enriched with the most splendid decorations of every kind"— which is Finegan's curious way of telling us that an official

315

"tomb of Christ" was established and tarted up in the reign of Constantine. Finegan includes a drawing entitled "Hypothetical Reconstruction of the tomb of Jesus," adding that St. Cyril of Jerusalem "could very well have seen the tomb as it was before the changes made by Constantine's workmen" —or, indeed, could very well NOT have.

3. He has no non-Christian or disinterested evidence. The principal exception to this (there are a few minor ones) is the Jewish historian Josephus, where Finegan relies on passages long discredited as forgeries and interpolations (two of Josephus' three Christian references are unknown to Origen, and have clearly been written in between the times of Origen and Eusebius). The use of Christian evidence, mainly Bible evidence, is of course a circular argument, since Finegan is getting material from the Bible and Church tradition, and then using it to prove the truth of the Bible and Church tradition. Many of Finegan's non-biblical early Christian sources are equally spurious or dubious: he treats Eusebius, a writer as credulous as Geoffrey of Monmouth, as though he were what Eusebius himself comically calls "authentic history"; he accepts as fact the legendary martyrdoms of Ignatius and Polycarp; he relies seriously on a jumble of apocryphal and pseudepigraphic writings such as the "Shepherd of Hermas," the "Letters of Barnabas," the "Odes of Solomon," the "Acts of John," the "Acts of Thomas," the "Sybylline Oracles," and such.

4. He believes that truth lies in the "earliest tradition" if it can be discovered. Finegan's assumption is the widely held common-sense one that myth is corrupted and glamorized history, that folk currency distorts and augments, and that the earliest form of a story will be the most historically accurate and the least supernatural. The only thing wrong with this widespread assumption is that it does not fit the evidence; wherever we are able to study oral transmission over a long period, the process is without exception the reverse: to make things more credible and less supernatural. Folk memory has

no slightest interest in preserving what we call "history," as Lord Raglan demonstrates in *The Hero*, and its "relics" are goods produced for a changing market. (Finegan observes, without comment, that Theodosius in 530 A.D. saw the bed of the healed paralytic at Bethesda, but that by the time of the pilgrimage of the Anonymous of Piacenza in 570 A.D. it had been replaced by the chain with which Judas hanged himself.) Finegan takes folk memory seriously: if there is "a tradition of very long standing" about someone someplace, it shows that he existed there; Finegan does not make the logical corollary that if there are heads of John the Baptist in Genoa, Damascus, and Constantinople, there were at least three John the Baptists. In regard to this personage, of all unlikely historical figures, Finegan is most sweetly reasonable: since John's parents were so old at his birth, he must have been orphaned early; an orphan child could not have survived alone "in the wilderness" (Luke 1:80) unless some such group as the Essenes adopted him. But Finegan admits that John was engaged in an "enactment of the role of Elijah . . . in surroundings associated with Elijah," which is his curious way of saying that the New Testament John the Baptist is a fulfillment of the Old Testament prophet Elijah, the requisite forerunner of the Messiah. As such, whether child or man, he could have fed himself on locusts and wild honey, or been fed by ravens, or lived on air, or done anything else that a supernatural being can do.

5. Finegan uses the material selectively, sifting out as true only what seems plausible to him. One brief example of this should suffice, again related to the figure of the Baptist. Finegan notes a story in "The Protevangelium of James" that when Elizabeth fled with her infant son John to save him from Herod's Massacre of the Innocents, "a mountain was rent asunder and received her." Finegan comments: "Legendary as this is, the reference is at any rate also to the hill country" —that is, it does not make the writer's point, that mountains cleave to protect those ordained to do the work of the Lord,

but Finegan's point, that John the Baptist grew up in the hill country around Jerusalem.

6. His book is a tissue of equivocations, half-statements, and hinted suggestions. There are literally hundreds of these, doing the work which real evidence would do in a work of genuine historical scholarship. Those on page 6 should serve as a representative sample: "it may be supposed," "is difficult to understand, unless," "it is at least possible," "is therefore at least hypothetically possible." The loveliest of these, to my taste, is Finegan's statement about the site at Nazareth, where no trace was found of the church believed to have been built there in the time of Constantine. "It is possible that an earlier structure was torn down when the Byzantine church was built," he writes, and indeed it is possible, since if it was torn down, it wouldn't be there. Like his illustrious predecessor, Dr. Werner Keller, the author of *The Bible as History* and *The Bible as History in Pictures*, Finegan sometimes prints pictures which a careless reader might fairly take to show more than they do in fact show. Thus he illustrates a debate on the location of the sycamore tree which Zaccheus climbed in order to get a better view of Jesus, with a photograph of an elderly sycamore with very low, climbable branches, as though it were the actual tree involved. He similarly prints a photograph of a "very large and very old" olive tree in the Garden of Gethsemane at present, as though it were a tree by which Jesus had prostrated himself and prayed. Finegan makes neither claim, but the pictures make the claim for him. He also prints two photographs of the "tomb of Lazarus," inside and out, without a word about any archaeological investigation into its authenticity.

7. He has a most impressive win-both-ways system. The model of this is the old joke about the torn umbrella: I never borrowed it; I returned it in perfect condition; it was torn when you lent it to me. For a simple example of the umbrella excuse, Finegan says of the early Christian pilgrimages to the

Holy Land: "While the genuineness of the sites is not proved by this alone, it is at any rate clear that Melito and the others would not have made their journeys if they had not believed that the places they wished to see were still identifiable and accessible." For a more complex example, there is Finegan's discussion of the site near Jericho of the Threshing Floor of Atad mentioned in Gen. 50:10. Eusebius located it as two miles west of the River Jordan, and Finegan comments: "The fact that the passage in Genesis puts the place 'beyond the Jordan' can be explained by supposing that the statement is phrased from the point of view of Joseph's party as they came up from Egypt. On the other hand, the sight may have been originally in Transjordan and transferred to the west side for the convenience of visiting pilgrims. It is not, however, mentioned in any of the ancient pilgrim itineraries." Finegan's characteristic form is equivocation, as when he writes of the tradition that Jesus was born in a cave: "In such tradition there was a recognizable tendency to localize events in caves, on the other hand caves have actually provided habitation and shelter for men and beasts in Palestine from ancient times until now." The most charming example of Finegan's win-both-ways argument is in connection with the theory of Charles Clermont-Ganneau that, since an ossuary found near the Bethany road had inscriptions naming an Eleazar, Lazarus, Simon, and Martha, the graves of the Lazarus-Mary-Martha family had been discovered. Finegan comments characteristically: "Needless to say, this interpretation has been contradicted by others, yet remains deserving of very careful consideration." I would add only a few remarks. First, that Clermont-Ganneau was a traitor to the noblest traditions of French *gloire*, since Lazarus is known (by the *Golden Legend* at least) to have been martyred in Marseilles, Martha to have domesticated a dragon at Tarascon and died peacefully in her Provençal bed, and Mary too, to have done great works in the Provençal countryside before her death there. Second, that making this sort of induction from common names, or saying that it deserves "very careful consideration," is on the order of deciding that a Mexico City graveyard containing inscriptions naming a Joseph, Mary, and Jesus is the last resting-place of the Holy Family.

8. His book is a tissue of logical fallacies, mainly non-sequiturs and undistributed middles. Melito, Bishop of Sardis, the first known Christian pilgrim to the Holy Land, says "accordingly when I went to the East and came to the place where these things were preached and done, I learned accurately the books of the Old Testament, and send them to you." On the basis of this explicit venture into Old Testament textual scholarship, Finegan erects the following: "From this statement we can conclude that the important places in Gospel history were actually being shown to visitors at that time, in the middle of the second century." Origen writes in *Contra Celsum*" in the third century (like Melito, he too had gone to Palestine in pursuit of Old Testament texts) of Jesus: "the cave in Bethlehem is pointed out where he was born and the manger in the cave where he was wrapped in swaddling clothes." Finegan concludes, most improperly, from this: "Origen is the first Christian to leave explicit eyewitness testimony of this sort to places of the Gospel history." He goes on later to improvise even more freely on the text, saying that Origen "speaks as if he himself were one of those to whom the cave had been shown," and adds further, "the characteristic formula, 'is pointed out,' doubtless attests a tradition of very long standing." Doubtless.

9. The work falls between two very different books, each valid in its own way. One is the traditional, modest, and secular "A Survey of Palestinian Archaeology" or "Daily Life in the Time of Jesus." The other is the frankly religious "The New Testament Retold for Modern Man," or "Sacred History of the God Jesus." For the second purpose, sacred history, the Gospels are probably preferable to anything Finegan could write. In his preface, he places himself with the early pilgrims "in contrast with the widely spread modern opinion" that the

artifacts of archaeology "are obviously not of the substance of the Biblical faith," adding his characteristic "but," that there is a sense in which they are. The first part of his subtitle, "The Life of Jesus," is used as a running head on the left-hand pages for most of the book, and it serves to focus the work precisely between the two reputable books it might have been.

10. The author is utterly oblivious to the Higher Criticism. He quotes Jesus' prediction of the destruction of the Temple in Matthew 24:2: "There shall not be left here one stone upon another, that shall not be thrown down." Finegan suggests this as the sort of sensible preaching against earthly majesty which Jesus would naturally make "when the disciples were impressed by the mighty buildings of the temple area." In fact, no informed schoolgirl teaching a Sunday school class in our century dares date this "prediction" (or, indeed, the earliest form of any Gospel) before 70 A.D., since no Jew would conceivably have publicly predicted the destruction of the Temple before it occurred (and, in fact, otherworldly Christianity itself, as a Jewish heresy, is inconceivable before the destruction of the Temple). Finegan does not even have any idea of the role of Testimonias (lists of passages from the Old Testament and its Apocrypha into which Messianic predictions had been read) in shaping the Gospel story. When Jesus, on Palm Sunday, orders an ass and a colt the foal of an ass in order to ride in triumph into Jerusalem (rather like taking two taxis), Finegan seems surprised: "He who otherwise, so far as we know, had walked all over Palestine, including the long steep ascent from Jericho, chose to ride at last into Jerusalem." But He is alleged to have done so by the Gospel writers because of the passage from Zachariah 9:9 in every Messianic Testimonia: "Rejoice greatly, O daughter of Zion; shout, O daughter of Jerusalem: behold, thy King cometh unto thee: he is just, and having salvation, lowly, and riding upon an ass, and upon a colt the foal of an ass."

11. For all his ministry in the Disciples of Christ, and his

never denying a New Testament miracle, the author seems to be a rationalist. Noting a statement by St. Jerome that John the Baptist is buried near the prophet Elisha, Finegan explains: "it may be judged not purely accidental if the disciples of John chose to inter him not beside Elijah, which would of course have been impossible according to II Kings 2:11, but in the place where rested the man who had inherited the spirit and mantle of Elijah, namely, Elisha." But in Christian belief John is not a conniving imitator of Elijah, but the true prophet Elijah returned to earth as the forerunner of the Messiah, while Christ himself (as his miracles clearly show) fulfills Elisha. Thus the adjacent tombs of John and Elisha were shown to Jerome's friend Paula as monuments to Elijah and Elisha, or John and Jesus, or any form of the basic Bible pair of Foreteller and Foretold.

For a somewhat pricklier example of rationalism, we have Finegan's statement that Jesus' healing, on the Sabbath, of the man ill for 38 years (John 5:8) "became one in a series of circumstances which led finally to the death of Jesus in the same city." Here some questions seem in order. Does Finegan believe that Christ was passively put to death because his acts offended pious and Sabbatarian Jews, or does he believe that as God He chose to sacrifice Himself to redeem mankind? Does he believe that the Jews of the time crucified all Sabbath violators and healers on the Sabbath? Does he believe in fact that the Jews killed Christ? In any case, Finegan does not seem to have much interest in the Resurrection, since his book deals with it in the most perfunctory of fashions, principally in a discussion of which of two Arab towns is the site of the ancient Emmaus. However, Finegan manages to be at once a rationalist (one who looks for rational explanations of supernatural phenomena) without being in the least a skeptic. In a book published in 1970, for example, he does not question the sort of thing which was questioned by that great doctor of the Church, Origen, in the third century. In his *Commentary on*

John, Origen says, among many other examples of skepticism, that casting the money changers out of the Temple without any resistance on their part would have been among the greatest miracles of Jesus, "if it really happened." In general, Origen argued for replacing the "sensible" Gospel with a "spiritual" one, and the historical Jesus by the Gospel itself, the divine Logos or Word. St. Augustine similarly wrote in the early fifth century, in "The City of God:" "Were it not for the authority of the Church, I should put no faith in the Gospels," and Augustine too turned to allegorical and spiritual readings of the Gospel stories.

Even such modern atheists as myself, if they are to take the Bible seriously, must transform it from spurious history into something more significant—spurious history could not have so changed the world. Christ's feedings and healings in the Gospels for example, are clearly not humanitarian but allegorical and tendentious: the True Bread of Christianity feeds, where other religions spiritually starve; the True Vision and True Way of Christianity enable the blind to see and the lame to walk, where competing religions leave them spiritually blind and lame, if they have not in fact blinded and lamed them. Does Finegan believe in Christ's feedings and healings, and if so, in what sense?

12. Finally, the author is touchingly romantic. John the Baptist, for example, is "he who fearlessly challenged Herod and Herodias." Finegan knows, as any student of archaeology must, that Jewish and Christian sites were built on earlier pagan sites, that even Bethlehem, the sacred city of David and Jesus, the House of Bread, was earlier the Canaanite Bit-Lahmi, and that Lahmi is apt to have been a Canaanite deity. But he cannot resist the idea, when St. Jerome reports that a grove of Tammuz overshadows Christ's birthplace in Bethlehem, that it is deliberate Roman Imperial profanation. He is enormously excited by the discovery in 1968 of the remains of "a first-century fishermen's quarters" underneath a Byzantine basilica

(associated with the House of St. Peter) at Capernaum on the Sea of Galilee. I assume (I have not read the report on the excavation in the "Israel Exploration Journal 18") that it was identified as fishermen's quarters by the presence of fishhooks, net sinkers, or such. But why the excitement? It may indeed have been the house of St. Peter, although the odds are rather considerably against it, since everybody living near the Sea of Galilee fished; the Sea is said to contain 40 different species of fish; Magdala on the same sea is identified in the Talmud as Migdal Nunaiya, "fish tower" and so forth. For a final example, take Finegan's pleasure at the discovery of an ancient walk, "believed to be from the Jewish period," on the way to Gethsemane from Jerusalem. Jesus "could have walked upon these very steps," Finegan exclaims. So indeed he could have, but he could equally have walked to Gethsemane upon the water or flown there through the air. If He is divine, He does not need Jewish flagstones to guide His steps.

In short, there is no archaeological or historical evidence whatsoever that a Rabbi Jeshua taught and fed and healed in Palestine in the first third of the first century, or even that he lived at all. But that is not what the New Testament has traditionally meant to Christians. It is the glad tidings that God became incarnate as man, was born of a virgin, was voluntarily crucified to atone for our sins, rose on the third day, and will return to judge the quick and the dead. No archaeological evidence would show any of that, any more than chemical evidence would show changes in the Eucharist. St. Jerome, in passages Finegan quotes, said that the Christian sites meant little apart from faith, and wrote approvingly of the Palestinian hermit Hilarion, who visited Jerusalem for only a single day, not wishing "to appear to confine God within local limits." As faith has decayed in our day, the Euhemerist passion for pseudohistory has increased, and the newspapers are hideous with accounts of expeditions looking for Noah's Ark or the Golden Calf, books on the man Abraham or the man Paul. The Reverend Dr. Finegan mocks his learning by adding to the number of such works. Is there, then, no real history connected with the Bible? Of course there is. The Jews and Christians who believed and WHAT they believed and practiced, are real history, not the doing of their divinities.

1970